ReEnchantment

The New Australian Spirituality

ReEnchantment

The New Australian Spirituality

DAVID TACEY

HarperCollins*Publishers*

HarperCollins*Publishers*

First published in Australia in 2000
Reprinted in 2000
by HarperCollins*Publishers* Pty Limited
ACN 009 913 517
A member of HarperCollins*Publishers* (Australia) Pty Limited Group
http://www.harpercollins.com.au

HarperCollins*Publishers*
25 Ryde Road, Pymble, Sydney, NSW 2073, Australia
31 View Road, Glenfield, Auckland 10, New Zealand
77–85 Fulham Palace Road, London W6 8JB, United Kingdom
Hazelton Lanes, 55 Avenue Road, Suite 2900, Toronto, Ontario M5R 3L2
and 1995 Markham Road, Scarborough, Ontario M1B 5M8, Canada
10 East 53rd Street, New York NY 10022, USA

The National Library of Australia Cataloguing-in-Publication data:

Tacey, David J. (David John), 1953– .
Re-enchantment: the new Australian spirituality.
ISBN 0 7322 6524 X
1. Spiritual life. 2. Social ecology — Australia.
3. Human ecology — Australia. 4. Aborigines, Australian —
Religion. 5. Religion and geography. I. Title.
291.4

Cover image: *Psychic Inertia* by Roxanne Oakley from the body of work
Scratching the Surface. Copyright © 1999.
Printed in Australia by Griffin Press Pty Ltd on 79 gsm Bulky Paperback

6 5 4 3 2   00 01 02 03

To my daughter, Ana Rose Gregory-Tacey

Contents

4: Spirit and Place

Sacred ground; the language of the Earth; the spirituality of embodiment, eros and nature; renewal through the feminine; two-way dialogue and cultural exchange; red spirit: the warm glow of the earth gods; ordinarily sacred: everyday reality and divine presence; Aboriginal spiritual receptivity to ordinary things; Anglo-Celtic spirituality of presence and embodiment.

5: Aboriginal Reconciliation as a Spiritual Experience

Out of the too-hard basket; the gain of loss and the art of sacrifice; the recognition and integration of evil; exploring the sacrifice; beyond Left and Right: the need for a radical centre; the indigenising process and the power of the land; indigenisation and deep cultural memory; blood-line ancestors, hoaxes and impostors; cultural materialism and the myth of white profanity; survival through integration and accommodation; Ned Kelly Dreaming: striving to redeem the invaders; spirituality, love and reconciliation.

6: Ecospirituality and Environmental Awareness

Sacredness as the key to environmental integrity; modernity's disenchanted universe; the cultural and scientific recovery of our spiritual bond with nature; a brief overview of the despiritualisation of nature; moral and spiritual dimensions of the popular ecological revolution; the New Age as a parody of our spiritual renewal; Eliade: the modern longing for re-enchantment; the circles of identity.

7: Youth Spirituality and Old Religion

Spirituality in youth culture: open, urgent, and political; the mass defection from established religion; a new outbreak of spiritual feeling; the crisis in understanding and the demand for inward knowing; the church in transition: from devotion to spirituality; towards a new theology of the Holy Spirit and divine immanence; taking risks with faith and tradition; the lonely path of individual spiritual experience; integrating the lessons of youth spirituality.

The spirits are all still there in the rain the wind the bush walkin' talkin' singin' dancin' in the land.

— Lionel Fogarty[1]

If I were indigenous or multicultural … you would suspend your sophisticated disbelief, and permit me my enchantment.

— Robert Dessaix[2]

We Aboriginal people do not have a monopoly on spirituality in this country; we have just been practising it a bit longer.

— David Mowaljarlai[3]

The Rise of Spirituality in Australia

Australian attitudes towards spirituality appear to be undergoing a profound and dramatic change. Not long ago, many of us in this country thought of spirituality in negative terms, as antisocial, irrational or unscientific, perhaps even as morbid. Spirituality received bad press, and consequently we have lived in a culture in which it was suppressed or ignored. "Until the last decade or so," Maryanne Confoy wrote recently, "most people thought of spirituality, if they thought of it at all, as something for other people".[1] Spirituality was rejected in favour of 'common sense', social reality, and an extraverted attitude to life; in other words it was regarded as 'otherworldly'. Almost all radical theories of human liberation in recent times (Marxism, feminism, psychoanalysis) have been reductively materialistic and antispiritual in character. Some of these theories are beginning to restate their basic arguments, with a view to including the transformative potentials of the sacred.[2] But for the most part, Australian intellectual culture has remained steadfastly secular, and this has driven a wedge between those who think about 'this' world and long to change it (the social reformers) and those who reflect on the 'other' world and long for redemption.

This typical dualism between spiritual and social worlds is false, and it has a debilitating effect on our revolutionary zeal — our desire to change the world quickly runs out of steam, because it is not being replenished or directed by the spirit. We do not have the mental capacity to bring about lasting change in this world until we have opened ourselves and our culture to the transformative possibilities of the sacred. The rational part of us lacks the resources to initiate real change, even as it seems to be motivated by pragmatic ideals. Nothing great or lasting can be achieved with purely secular motivations.

Yet many of our progressive thinkers remain terrified of religion because they associate it, often with good reason historically, with fundamentalism, fascism or destructive emotionalism. It is a habit of the secular mind to constantly point to the negative and abusive expressions of the religious instinct, and having our noses rubbed in these negative expressions is supposed to cure us of the desire for a religious life. But although the religious instinct can be manipulated to serve evil purposes, it is nevertheless a powerful force that must be aroused if any society is to achieve greatness. The transformative energy in self and society comes not from positive thinking, social legislation or secular politics, but from our discovery of the spiritual dimension of life, which gives us the courage to change, trusting in a deeply secure foundation.

THE SITES OF SPIRITUAL RENEWAL

Spirituality is making a comeback, although it is still too early to track this development in great detail. Every now and then, we hear prophetic comments about this cultural change, such as this from Hugh Mackay:

> Caroline Jones' An Authentic Life *is a disarmingly intimate chronicle of the culture-shifts taking place in our society, as many Australians switch from the twentieth century's rationalist focus on 'seeing is believing' to a more ancient, essentially religious position that 'believing is seeing'.*[3]

This shift is certainly taking place, but it is so diffuse that it is difficult to define or name, especially in view of this culture's continued official protest that it is secular and non-religious. Broadly, the areas that appear to be giving rise to a new spirituality in Australia include the experience of nature and landscape,[4] the environmental emergency,[5] Aboriginal reconciliation,[6] the visual arts,[7] popular life-history and story-telling,[8] biography,[9] autobiography,[10] public interest in Eastern religions,[11] contemporary youth culture, progressives in the churches, the therapeutic and mentalhealth professions, workplace relations, human resources and industry leadership, social analysis,[12] the naturalhealth movement and the re-enchantment of gardens and herbs, the popular men's movement,[13] the spiritual women's movement,[14] and a kind of generalised hunger for personal and cultural renewal.[15]

In other fields, spirituality is becoming an important issue in theory of culture and society,[16] education theory,[17] theory of personality,[18] theoretical physics,[19] anthropology,[20] Australian theology,[21] feminist theology,[22] postmodern theory,[23] Aboriginal cultural studies,[24] outdoor education,[25] and nursing and health studies.[26] (The references provided in the notes for these sites of spiritual renewal are highly selective; their purpose is to indicate activity taking place in the field, not to provide comprehensive listings. Some overseas titles have been included, to point to international sources that are now influencing debates here in Australia. But also note that some overseas titles on spirituality are written by Australian authors.) It would be wonderful to discover a thorough, non-sectarian study of the spiritual renewal taking place in Australian public and professional life, but no such study yet exists. It is still too early, and the renewal is too vast and covers too many disciplinary fields to be encompassed by any single researcher. But there are interdisciplinary postgraduates working on certain aspects of the bigger picture, including Simon Harvey and John Fisher, who are mapping parts of the new public story that is emerging.

The cartoons, drawings and prayers of the artist Michael Leunig have, almost single-handedly, whetted the nation's appetite for spiritual exploration. Leunig deserves to have an entire book written about his long career, its influence upon the arts and social attitudes, and his momentous lifting of the bans and repressions on Australia's hidden spirituality. The creative arts and literature in this country have always been concerned with spiritual themes and interests, and we need only mention the names of Leunig, Arthur Boyd, Peter Sculthorpe, Patrick White, Les Murray, Judith Wright and Tim Winton to confirm this point. But it remains a curious problem, and a symptom of the divided nature of the Australian psyche, that the spiritual themes of our artists have been ignored, denied or repressed by the intellectual-critical culture that pretends to interpret the arts for the nation and for its educational institutions. The art historian Jane Magon is attempting to unravel and redeem the lost spiritual dimension of Australian art.[27]

I will explore later in this book the problems that arise when an ostensibly secular society, led by sophisticated and non-religious ruling elites, is confronted by the fact that most of its important artists are visionary or spiritual in character. The work of our major artists subverts the pose of secularism that governs the nation's outward style, so that the arts constantly put forward a challenge to our society, a challenge that is rarely integrated by society. This creates a deep-seated tension in Australia between the artists and the intellectuals, since the artists are advocating (re)enchantment from the depths of a prophetic imagination, while the intellectuals are promoting disenchantment and an ironic vision of the world. Tensions and frictions abound in Australian cultural history, where the artist's vision of a deeply spiritual inner life comes into collision with the official national persona: young, free, aggressively secular and postreligious. Veronica Brady deserves special mention for her relentless struggle to bring forward the repressed spirituality of the arts in Australia, and to expose the systematic denial of the sacred that takes place in secular high culture. In the realm of broadcasting and media, Geraldine Doogue and Caroline Jones have worked extremely hard to lift the bans on the sacred and to introduce this subject into 'normal' public discussion. One is no longer dubbed a freak or a clown if one talks about spirituality.

AUSTRALIA DISLODGED FROM THE COMFORT ZONE

Those who have recognised the presence of spirituality in Australian life in the past have often argued that it is *un-Australian* to talk about it.[28] Even today, some people argue that Australians are naturally reticent about religious matters, that we are shy about spirituality, and such people often hope we shall remain that way. Behind this attitude, I think, is a fear that too much talk about religion will prove to be socially divisive and that our democratic life might be unsettled by outpourings of religious emotion. However, our social conditions have dramatically shifted in recent years. There is a real crisis of meaning in the community, and the problems associated with constant social change — the erosion of the old public morality, the breakdown of family structures, high levels of unemployment and instability in the workplace, and the public emergencies created by drugs, alcohol, crime and increasing suicide — have shaken this country out of its former innocence and urged us to take stock of 'what really matters'.

In other words, the social stability of the comfort zone that protected the old Australia from introspection and that enabled Australians to be relatively quiet about spiritual matters has been radically undermined. We can no longer afford to remain silent about matters of meaning. Nor can we afford to sentimentalise the 'old Australia', in which problems of the spirit were rarely discussed and in which the 'true Aussie' never fussed about such matters. People who idealise the relaxed social conditions of the past are refusing to engage the urgent crises of our time, and failing to see these crises as a cry for clarification and affirmation of human and social meaning. Speaking about our innate hunger for spiritual meaning, David Millikan has said that "there is a distinctive quality of capacity in us all which creates a restlessness with the limitations of our present life".[29] This spiritual restlessness is dramatically accelerated when society goes through a period of critical instability and uncertainty.

Often, what inspires spiritual search in Australia today is a profound disillusionment with the present social system, especially in the fields of politics, social leadership, industry, health, law and education. The search for new values and visions is frequently sparked by frustration, disappointment or anger at the current state of secular society. This is why the new spirituality can hardly afford to be otherworldly: it is concerned with discovering new and better ways of conducting life and community. Bishop Spong has observed that spirituality "speaks of a discontent rising out of the human situation that compels us to venture into the unknown".[30] Our new social discontent, although at times rancorous and disruptive, is a 'holy discontent' in that it represents a protest against the conditions of our all-too-human world, as well as a search for abiding spiritual values that can provide a new stability and unity to society.

THE POSTSECULAR ENLIGHTENMENT

The spiritual reawakening will challenge and overturn many of the principles that have governed our society during the long secular period, which has taken its promptings from humanism and the Intellectual Enlightenment. The secular period ushered in many positive and valuable changes, as our society came to terms with the material dimension of the physical universe. But the quality of life itself has been dramatically eroded by our obsession with materialism, which has delivered a spiritual emptiness even as it has struggled to improve our social conditions. We are about to experience what could be called a 'second' enlightenment, a postsecular enlightenment, where religion and spirituality will return to centre stage and where secular materialism will appear out of date and anachronistic. However, with this new religious enlightenment, the sacred will be experienced in radically different ways from the past. The new awareness will not champion premodern religious categories but, rather, will introduce new and altered concepts of the sacred. That is why, in my own work, I stress the need for a postsecular and postscientific spiritual awareness, not merely a return to mediaeval or archaic attitudes.

RESISTANCE AND CONFLICT AT THE END OF AN ERA

Needless to say, in an officially secular society, the return of the sacred will be met with resistance and denial from numerous quarters, and we are currently on the cusp of a testing in-between period, where a clash of paradigms will become evident. I see this especially in the universities, where a growing number of students are calling for serious consideration of spiritual values but where established academia holds firm to its rationalistic enterprise and to its secular fund of knowledge. As the old paradigm crumbles, institutional resistance will stiffen, and we see this also in high culture's scorn towards popular experimentation in religious life, which is frequently dismissed as 'New Age' nonsense, and in the mainstream media's cynicism towards the new public interest in spirituality.

Many of our institutions do not know what to make of the popular rise in spirituality, and seem to hope it is a cultural fashion that will quickly disappear. This is ironic, because these same institutions, governed by an economic rationalism that speaks about consumer needs and niche marketing, argue that their primary goal is to meet the demands of their clients. However, a radical change in official cultural attitudes will be needed before many of our institutions can ever hope to deliver the kinds of discussions for which people are calling at the present time.

Having said this, it also has to be admitted that the new momentum towards spiritual awareness is so intense that some of our secular institutions are changing their orientation and attitude. For instance, the Vice-Chancellor of Griffith University, Professor Roy Webb, recently made this significant announcement:

> In the past Australian universities have, with some important exceptions, largely seen themselves as secular institutions, pursuing the preservation, transmission and development of knowledge without much reliance upon, or regard for, and sometimes even with hostility towards, the religious and spiritual dimensions of life.
>
> At its most severe, the secularisation of our universities proceeded on the assumption that the

paradigms of religion and of scientific rationalism were in fundamental opposition; that sooner or later the domain of religion would be crowded out by the ever-increasing explanatory power of rationalist endeavour.

I believe that we can now say that the most extreme episodes of secularism have passed.

The re-emergence of emphasis on the spiritual, moral and ethical dimensions of life is evident in the Australian community in a number of encouraging ways, although there is still enormous distance to be covered.[31]

This is perhaps the most visionary expression yet from a leader of a secular university, who has obviously sensed the change of moral climate in the wider community and who may also be alert to the new, friendlier attitude to spirituality in the contemporary sciences, environmentalism and mental health. But I suspect that at least some of this vice-chancellor's staff would want to challenge his announcement that secularism is in decline and a new religious dispensation on the way. For staff who have trained in secular ideologies and whose intellectual authority is based on their strict adherence to secular materialist principles, such an announcement would come as a tremendous shock and would be met with keen resistance.

I meet many people who are impatient with the old paradigm and who demand instant change, and while I share some of this impatience, I also think it is necessary to respect those who are working in the old paradigm. Patrick White once described rationalists as "admirable people, really, though limited".[32] I think we should challenge those limitations at every possible opportunity, though not attack the integrity of the people who are bound by them. I am not looking for a bloody revolution, but look forward to increased dialogue and engagement.

We need much more discussion in this country about spiritual issues, because the silence is enforced and uneasy. We should not be afraid to put a contrary view to any established authority, even to the self-appointed voices of 'enlightened' Australia. Secular and/or cynical authorities do not have the right to mock what they cannot as yet understand. Tolerance will be required as we negotiate our way through the future terrain, through the clash of paradigms from which none of us, finally, can escape.

THE NEED FOR INCLUSIVE AND ANTIFUNDAMENTALIST SPIRITUALITY

The new religious vision will be, it is to be hoped, the opposite of fundamentalist, as long as it develops consciously and with creative leadership. However, if it develops unconsciously and without cultural support, it could readily lapse into an inferior social movement, giving rise to a populist right-wing backlash or to resurgent fundamentalism. "The more unconscious we are of the religious problem in the future, the greater the danger of our putting the divine germ within us to some ridiculous or demonic use".[33] Like Jung, I believe that religious impulses, if understood and integrated, can lead to health and renewal, but if not understood can lead to personal illness and social pathology.

What we have recently glimpsed in politics in the One Nation party — namely, an intolerant, divisive, and totalitarian political movement — we might see in the future in the religious domain, unless the nation comes to grips with its own repressed religious life. Walking around the university campus, I see disturbing signs of a rise in religious fundamentalism, encouraged by poorly educated ministers, and I believe these activities will increase unless the official culture on campus attempts to address, and to educate, the religious life. Arising from a blandly secular nation and its dark inner life, we could readily imagine the emergence of a group called 'One Way', which might tap the unexpressed religious impulses and give them negative form. Such a group might seek to impose upon all of us, and especially upon our youth, fundamentalist, intolerant images of the sacred. We already see such fanaticisms emerging in religious cults and fringe groups, which always seem to decide that they alone have access to absolute truth and that subordination and conformity to their ideology is the only path to that truth.

I would predict more religious fanaticism and intolerance until we can bring our repressed religious life into the open and express the non-rational forces that underpin it. The non-rational becomes dangerously active only if we lack the cultural symbols to express and nurture it. Paradoxically, inferior religiosity can be cured only by public and expressive contact with our religious impulses. The cure is homeopathic: like cures like. Someone who has been the victim of a dangerous religious cult is best cured not by winning them back to ordinary, disenchanted consciousness, to 'normality' as we like to call it, but by deepening and developing their religious impulses, by educating the religious instinct. It may seem peculiar to some, but to express religious life consciously and to celebrate it publicly is the best insurance policy we have against future outbreaks of morbid or infantile religious passion.

Most of us who are open to religious experience are at times gullible and naive. If we do not have the courage to face this spiritual life consciously and with intellectual integrity, it could overtake and consume our rationality, and we will be the victims, rather than the beneficiaries, of the new spiritual dispensation. Education, as long as it can break free from the old rationalistic mode, becomes vital in the task of discovering personal balance, psychological equilibrium and cultural well-being. According to recent research, an overwhelming majority of secondary school teachers (both in secular and in religious systems) believe that spirituality is a vital ingredient in the education of youth.[34] All of us need to educate our spiritual impulses so that they contribute to rather than undermine the cultural context in which we are operating.

This is why we need dialogue and interchange — so that we can integrate the newly rising spiritual contents into our culture, rather than hold them back and condemn them to a marginal existence. The worst thing our institutions can do is remain silent and refuse to enter the fray, as this will only breed the kind of resentment and anger that will lead to violent disruptions and fanatical oppositions. If we force a showdown between spirituality and rationality, both will be the losers. Rationality without spirituality leads to dryness, inhumanity and lack of meaning, a scenario reported by many of our depressed and suicidal youth. Spirituality without rationality leads to emotionalism, superstition, wild enthusiasm and fanatical loyalties. Both need to be brought together in a meaningful way; we need reason and passion, *logos* and *mythos*, economics and mysticism, to keep society balanced and sane. If allowed to participate creatively in culture, the new religious awareness will become a real agent for change and positive transformation.

AUTHOR'S NOTE

This book scratches the surface of our culture, peeling back the secular mask to reveal the possibilities for spiritual renewal that are already to be found in Australian experience. It extends several of the themes of my earlier book *Edge of the Sacred*,[35] and it also develops the theme of spirituality which ran through *Remaking Men*.[36] *Edge of the Sacred* was a sort of brainstorming source-book, containing many embryonic themes and ideas that needed further elaboration. This book is not settled or systematic either, because the changes in Australian awareness that I am interested in tracking are many and diverse, and it has been impossible for me to remain within the confines of any single discipline or intellectual view. When consciousness changes, all fields of human experience are influenced. Now is a time for a generalist and multidisciplinary approach, because the old specialisations and labels no longer reflect or contain the exciting diversity and complexity of our changing cultural spirit.

As ever, I mix together the styles and methods of psychology, religion and personal reflection, while also drawing at times on literature, history, anthropology and ecology. My main intellectual influences are Jung, Yeats, Eliade and Bede Griffiths, although here I simply adopt their point of view rather than intellectually explore them, because my main concern is to apply religious awareness to different aspects of Australian life and society. In some ways, this book represents a sociology of spiritual experience, or an attempt to merge mysticism with history. I am never concerned wholly with the inner world or the outer world, but try to deal with both at once, which is, after all, the way we have to live life.

I am aware of the risks of writing outside established conventions, and especially of mixing scholarly methods and styles with spiritual explorations. In particular, moving close to the prophetic mode in Australian society, when our society officially views prophecy with suspicion, is a hazardous undertaking. However, it is only through such risk and adventure that our culture can break out of the imprisoning secular mask that currently confines and limits it. In this task, I am joined and supported by most of this country's creative artists, by some of our intellectuals, and by some of our religious leaders as well.

OPENING A DIALOGUE BETWEEN NEW SPIRITUALITY AND OLD RELIGION

Edge of the Sacred was concerned with the phenomenon of new spirituality arising in Australia, and while it was generally well received, several reviewers from the religious community called for further consideration of the links between new spirituality and religion. Associate Professor James Tulip in Sydney wrote that "Like Harold Bloom in *The American Religion: The Emergence of the Post-Christian Nation*,[37] Tacey ignores mainstream religion".[38] Tulip clearly doubted that vibrant spiritual life could bloom without religious roots, but he found the prospect of an Australian spirituality exciting. Tulip wrote that "Australians have deeply internalised negative attitudes on religion and suffer from a self-inflicted repression on this matter". What the future held in store was a difficult question, but he felt that the Australian cultural situation "promised a future of surprising developments". In Perth, Sister Veronica Brady wanted to know how this new spirituality related to Christianity, and how we could know it would work for the social good, rather than for evil.[39] Brady seemed suspicious of the new talk about 'spirituality' (ie. disconnected from religious morality), and wondered if it gave rise merely to personal highs rather than to social justice and moral commitment. This, indeed, is the view many people in the churches have of the popular spiritual revolution.

In Melbourne, Professor Kevin Hart pondered similar problems and questions, asking if the new spirituality represented a resurgence of gnosticism. Like Veronica Brady, he was worried that the do-it-yourself spirituality might be more interested in the pursuit of personal ecstasy than in morality and the common good.[40] However, Hart conceded that we were indeed in a spiritual crisis, that "the churches today seem unable to speak with authority about our spiritual anxieties and longings", and he placed himself in sympathy with alienated moderns when he acknowledged that "it is pointless to call for a return to organised religion, for the sacred is not churchy". In Canberra, Reverend Stephen Pickard asked whether this new Australian spirituality was pre-theological.[41] What did it have to say to the churches? At the time of writing *Edge*, I could not respond to these questions; I was tracking a nascent, primarily land-based or ecological spirituality that operated on a different level from organised religion and that was, in part, a reaction against it.

Partly prompted by reviewers and also motivated by my own developing interests, I now find myself exploring the implications of the newly arising spirituality for religion and morality. This seems like a logical next step in my work. If spirituality, as I have claimed all along, is primarily about connectedness, about our links with nature and cosmos, then what about our links with tradition, history and our religious ancestry? We might see the modern Western world as basically secular, but it wasn't very long ago that everyone belonged to one religious tradition or another — or, at least, everyone had to wrestle with religious questions, if only to reject them. During the secular period, these religious questions were anaesthetised or put to sleep, awoken only in those unlucky enough to experience a life crisis or some emergency that again brought 'religion' to the fore. Today, we often have spirituality without religion, but as our new spirituality matures, it sends down roots into the historical past. It starts to ask questions about what brought it to birth and what came before it. These questions lead naturally into reflections on religious tradition, on the crisis facing the churches, and on the apparent separation of popular spirituality from the institutions of faith.

Although spirituality is often idealised today, it can lead to personal and collective disorientation if a larger, cultural solution is not found for the newly arising spiritual contents. Ironically, we can feel ourselves getting closer to nature, impelled to hug trees, while we grow more alienated from society and our fellow human beings. This social isolation is crippling unless we do something about it. It seems to me that the spiritual longing for interconnectedness must lead eventually to some kind of social reckoning, to a desire for human community and a renewal of community bonds. The spiritual wanderer finds him- or herself ineluctably drawn to communities of faith, realising that the isolated path works only for a time and then must give way to something greater. This is not just a matter of taming personal spirituality so that it fits in neatly with existing or conventional religious forms, especially at a time when traditional religions, both Western and Eastern, are themselves in crisis and in dire need of transformation. We must not end our personal journeys by fusing uncritically with any church, temple or creed. Traditions need to be challenged and revivified by precisely the kind of spontaneous and vital spirituality that we find in the community today.

The interaction between spirituality and religion is of necessity an explosive and emotional one, in which the progressive spirit of the new collides with the conservative spirit of tradition and its resistance to change. To paraphrase Jung in a different context, I would say that the meeting of new spirituality and old religion is like the contact of two chemical substances: if there is any reaction, both are transformed. To practise the creative art of religion is to maintain a delicate and precarious balance between the unique spirit of the individual and the claims and demands of one's chosen tradition. This, above all, is the Australian stamp upon our spiritual experience: to preserve the integrity of individual difference and the right to disagree, even as we attempt to fit in and connect.

1

Spirituality and the Return to Mystery

But the true God, as distinct from the gods we create according to our own image, is totally other, even though at the same time totally inner, the hitherto unknown truth about ourselves.

— VERONICA BRADY[1]

WHAT IS SPIRITUALITY?

What is spirituality? It is difficult to offer precise answers, since spirituality eludes the kind of rationalistic knowing that arrives at simple definitions. But we can talk around the subject and provide some hints and descriptions. Spirituality is a desire for connectedness, which often expresses itself as an emotional relationship with an invisible sacred presence. To those who experience this relationship, it is real, transformative and complete. To many others, spirituality is said to involve a 'leap of faith', or 'blind trust' in the nature of reality. But blind trust or leaps of faith are hardly on the minds of those who have allowed themselves to be brought into a relationship with the sacred. These secular clichés are important only to the outsider's perspective, which is always looking for slightly condescending and judge-mental ways of describing what appears to be beyond its grasp. The secular mind can become furious if it imagines it is missing out on a significant part of the experience of life, so that its condescending attitude towards spirituality is also tinged with envy.

But spirituality is not beyond our grasp; in fact, it is the normal way of being. In tribal and indigenous societies, spirituality is an entirely natural mode of being in the world, and it is still available to modern people as well, if we can open ourselves to this dimension of experience. I think spirituality should be seen less as an unusual 'achievement' of a special or gifted human personality, than as a natural state to which we always have access, if we manage to relax our conditioned defences and resistances long enough to admit the presence of the sacred. Spirituality is our birthright, not some kind of bonus or added extra to life. From this religious perspective, secular or disenchanted 'normality' is really the unusual condition, the exception to the rule, the aberration.

Spirituality is assumed by the rational mind to be some kind of escapist madness or quaint delusion. But there is nothing escapist about the desire to relate to the core of living creation, nor is there anything deluded about a relationship that can provide stability, surety and well-being in a world that suffers from relentless change and where time-honoured truths are regularly undermined or debunked. Today's longing for spirituality is above all a desire to find a stable point in the teeming chaos that modern life has become. The social world and its institutions receive less and less of our faith and trust, and understandably, we are looking beyond society and towards the eternal realm for that sense of moral foundation that was previously provided to us by a stable social order.

Spirituality rises as society goes into moral and cultural decline, not because spirituality is a sign of that same decadence but because it represents a positive reaction against it, a striving towards a new kind of order in a disoriented world. However, we cannot afford to be too naive in our search for order through spirituality, because the nature of the sacred exceeds all human understanding, and sacred truth itself is never static and is always full of surprises, at least to the rational mind. So while we look to spirituality for stability, our search, if it is too naive, can give rise to mindless fundamentalism or to sentimental distortions of the character of God and the nature of divine truth. On the other hand, if we are too sophisticated, we would never begin a spiritual search in the first place, but would simply join the many who have opted for existential despair, cynicism and nihilism. We need to be sophisticated enough to avoid falling for stupid answers to spiritual questions, but naive enough to be inspired by hope and to expect to discover spiritual truth if we seek it. The desired innocence is not a 'first' innocence, which has not known sophistication, but a 'second' innocence, which comes after we have tasted sophistication.

SPIRITUAL INTERCONNECTEDNESS AND THE END OF MODERNITY

Mostly, we obtain only fleeting glimpses or momentary intuitions about the greater mystery to which we are connected and in which we are profoundly situated. Spirituality is the art of gaining access to this mystery and of relating our lives to it in meaningful and transformative ways. In describing spirituality, the key word that comes to mind is 'interconnectedness'.

Spiritual experience replaces the isolation of the individual ego with the unitary awareness of the larger or cosmic self. That cosmic self is personified in the world religions as Christ, Buddha, Atman and so on, and the disciple or follower of these religions seeks to achieve harmony with the universe through identification with the charismatic founder of their respective tradition.

Spirituality was thus traditionally a goal or product of religious devotion, but increasingly, as we shall see, it is being separated from religion and experienced as a reality in its own right. In the postindustrial world, the Internet and the World Wide Web embody some of our secular hopes and dreams about 'interconnection', but even on the Web, it has become apparent that spirituality looms large and that the new technological interconnectedness is being experienced in a quasi-mystical way.

Spirituality is a feeling of being connected to a greater or larger whole, and an awareness that in the part or fragment, the radiance of the whole shines forth. The rise of spirituality in our time signals the end of modernity as we know it, for the special insignia and persistent theme of the modern age has been alienation and isolation. One reason why spirituality is returning today could be that our contemporary experience of alienation is so relentlessly overwhelming that it has activated the desire for 'belonging' or 'interconnectedness' as an emotional counter-response. The more alienated the self becomes, the more it craves that ancient, repressed experience of being dynamically related to everything around it by virtue of the presence of an indwelling, unifying spirit in all things.

Karl Marx believed that only a total revolution in society and politics could alleviate the alienation inherent in the modern condition. I think Marx was right that a major revolution was needed to oppose our entrenched alienation, but since the socialist revolution has stalled in the West and proved disastrously catastrophic in the East, it may be that the revolution that will bring about the desired transformation in society will be a spiritual one. Like Marx's socioeconomic revolution, the spiritual revolution is spontaneously welling up from below, from the hearts and desires of ordinary people who have become sickened by modernity and frustrated by its undelivered promises of liberation. It is also, like the Marxist revolution, largely in opposition to the ruling elites, who remain committed to the ideology of modernity (and, ironically, often to Marxism itself), and are highly suspicious of the new populist movement in which spiritual sustenance is being sought.

The ruling elites dislike the popular interest in spirituality because it involves an appeal to a cosmic authority that is greater than their own. The secular intellectual culture, which has everywhere been permeated by various strains of Marxism, political feminism and cultural materialism, is desperately uneasy with spirituality and tries to pretend the rising movement is just a passing cultural fashion. The intellectual elite remains committed to a 'postmodernism' which is really just more of the same — ie. the extension of the disenchanted and reductive logic that was already enshrined in modernism. Authorities within our ecclesiastical church culture are also relatively uneasy about popular spirituality, because it seems that more and more people are assuming spiritual responsibility for their own lives, thus challenging the authority of the clergy and the 'one true way' of established religion.

What is decidedly 'postmodern' about the new spirituality is that it is plural, diverse, fragmented and decidedly eclectic. People often borrow religious insights from the West and spiritual practices from the East. We are interested in the vision quests of North America and the initiatory rituals of the South Pacific. There is an almost carnival or festive atmosphere about the conduct of this spiritual adventure. The postmodern intellectuals ought to be proud, at least, of this global and multilayered aspect of the contemporary spiritual odyssey. The environmental and ecological experts have also noted that popular spirituality is very friendly towards environmentalism, and that the new sense of spiritual wholeness is profoundly connected to a new, organic vision of wholeness in which humanity's creaturely pact with nature and dependence on the natural order is celebrated and affirmed. This is especially true for the new spirituality of young people, as I will go on to explore.

Spirituality admits that our normal experience touches constantly upon, and is in turn touched by, the presence of eternity, a presence that seems to love and nurture us and lead us towards our individual human destiny. I take seriously the idea that the divine is present with us and that it stands within the real, and within the human, as the spiritual guarantor of this reality. What we do matters, our lives have meaning, precisely because the temporal, the spatial is loved and supported by the sacred. Or as William Blake put it so memorably: "Eternity is in love with the productions of time".[2] If we are beginning to experience again the love that eternity has for time, and the love our creator has for ourselves as creatures, then this cannot be reckoned a cultural regression, but only an advancement to a new and better state of human awareness. Although we live in a world that pretends to have experienced the so-called 'death of God', our intellectual resistances do not have an impact upon the sacred itself, which is always prepared to receive our acknowledgement and to work with us in the deepening and redemption of our lives. Spirituality is not a marginal experience, but is pivotal and central to human existence; it is only our embarrassment or arrogance (or a mixture of both) that relegates it to the margins.

NEGATIVE ASSOCIATIONS OF SPIRITUALITY

I have already outlined some of the negative associations of spirituality, linked to resistances of the rational mind and also to the defensive mechanisms of ruling elites and institutional authorities. But it is also true that the term 'spirituality' carries a lot of traditional baggage, and a great many people whom I respect would probably have a negative view of the word. For some people, 'spirituality' is associated with otherworldliness, and the word cannot be won back from this negative definition. In the past, spirituality was often viewed as esoteric, private and internal, nothing to do with the world. As such — or so many intellectuals have concluded — spirituality is irrelevant to real life and a menace to society.

To be fair to this modern prejudice, much of what has passed for spirituality in history has indeed been marked by transcendentalism, disdain for the world, and a negative attitude towards the body, sexuality, nature and passion. This is where the important new work has to be done, and where contemporary and future theology must redeem spirituality from its own negative history. In several chapters of this book, I will explore the crisis in traditional spirituality as a crisis in engagement, a refusal to fully acknowledge and encounter the incarnational thrust that is found in religion itself. In other words, not religion but human nature is responsible for the general impression that spirituality is escapist and delusional.

But the new spirituality poses an interesting series of tensions between the internal and external domains. Although spirituality is often seen as personal, a conversation with the deepest recesses of one's own inner being, it is hardly a 'private' affair if this internal conversation is now regarded as universally important and globally relevant. The traditional humanist prejudice that spirituality is purely subjective, a kind of sophisticated form of navel-gazing, is completely undermined if we accept that deep within the self is a collective spiritual reality that connects and binds us all. In other words, at the heart of our subjectivity is an objective psychospiritual reality that has been known in theology and mysticism as the soul or spirit.

Although our modern mechanisms and techniques for accessing this inner reality seem very subjective and personal — and these techniques include psychotherapy, meditation, poetry, retreats, wilderness experiences and the like — the reality we contact, if we are successful in our search, is the opposite of subjective. We arrive at a transpersonal dimension with immediate and enormous ramifications for society, politics, the environment, theology, relationships, developmental psychology, education and health. What may start off as navel-gazing can end up as social revolution, since when the ground of our being is touched and stirred, that spirit is the same spirit that energises and activates the whole of creation. Fake spirituality may well be masturbatory and private, but true spirituality always engages with the world and is unafraid to meet and transform it.

TENSIONS BETWEEN RELIGION AND SPIRITUALITY, OR FORM AND MYSTERY

Spirituality is especially difficult to define because it is largely what we don't know about ourselves. I distrust those who claim to be experts on spirituality, and those who have dogmatic or technical knowledge about this subject, because it is still largely a mystery, a deep source of unknowing. We must approach this subject with humility, awe and reverence, not hubris or certainty, because when we are most certain about spirituality, we are most certainly removed from its essence. The sacred is not synonymous with our images or conceptions of the sacred, and to pretend that our images of the divine are the divine reality itself is idolatry rather than religion. Sometimes religious knowledge can become a barrier to spirituality, and spiritual practice would then consist of sacrificing what we thought we knew about this subject.

I oppose all kinds of fundamentalism, believing that the healthiest approach is to emphasise the Unknown God, and acknowledging that the deepest human urge is to befriend and forge a relationship with this hidden source. Our relationship with the sacred makes God known and visible, and this is the primary task of religion: making known to ourselves, to others and to the wider community the covenant between ourselves and our God. We have a moral and civic responsibility to make the sacred known, so that this dimension of our experience can be raised to consciousness and celebrated throughout society. But the process of 'making known' can backfire on us, since religions can lose touch with the spiritual meanings they enshrine. If the Unknown God becomes too known and familiar, if our religious ceremonies and rituals become mundane, if we lose touch with the spontaneous creativity of the spirit, then religions no longer serve as carriers of the sacred. When our religious images become ossified and overproduced, they are more reflective of the sociopolitical human order than of the mysterious and the sacred.

In our relationship with the sacred, it is inevitable that we will end up projecting aspects of our own human and social character upon the face of the Divine Other, so from time to time, religious upheavals become important in enabling us to recover our connection with the living sacred. If these creative upheavals do not occur, religion can readily degenerate into a social habit or custom with little or no spiritual substance. This is the problem we face in our own time, where our religious codes too often mask the spiritual revelation they are designed to communicate. Religions have to be prepared to take risks, to listen to the prophetic voices, to stay in touch with the people, to remain open to nature and to grace. Otherwise, they will petrify, become self-serving, and lose their divine spark under the dead weight of institutional power.

The creative spirit is a headache for institutional authorities, since it is often at odds with our religious forms. The spirit is profoundly iconoclastic, original, radical and challenging. It readily reminds us that our images of the divine are human, and conditioned by historical circumstances. The spirit is a trickster: it bloweth where it listeth; it often finds institutional forms inhibiting, and it can perform extraordinary deeds, infuriating the religious authorities of the day. Christ himself was persecuted and crucified by the religious and political authorities of his day, which should remind us that spirituality and religion, while seemingly closely related, are often viewed as hostile enemies in a life-and-death struggle. Christians have often projected the recalcitrant side of religious institutional life upon the Jewish establishment, but the fact remains that any institution, Christian, Jewish or otherwise, is likely to find itself at odds with the demands of the living spirit.

In the past, many of us believed that spirituality was a product of religious life and devotion, but we are having to face the fact that spirituality itself is larger, greater and much older than any organised religion. Spirituality is the primary category, the baggy monster, whereas religions are discrete categories of the spiritual realm. It is a devastating experience for any religion to have to admit that it no longer contains what it is meant to contain, which is why 'spirituality' outside its own precincts is often regarded with suspicion, even with overt hostility. This is the major reason why creative spiritual thinkers are often branded as heretics, why mystics and visionaries are feared, and why spiritual ferment outside the established boundaries is often rejected by religious authorities.

The history of the church in the West is littered with instances of excommunication, banning and banishment of creative individuals. These people are at first feared because of the threat they pose to established authority. However, years later and often after their death, such individuals are sometimes reconsidered by the church, which may decide that they have made a creative contribution. The transgressor may be posthumously canonised as a saint or revered as a major religious figure or inspired thinker. Somewhat cynically, we could say that once such transgressors are dead and no longer pose any real threat, the church can afford to idealise them and place them on a pedestal. This is cold comfort, however, for the indignities, persecutions and loss of identity suffered in the lived experience of their creative mission.

This persistent problem has to do with the difficult relationship between form (structure) and mystery (substance), or between officially recognised revelation and ongoing spontaneous revelation. As long as God and the spirit remain alive, they will continue to speak to us in new and challenging ways. When the living spirit dances and beckons, religious stalwarts will always become annoyed. In Christianity, much emphasis is placed on the historical person of Jesus, because such emphasis leads to the fond hope (or illusion) that a religion based on this figure can be stage-managed by the church and can be contained by dogmas and precepts. Such certainty is profoundly illusory, since we know so little about the historical Jesus, and what we do know has been filtered through the transformative lens of legend and myth. But the idea of a living Cosmic Christ who might at any moment be discovered in some new context or shape is far more troubling and difficult to handle, since to figure such an enigmatic reality into the religious equation would require of our institutions an openness to ongoing presence and mystery. Almost by definition, then, religions can accommodate the spiritual only if they can accommodate change. Since they are generally resistant to change, they are at the same time resistant to the creativity of the living spirit.

Religion and spirituality thus face each other as paradoxical twins. Without religion, we have no organised way of communicating or expressing truth, no sacred rituals to bind individuals into living community. Yet without spirituality, we have no truth to celebrate and no contact with the living and ongoing nature of divine revelation. We need both — form and substance — but each can attack and cancel out the other if the conditions are not propitious. We encounter the terrible irony that our attempts to make known the unknowable mystery may have the effect of rubbing out that mystery and alienating us even further from the living depths of the sacred. We live in times where spirituality is privileged and where religion is under attack, which is to say that spirituality holds our hopes for interconnectedness, and religion stands accused of mere institutional authority. This is the mood of our age, and we must respect it, but it is still not clear what will bind society together or provide the foundation for community.

WHEN 'MYSTERY' IS READ AS 'MYSTIFICATION'

The greatest Western and Eastern traditions of spiritual wisdom insist on the inability of rational knowledge to comprehend or grasp the essential mystery. Unfortunately, this emphasis on unknowability, mystery, and styles of paradox and poetry has given rise to the suspicion among the intellectually enlightened that religion is some kind of hoax or system of thought designed to confound and ridicule common sense. Some materialistic 'liberators' of humanity have decided that we can do without religion altogether, saying that it represents a political trick designed to keep the bulk of humanity in a state of oppression. In other words, when the spiritual transformations religion is meant to achieve have not been taking place, the methods and techniques of religion have been regarded with scorn and derision. When religion is judged hollow by society, it becomes far easier to undermine, which is all the more reason why religion must actively seek out spiritual content.

Religion is not designed to trick people, oppress them or contradict the life of the mind. The whole point of spirituality is to *transcend* ordinary human limits and conventions and to aspire to a relationship with the sacred. But if the metanoia or transformation of one's own life and being do not take place, then some are bound to imagine that religion is 'opium for the masses', charlatanism, or some collective sorcery driven by malign political purposes. We live in a time that has forgotten the meaning of religion, and so everything today has to be carefully and tactfully explained to a largely disbelieving public.

As Karl Rahner has said, modern theology has to be addressed to the unbeliever, and to the unbeliever in the theologian, rather than to an imagined captive audience. There can be no 'preaching to the converted' any more, since the world itself has converted to secularism and its common sense. Religion has to fully understand its defensive position, and exploit this as a potential strength rather than regard it as a weakness. If it contains truth, then that truth has to be boldly announced and explored. Containing truth as it does, it can afford to take risks in order to win back credibility.

WESTERN RELIGION'S FATAL ATTACHMENT TO MAGICAL THINKING

Western religion has never fully recovered from the attack made upon it by the scientific enlightenment. The moral and cultural authority of the churches has been in decline since the late mediaeval period, and religion has not been able to claim a monopoly on truth since at least the dawn of the scientific era. But I believe that the most self-destructive strategy ever adopted by Western religion was its insistence upon the literal reality of its mysteries and miracles. It felt that its mysteries (the creation of the world, the resurrection, the immaculate conception) could be true only if they were literally true; it disregarded the truth of metaphor and symbol, opting instead for the truth of fact and history.

As the Western intellect developed and as science gained in strength and reason, the claims of religion seemed far-fetched. Religion had rejected the truth of *mythos* (story) for the truth of *logos* (reason), and yet the science of *logos* would rapidly transcend and debunk the claimed truths of religion. In a sense, religion had actually undermined itself by literal thinking and fundamentalist claims, and by abandoning its true foundation in myth, metaphor, narrative and story. In time, very few self-respecting thinking persons could subscribe to the impossible claims put forward by religion, which rapidly lost the support of the intellectual classes and has never managed to recapture it. Instead, religion looked for support from the uneducated classes, hoping that they would keep faith with its tenets and claims.

This is an astonishingly weak and negative strategy, and religion in the West has never yet made a decent attempt to win back the best and the brightest in society. The church responded to this crisis by increasing its threats of the moral retribution that would befall those who failed to maintain the faith. Especially in the nineteenth century, it used coercion, guilt and the rhetoric of damnation to maintain its flock, thereby making itself an enemy of reason, social progress and individual liberty. For many creative thinkers, the church has become synonymous with oppression. It could not, by this stage, revert to its grounding in *mythos*, having gone too far down the pathway of literal claims and historicity.

The church needs to educate itself beyond its own magical or literal thinking. In other words, in rejecting the world of philosophical education, it also neglected to educate itself beyond its own early forms of reasoning. Its theology, dogmas and tenets are still embedded in an archaic pattern of thinking, whereby something cannot be regarded as 'true' unless it is literally so. Ironically, in the West, the church suffers from a fundamental problem: an essential lack of faith in the reality of spirit. In order to believe in spirit, the church has to have miracles and wonders performed by its charismatic founder, and the claims of spirit have to be constantly demonstrated or acted out, in material reality. So, for instance, the eucharistic wafer cannot be an effective sacrament unless it has been magically transformed into the substance of the redeemer. There can be no effective or real resurrection unless the body of Christ has literally risen from the grave and ascended into the sky. The child in religious education class is thereby prompted to ask: "To what planet, moon or star did the body of Jesus ascend?" If the most important elements of Western religion have been couched in such infantile literalism, it is little wonder that the religious stories of the West have been treated like nursery rhymes or fairy stories, things we outgrow and leave behind. Western religious claims have also become something of a laughing stock to the clergy of the more sophisticated Eastern religions, who look upon such claims (especially the claim to exclusive and absolute truth) with faint amusement.

Why should the resurrection of the spirit be dependent on the idea of a broken body or corpse floating into the sky? Why should the idea of spiritual purity be dependent on the idea of a literal virgin birth? Why should the idea of spiritual purpose in creation be dependent on a seven-day creation story? No matter where we turn in Western religion, we find a conflation of spiritual idea with literal assertion, suggesting to me that the church has at every point needed props and proof of faith. The myths of religion are no less 'true' if they are separated from their literal proofs. If treated as symbolic statements, as claims of the living spirit, they are freed from their cumbersome logic, allowing adult awareness to appreciate and be guided by these truths again. The overwhelming imperative, it seems to me, is to return religion to mystery and restore its claims to the mysterious depths in our own lives. Here, the need for proof fades away and the truth status of religion is restored to its rightful place.

Apart from the problem of magical thinking, it is the Western dualism between the body and the spirit that continues to mar and undermine the church. Actually, these are different expressions of the same problem, which is a refusal to acknowledge the holistic, organic and complex nature of our reality. We no longer need to imagine the spirit in the old way, as something antithetical or contrary to matter, flesh and the body. There is little point in moralising against the body to a culture that has experienced a sexual revolution. Similarly, it is tragically out of step to insist on a patriarchal religion, at whose pinnacle stands a Father God, in a cultural period that has witnessed the revolution of the feminine and the female. It is also self-destructive to insist on belief in an external deity in an age that is hungry for direct experience and inward understanding. All of these problems have led to the demise of religion, and have forced an unnecessary separation of spirituality from religion, leading many people, perhaps the majority, to the conviction that they cannot trust organised religion with their spiritual lives. Most of the problems raised here will be revisited and extended in subsequent chapters.

THE LOSS AND RECOVERY OF SPIRIT

In Eastern meditation practice, there is a chant that says: "First there is a mountain, then there is no mountain, then there is". Meditation practice first observes the ordinary world, then dissolves it in cosmic unity, and then returns to the world again with renewed insight. In the West, it is not a mountain that keeps appearing and disappearing, but spirituality. First we had spirituality (largely encased in religious tradition), then we had no spirituality (during the triumph of scientific materialism), and now we have spirituality again (looking for a new home, but not sure where it can be found).

This little three-part story could describe the history of Western culture, with its dramatic shift from the premodern religious world view, through secular humanism and reductive materialism, to contemporary postmodern science, with its renewed interest in the sacred potentials of matter in particular and of human experience more generally. This narrative is also the story of my own life, from childhood religious belief, through intellectual enlightenment and disbelief, to present eclectic and pluralist spirituality. And this three-fold pattern is the history of Australia, from traditional Aboriginal animism, through white Australian sceptical materialism, to the present postcolonial and postmodern era where so many of us are talking about the 'spirit' of place, earth spirit, ancestral spirit, and even the spirit of things. After a relatively brief period of cultural exile, spirit has come back to haunt us, and it looks like being back to stay.

At each of the three stages in our cultural and personal journey, spirit has a different character and meaning. At the first stage, spirit is most often literal, palpable, fixed, absolute. In ancient times, people spoke about spirit, invoked the name of spirit, and built churches upon spirit, in a certain or absolutist style that will probably never again be available to any of us, except fundamentalists. The stage of tribal religions and of 'exclusivist' definitions of spirit is over. At the second stage, ushered in by intellectual enlightenment and secular humanism, spirit is viewed as illusory, fake, even delusional. Writing about the prospects for religion, Freud speaks only about the "Future of an Illusion". At this second stage, spirit is at best a sociopolitical fiction designed to make society 'work', with moral values and the bonds of community founded upon an imagined, entirely invented transcendental authority.

At the third stage, now arising from postenlightenment science and various other cultural and popular sources, spirit is real again, but a different kind of real: fluid, expansive, non-exclusive, changing, metaphorical, non-literal. But above all, spirit is alive again, and this affords us an opportunity not only to reconnect with the sacred as the basis of reality, but to reconnect with the past as well, to link up with our previously estranged and alienated premodern religious point of view. This reconnection, however, has to be carefully negotiated. It must not be a full-blown reversion to the past, for that would constitute a cultural and historical regression, and the secularists' worst fears about a sudden return of religiosity (with intolerance, bigotry, religious wars, and rivalry between competing faiths) would be realised. Religion in this third stage, based on a new experience of spirit, must recognise the sacred in all its manifestations, and renounce the time-honoured fantasy that only one religion — usually one's own — has been chosen by God and ordained from on high, and that all other religions are false or monstrous.

Our intellectual high culture is still largely caught up in the second stage, with its negative, suspicious or reductive views of spirit and its almost allergic response to organised religions. There are some so-called 'new paradigm' thinkers on every university campus, but they do not always attract attention to themselves, for fear of being dismissed as mystics or religious fanatics. The problem is that stage-two thinkers do not know how to identify, recognise or respect the third stage, and cannot distinguish between stage one and stage three, so every postmodern new-paradigm thinker is likely to be regarded by mainstream academia as a premodern mystic. This, of course, is how Jung was treated, and persecuted, by the Freudians and other intellectuals in his own day. Even today, Jung continues to be denounced as a lunatic or a mystic by those who fail to appreciate that there is a further stage of spiritual development beyond the modern condition.

But from the perspective of stage two, any talk of 'spirit' is as crazy as any other. The intellectually enlightened look down their noses at what they see as religious ignorance or superstition. According to Thomas Kuhn's analysis of 'paradigm shift', any change of mind or heart involves massive upheaval, and a new paradigm always meets considerable resistance at first. Ironically, the academic tradition of so-called 'free thinking', originally established as a critical discourse in opposition to mediaeval religiosity, has itself become a dogmatic 'church', in which the tenets and assumptions of cultural materialism are rarely examined or questioned.

In some ways, more progress can be achieved with the general public than with academia, since the public has an honest hunger for truth and is not fettered by professional prejudice or ideological obligation. Ordinary people are not card-carrying members of stage-two thinking, but are free to pick and choose as they see fit. They have already started their own separate search for meaning, dubbed the 'New Age', which is frowned upon by both academia and ecclesia, since people have started to take questions of meaning into their own hands, independent of professionals in either Church or university. If intellectuals or theologians will not take the lead in defining a new sense of spirit, then the amateurs will do it for themselves.

GOD MADE MAN AND MAN MADE GOD: THE NEW RELIGIOUS AWARENESS

At the third stage of consciousness, do we say, with stage-one thinking, that God made man, or do we say, with secular enlightenment, that man made God? I have thought about this a great deal, and my view is that we must say both at once. It is a question not of either/or but of both/and. At the stage of postenlightenment, life can be understood by way of paradox and complexity. The simple faith and fundamentalism of stage one, where God is the sole player in the making of human and social reality, must be sacrificed in the name of increased awareness and sophistication. At stage three, we take with us the knowledge and learning of stage two, where we discover that everything in society — politics, the arts, theology, culture — are human constructs or at least are conditioned by historical and psychological influences. Nothing comes to us absolutely; rather, human reality is continually refracted and filtered through the lens of time and place.

This need not imply that we have no access to ultimate truth, only that truth comes to us in culturally conditioned form, as indeed it must. In Jung's psychology, the archetypes that constitute human reality have their roots in the eternal mind, but they are always conditioned and influenced by history and society. This is simply a modern version of neo-Platonic theory, where the bases of reality are eternal and divine, but where these divine ideas cannot be known directly, only in mediated form in time and space. The immortal nuclear element gives our religious philosophies their conviction and moral authority, but the sociohistorical encasement gives them their apparently arbitrary or constructed quality, which then causes literal-minded persons and materialists to say that they are 'mere constructs', not divine revelations of an absolute truth.

Archetypal images, religions and mystical systems are absolutely relative, but they are also relatively absolute, because the field of cultural ideas and expressions is the only field through which the Unknown God can be manifest and heard. When the sacred participates in the real, it steps into history and inevitably loses its absoluteness to take on the conditions of the relative. Perhaps this is what is meant by the 'sacrifice' of the Son by the Heavenly Father; God sacrifices His life to the relativities of time and space. The sacred loses some of the blazing white light of eternity by becoming colourfully real.

In the new enchantment, we understand the cultural field as a joint cooperation of God and humanity, and social reality as a co-creation of eternity and time. The constructed nature of social reality no longer indicates the absence of God or philosophical nihilism, since we now look upon our reality in a new way and appreciate it with a new awareness. Relativity does not confirm that there is no Absolute God; rather, relativity confirms that the sacred is continually, in diverse and plural ways, incarnating itself in the real. Relativity must therefore be distinguished from relativism, in its nihilistic aspect. The French scholar Rene Girard puts it best when he says: "[we must] admit that truth can coexist with the arbitrary and perhaps even derive from it".[3] We should learn to celebrate the arbitrary and the relative, because only in this way can we know the sacred; only in this way can the divine enter the real and transform it by its radiance and truth.

God is no longer conceived as a distant powerful figure who intervenes in human affairs from 'above' or who works upon us from outside creation. Rather, God is seen as the divine presence within nature and the powerful force that works towards wholeness and holiness at the heart of human creativity. What we do in life and society not only springs from us, but the best of what we do arises from a mysterious moral force that we can refer to as God. We use the old word again to refer to our new experience of the sacred, even though for some the word 'God' is irrevocably fused with premodern thinking. But the word 'God' means different things today, since the modern period has undermined the old parental and magical image of deity. In the wake of the huge cultural depression caused by the collapse of the old God image, 'enlightened' humanity was too depressed to notice the still-small voice within, or to observe the miraculous dimension of the so-called ordinary world. We were so shaken by our new dispensation that everything seemed shockingly arbitrary and without purpose, and we concluded that there was no God. We were so appalled at the loss of the old enchantment that everything seemed shockingly ordinary, man-made and arbitrary, and we concluded that there was no sacred design or higher order. Then, after a long period of mourning and instability, we have begun to see the presence of God again, often where we least expect it and always with astonishment and surprise.

In the new enchantment, we cannot afford the fatalism of the premodern period, which often insisted that society or personality could not be changed because everything was already as it should be, any meddling representing interference with God's will. The new position, on the contrary, would recognise that social and political forces are always conditioning our reality, and that to reach the divine presence and listen to the divine voice might involve an enormous amount of shedding and deconditioning of our reality, including our religious reality.

At the beginning of the new millennium, we are almost crushed by the sheer weight of what still has to be born and discovered, what still has to emerge in our search for truth and meaning. For the time being, we are stuck with a 'spiritual' language that reminds many of an absolutist religious regime that has already passed. But the suggestive and colourful terms 'spirit', 'soul' and 'God' are still with us, and despite the unfortunate baggage they carry, they are the best terms we have for describing the realms of experience to which art, prophecy and our deepest intuitions continue to point.

2

Australians in Search of Soul

WHAT IS SOUL?

What is soul? According to the perennial philosophy that modernity has rejected but which will return as we recover our wisdom tradition, soul is the middle term between the body and the spirit. A neo-Platonic scholar writes that "Soul is the intermediary between the Nous (mind of God) and the sensible universe".[1] The human being consists of body (in Greek, *soma*), soul (*psyche*), and spirit (*pneuma*), and soul is vitally important in bringing all three into working relationship and, thus, in bringing about wholeness of character and society. The Western myth tradition often imagines the soul as a golden bowl, chalice or cup, and the soul could be conceived as a container or vessel of the spirit, or that part of the person which captures the divine essence and gives it residence and embodiment. In our modern-day sports culture, the winner's cup or trophy is the contemporary reminder of the sacred vessel or soul-container that symbolises the spiritual boon bestowed upon those who excel at the game of life. The winner's cup symbolically represents the elusive soul that gives spiritual meaning to life. In psychological terms, soul is personality and creativity, the dynamic life within, inspiring the body and giving purpose and direction to our actions. Without soul, the body lacks animation and the spirit remains remote, otherworldly and beyond our reach.

CULTURE AS SOCIAL DREAMING

For human society, soul can be broadly summed up as 'culture'. Culture is our social dreaming, our way of reflecting and embodying the imaginal life of the community. Culture is also the way in which a society reflects its own meaning and direction, its sense of belonging to a specific time and geophysical place, and its belonging to eternity and the sacred. There is always a religious dimension to any living culture, because culture has to grapple with the big questions, which are invariably theological: what is the purpose of life? what is my place in the scheme of things? what is the point of human community? what should community serve? These questions can be successfully answered only if society discovers a primary Other world before which it can orient itself and beside which it can find its own secondary or relational role. It is only when society imagines itself to be the primary reality, the master rather than the student of life, that things can go horribly wrong and our humanity can become demonic.

The discovery of an objective sacred presence is the beginning of all culture and the foundation of all human ethics and personal morality. This objective essence gives us our self-definitions, our self-descriptions, our values and our visions. But this objective essence cannot be formulated by any one individual; it requires time, history and tradition. Moreover, this sacred presence has to be reformulated and rediscovered over and over again, so that it is constantly made new in human society. This is the true work of culture, which grounds the reality of spirit in the embodied life of the community.

In this sense, a society with fine arts and crafts is not necessarily a society with culture, especially if the arts do not affect the everyday lives of ordinary people, remaining above or outside the normal range of experience. Culture involves aesthetic awareness and beauty, but it is more than mere aesthetics: it is beauty with soul, or form with spiritual content. In Aboriginal philosophy, culture is the social and aesthetic embodiment of traditional dreamings and religious values. It is almost synonymous with religion, but it is wider and broader than religion, since 'culture' includes many ordinary and everyday things that would not necessarily be designated as religious. A person with culture is a person with ceremony, song, ritual, but also a person who has a sense of deep spiritual orientation in ordinary life and common activities. This orientation gives direction and meaning (soul), but also integrity and authenticity (human worth).

WHITE MAN GOT NO DREAMING

Outside us, society functions in an external way, its collective eye does not know interiority, it sees only through the lens of image, impression and function.

— *JOHN O'DONOHUE*[2]

While growing up in central Australia, Aboriginal people often asked me whether white society had any culture. They could not see much evidence of culture (as they defined it), and asked whether it was more apparent to those inside white society. At first, I was unsure how to respond to this, but gradually it dawned on me that these Aboriginal people were asking whether we had any living spirituality, any cosmology that gave bearing to our lives and larger design to our individual activities. While some of us were 'cultured', in a narrow sense, as a result of education or class privilege, we did not 'have culture' in the cosmological sense to which the Aboriginals alluded. I indicated that some of us followed Christianity, but church attendance hardly constitutes living in a spiritual cosmology. Perhaps, I reflected, Christian religion meant something infinitely more in the past, and presently we were witnessing Christianity in a weak and ineffectual phase. Reluctantly, I had to conclude, especially in view of the commercial greed and shallowness of white society and its obsession with material acquisitions, that we did not have any culture in the Aboriginal sense of the term.

I think white Australians would agree more readily today with the Aboriginal accusation that we have no spiritual culture. As a nation, we have concentrated on the development of the material level of reality, striving to meet the physical needs of our bodies. The soul appears to have been left out of our calculations, at least publicly and officially. In the encounter between Europeans and Aboriginals, we discover a meeting between a European society that is high in technology but low in spirit and an Aboriginal society high in spirit but low in technology. This encounter will radically change and transform both societies. Aboriginal society will be changed forever by advanced technology, while European Australia will be constantly reminded of its own spiritual impoverishment and lack of soul.

In recent times in Australia, a standard remark or quip was to say that the nation's capital, Canberra, had 'no soul'. The implication was that Canberra seemed artificial, lifeless, unrelated to the ground beneath it, lacking in history, human community, organic vitality or spiritual direction. We are now having to admit that much of white Australia suffers from the Canberra complex: it lacks soul, interiority and depth. What once we projected onto Canberra we now must accept as a metaphorical state for all of Australia, with all our towns and cities simply the outer suburbs of a chronically soulless nation, driven by bureaucracy, rationalist economics and materialism.

We have an enormous challenge to meet: how to re-enchant our disenchanted secular society. The first signs of re-enchantment are already upon us. There is the realisation of our spiritual emptiness beside the spiritual richness of traditional Aboriginal culture, even though that culture has been seriously damaged by its encounter with the colonisers. But even in its brokenness, and especially in its recent attempts at cultural renaissance, Aboriginality remains a symbol of spirituality in the Australian mind. A further sign of re-enchantment, or perhaps a precondition for our nascent search for re-enchantment, is our relatively recent sense of being unfulfilled by our materialistic lifestyles. More and more Australians are realising that life is not as rewarding as they have typically asserted it to be. Our generally glib exterior, which asserts that everything is fine and 'she'll be right', is being challenged by a new desire for deepening and interiority. The 'lucky country' seems to be running out of luck, or maybe it is just discovering that there is a greater fortune to be had. As more people realise that they have been living on the surface of life, they will begin the search for a missing richness, which is characterised by such words as 'soul' and 'spirit'.

BRINGING DEPTH TO THE SURFACE

We Australians have been skating around on the surface of life for some time, and cracks are beginning to appear in what we thought was our solid psychological and social earth. Some people are falling into the cracks and being forced to explore the depths below, often leading to painful but transformative confrontations with the sacred. The habitual surfaces of life are being exposed as thin and fragile, and as incapable of supporting us in the old way. Or is it, perhaps, that the depths have come up to the surface, disrupting the layers of social conditioning that have repressed the sacred for so long in Australian public life?[3]

It is typical of the human personality, especially in a secular and emotionally defended culture like ours, to resist the reality of the soul and its call to the depths. Hence, a great many people will vehemently deny my assertion, that life as it is currently lived is not as rewarding as we claim it to be. In the past, some reviewers of my work have accused me of projecting my personal dissatisfactions upon other Australians, claiming that the majority are profoundly happy with their lot. But the soaring suicide figures suggest otherwise, as do the alarming statistics relating to depression in our society, and also the growing interest in spiritual exploration. Our denial of this restlessness and dissatisfaction arises from the sophisticated defence mechanisms of the habitual ego. The rational ego wants to protect the status quo, seeking to avoid the challenge of spiritual change and transformation. It clings to and defends what it knows.

The human ego at first views the soul and its depths as the enemy and antagonist of life, since the ego cannot see how those depths could actually support and sustain it. However, once the ego acquires maturity and wisdom, it recognises that its own life is completely dependent on a greater, invisible or symbolic life, and that recognition and acceptance of this dependence is a sign of high culture and awareness. The infantile ego that is bound up in itself views the soul as absurd, an embarrassment, but the mature ego realises its indebtedness to a mysterious hidden source.

The ego is part of a much larger energic and spiritual system, and its life is bestowed upon it by that larger system. Therefore, even for very practical reasons, it is wise for the ego to develop an ongoing relationship with its source and creator. This relationship could be described as *sacramental*, because the ego must learn to sacrifice aspects of itself to the larger reality, which in turn replenishes and renews the ego. The ego and the soul are interdependent: the soul needs the ego for the outward living of its life and for the incarnational expression of its spiritual essence, while the ego needs the soul for its energy, its passion, indeed its very existence.

The ego also needs the soul for direction and meaning. Without the support of the soul, the ego cannot know what its activity is for, or what it means. The busy ego can suddenly be arrested in its tracks, or paralysed by meaninglessness, if it does not feel that its effort and toil relates to a larger good and is somehow validated by an authority beyond itself. As in the experience of the individual, so too in the experience of the nation — a 'life crisis' can overtake us, rendering life directionless until various realities have been confronted and dealt with. In moments such as these, the ego, in its suffering and pain, realises that it is not the master of the house, that larger realities are at work and in control of us, and that it is not until these larger forces are propitiated or served that life is able to move forward in its natural course. The surface of life will not be restored until links have been (re)established with the depths. I think this is why so many Australians, especially young Australians, are talking about the need for spirituality today, and why we are looking for a new orientation and purpose.

THE HISTORICAL CONTEXT FOR SPIRITUAL HUNGER

Why has this new quest or hunger come about? What has happened, socially and culturally, to bring about this spiritual crisis? I think many people feel that we are running on empty, our spiritual fuel gauge having registered 'low' for some time. Warning signals are evident in all walks of life: depression is now so prevalent that some one in five Australians suffers acute or chronic, often undiagnosed depression. We read of mid-career professionals with chronic fatigue syndrome, unable to continue in their chosen careers because there is nothing left in their energy reserves. We find young adults, even teenagers suffering from burnout and exhaustion. Their burnout is not merely personal, because they have hardly had the chance to become exhausted; rather, their exhaustion is transpersonal — they are suffering the loss of energy felt by the collective soul, and are registering this loss in a personal way.

These problems are not just personal health problems but are also expressions of the psychic health or spiritual illness of the entire community. When depression and fatigue reach epidemic proportions, we know that our psychic energy has become alarmingly depleted. Journeys into the deep unconscious to recover this elixir of life are spiritual journeys, rightly regarded as heroic, dangerous and vitally important.

Our spiritual energy will not be recovered until we have had serious public discussions about the values and visions that can give life purpose and meaning. We will need then to develop rituals and spiritual exercises to ensure that the culture is renewed, and keeps on renewing itself, through its reconnection with the archetypal forces. As I have argued, the human ego needs to feel that it is working for, and supported by, a higher good or some greater authority. It needs to believe that there are visions and values worth living for and, in times of social emergency, worth dying for.

In the past, these visions and values were supplied by church or state or workplace, and included such key ideas as freedom, democracy and equality; political destiny and contribution to the common good; right action and morality; and spiritual reconciliation with the divine creator. Moreover, these motivational values have been inspired not only by the secular state or the religious institution but also by the institution of the family, whether extended or nuclear, which has served as a vessel for a greater authority. If the job was difficult and the pay lousy, the average person could console themselves with the thought that everything was somehow justified by his or her contribution to the family, or the common good or the church or the state.

But as we know, the great institutions of society have been profoundly shaken by recent history, and today, a great deal of public cynicism attends to our perception of these institutions. National politics is felt to be mean and petty, motivated largely by the personal ambitions of flawed and all-too-human politicians. The nation's politicians are felt to be without vision or purpose, and this means that they, and their governments, cannot represent a higher authority that inspires faith or commitment in its citizens. The churches have faced an even more radical loss of public confidence. The overwhelming majority of Australians find the churches unappealing and irrelevant, because the churches do not speak a language that the modern world can understand. Many people have begun to separate the very concept of 'spirituality' from the structures of organised religion. In the arena of business and industry, managers, financiers and entrepreneurs are often viewed with considerable caution or suspicion, since they are felt to place their own commercial concerns before those of their clients. The family unit is no longer infused with spiritual meaning, and while the extended family has largely been dissolved by changing social conditions, the nuclear family today is no 'safe haven', often representing a battleground for the expression of competing ambitions, personal desires and, sometimes, aggression. In today's world, virtually nothing has remained immune from the disillusioning forces of modernity; nothing has escaped the appearance of being arbitrary, contrived, and corrupted by egotism or human vice.

I think this provides the wider social and cultural collapse that has inspired the spiritual searching of our time. We are urged to discover new sources for spiritual idealism, since the old cultural forms can no longer contain the authority of the sacred for us. Our advanced state of disenchantment is, perhaps paradoxically, bringing about a desperate search for re-enchantment. This search will give rise to new and original meanings, and cultural revival will be imminent as we search in the mythic underworld for the lost elixir of life. Certainly, our institutions need to be renewed, and our human community revived, by reducing our egotism and reconnecting with values that lead us beyond our material desires to a larger and purer source. But meanwhile, our culture is depressed, and we must follow this depression down into the psychic depths, below the surface of our normal lives.

LEARNING THE ART OF SACRIFICE

To recover the lost vision or integrity will involve us in what psychotherapy calls introspection and reflection and in what religion calls *sacrifice*. To go where the depression points means that we can no longer go where the ego wants us to go. This leads inevitably to quiet brooding, to careful consideration of our situation, and to contemplation. There will be a marked need to sacrifice elements of our habitual world for the sake of spiritual integrity and growth. But how are we to best conduct the necessary sacrifices?

In the past, in times of social crisis and uncertain public direction, we conducted sacrifices in foreign theatres of war, and those sacrifices were so important to the life and identity of the nation that Australian history marks our very coming of age from adolescent colony to mature nation by reference to these wars. In every city, town or village in Australia, we have erected public shrines to the men and women who gave their lives for national ideals and inspirational values. We respect and celebrate the fact that men and women shed blood in the service and establishment of these values. In other words, their deaths and sacrifices have *made sacred* these national values, and even though Australia is a basically secular society, it freely recognises and salutes the religious dimension of war sacrifice.

It is astonishing, actually, how freely and willingly the secular nation engages in the religious dimension of war experience, although it is questionable whether this religiousness is Christian. It seems to me to be a kind of pagan religiosity, or a secular version of Mithraism, that militaristic religion much favoured by the Roman legions and other ancient men of war. Australian militarism is governed by the archetypal image of the young male hero involved in a rite of passage into manhood, and whose war effort leads not only to his own assured manhood but also to the masculine stability of his nation. If the young hero is killed in action, he immediately becomes enshrined as a mythic hero, who sheds his blood so that the gods might be propitiated and the sun might rise again the following morning. This folk or civic religion is martial, secular, heroic, sacrificial, and deeply embedded in the national psyche of Australia, especially in the culture of masculinity.

Some are saying that at this point in time, we need another war; another war will clear our heads and set the ship of state back on its course. While it is true that we need to perform a sacrifice, it is by no means the case that we need another war. In any case, Vietnam taught us that war experience is no longer a valid rite of passage for Australia or for the young men who go away to fight. Educated opinion has shifted against war experience, and rightly so. We must not rely on killing and destruction to set us right with the sacred, nor use the blood sacrifice of young soldiers to recover our relationship with the forces of the cosmos. Although war is a convenient precedent, and although we have an entire military industry to support and underwrite this archetypal procedure, we must not be seduced into this dangerous pattern. Australian culture, which has been predominantly patriarchal, has not yet shown that it is capable of styles of sacrifice that take place outside the familiar militaristic mode. The kind of sacrifices that we need at present are not macho-heroic but delicate, sensitive and reflective. We need to sacrifice much of our robust and secular exterior so that soulful depth and spiritual interiority can be attained. We do not need more of the ANZAC myth. Rather, we require more poetry and wisdom, so that our national character can become more expansive and inclusive. Moreover, our sacrifices need to be conducted at home, not just in foreign theatres of war.

One major public sacrifice, which is not at all popular in our colonialist, land-grabbing society, is to return land, dignity and value to the much-maligned Aboriginal people. This crucial sacrifice is one that many Australians are resisting, but resistance is futile, because we will never achieve peace in this land until these colossal wrongs have been addressed. Another, very much related sacrifice involves restoring dignity and respect to the land itself. Instead of taking greedily from the land to support our short-term consumerism, we must start to think of the land itself as a living subject, a sensitive ecological reality with its own needs and demands. We are called by historical and environmental realities to renounce our ego-centredness for an *ecocentric* view of the world. We have to sacrifice our mastery and conquest of nature for a new attitude based on holism, relationship and cooperation. This sacrifice would ensure not only the health and integrity of the environment, but also our own long-term human survival in a living green world.

On another level, we must sacrifice to the soul itself, and return value, integrity and meaning to the interior reality. What on earth is soul? asks the official Australian persona. But the silent and deep Australian heart knows about the soul, and it knows how to answer this question. Soul is the centre of the human person, the centre of authenticity and meaning. Soul is the container of the spirit, the dwelling place where spirit is received from the cosmos and integrated into our own individual lives. We must learn to honour the soul in our personal, social and political lives, because this is the level from which purpose, meaning and self-esteem comes. It is not enough just to 'have' soul; we must also recognise it, activate it or, to borrow from Aboriginal culture, 'sing it up', so that it can flow freely towards us, just as we learn to maintain and restore its life.

SUBVERSIVE AND UNCONVENTIONAL SPIRITUALITY

But if it is true that the ruling Australian consciousness has run out of energy and ideas, and that the only path to renewal is a 'recovery of soul' through acts of sacrifice and vision, how will our secular society see the wisdom of such recovery and begin to seek it out? The workaday mind will probably reject recovery of soul as regression, weakness, futility. There is no guarantee, finally, that a secular society will willingly engage in what are, after all, religious acts of sacrifice. I think this is one reason why our so-called 'secular' society is in the process of transforming itself. It realises, in its inarticulate depths, that there is no future in secularism, and it is changing its own character to prepare for the ritual atonements that must take place.

On the face of it, changing a secular society into a spiritual community would seem most unlikely, perhaps even impossible. It would be impossible if the official persona of the nation were the only real dimension of the national being. But there is much more below the surface, and it is here that change is taking place. Structural change can and does take place without the ruling ego's consent. Australia is experiencing what can only be described as a grassroots spiritual renewal, and this is occurring quite spontaneously, without institutional guidance or governmental support. In fact, the major institutions, whether we turn to church, state, education, health or law, are considerably wary of this spiritual revival, in some cases decidedly opposed to it. But the renewal is happening anyway; it is not asking for approval from the ruling institutions, but is realising itself in spite of them.

Key features of the new Australian spirituality would include its uncertain and obscure nature. It is not too sure of itself, and it does not yet know what to make of itself, because it is not getting any affirmative mirroring from mainstream public society. It is also fragmentary, individualistic and personal, since there are as yet hardly any collective identifications to which it can be attached. Because the public life continues to be governed by an opposite kind of authority, spirituality is operating mainly in the personal arena, where there are fewer resistances to the reality and claims of the sacred. Secretly and subversively, the secular society is being undermined from within, like some kind of communist plot of the spirit destined to undermine the rapacious capitalist system.

This psychodynamic movement helps to explain why so much Australian spirituality is unconventional and eccentric. After reading my book *Edge of the Sacred*, a cleric telephoned me to ask why the new spirituality in Australia was not putting bums on pews. It is often difficult for churches to imagine that they do not have a monopoly on the sacred, and when they see a spiritual revival taking place just at the point where churchgoers' numbers are rapidly declining, this is a serious blow to morale and credibility. But the new Australian spirituality is actually a protest movement against the established national ego, and anything directly connected with the social establishment, including the traditional churches, will be rejected in favour of a far more radical style of spirituality. Perhaps this is one reason why the new churches, such as the apostolic and charismatic, are thriving, while the traditional churches continue on a downward trend. Moreover, Buddhism, Hinduism and Islam are finding many new followers in Australia, and this may be part of the same pattern of search for a radical spiritual style. Buddhism, at last count, is the fastest-growing religion in Australia.

Another key feature of the new spirituality is that it is not intellectual or verbose, because the new psychodynamic need is to find an outlet for those parts of the spirit that are not nourished or fulfilled by the rationalistic consciousness of the nation. Therefore, churches that practise silent meditation seem to be faring well, while the Eastern ashrams teaching yoga, contemplation and spiritual exercises are filling up with defectors from the conventional churches. Catholicism has declined, but it maintains its reduced ground, partly because of the strong emphasis on ritual and sacrament, which feeds the hunger of the spirit. But any church that appears too rational or verbal and whose image of God is too familiar, such as the low Anglican and Protestant churches, is suffering greatly, and may be utterly destroyed by the new Australian preference for mystery and ritual.

Australians will not attend churches simply because they need the support and the funding, and one of the authentic features of the new spirituality is that it will service the spiritual and emotional needs first and the institutional requirements second or not at all. The Anglican Archbishop of Brisbane, Peter Hollingworth, recently reflected on the spiritual problem of Australia:

Everywhere one goes there are vast numbers of people who have been through Christian traditions and who

*have said 'not for me, it is too narrow, the framework
is not enough for me to tell the story of my life. The
analogies and the metaphors are too constricting and
restricting, and I will do it myself in some other way'.
Our churches are pretty empty and they are not likely
to break new ground unless we do something about
addressing what is a very real issue for the post
modern generation.*[4]

It is a sign of the realism and integrity of the church
that it is able to face these issues with unsentimental
directness. But we are realising in Australia what historians of culture have always known: that spirituality is
a larger social category than formal religion, and the
decline in formal religious practice tells us very little
about the spiritual interests and preoccupations of the
Australian people, apart from the fact that these interests
are not being pursued in conventional ways.

With regular church attendance in Australia down to
between seven and twelve per cent of the population,
and with so many people following personal views and
experiences of spirituality, it would seem to me that
secular spirituality is a powerful religious force in this
country, perhaps even the religion of the silent majority.
But how can it be quantified or surveyed when most
institutions fail even to recognise its existence? There is
an enormous amount of searching going on, and I do
not think the decline of religious institutions should
make us believe that there is a reduction in religious
feeling or intensity in this country. As I have intimated,
our 'secularism' is probably the greatest illusion of all;
it is a bland category concealing more than it describes.
With the introduction of the category 'secular
spirituality', we problematise the very basis of Australian
society, revealing the paradoxes and inconsistencies
found at its heart.

Publicly and officially, Australia has performed very poorly in the spirituality stakes. Our churches are based on cultures of belief and devotion, not spirituality, and they have mostly discouraged, rather than made possible, individual experiences of the sacred. It would seem to me that experimentation in the spiritual realm, not just 'receiving' conventional church dogma, would suit the temperament and enthusiasms of Australians. Also, religious institutions here have been very slow to adapt themselves to the reality of Australia. Our society has relied for too long on the soul that was imported here from Europe and other foreign places. Our churches are the Church of England in Australia, the Church of Rome in Australia or the Church of Salt Lake City in Australia. Where is the Church of Australia? Interestingly enough, the Australian Constitution actually forbids the establishment of a national church, sensing perhaps an improper marriage of church and state and fearing systemic intolerance, religious prejudice and spiritual monopoly. This ban may have started with a noble intention, but if it ends up denying this country its public spiritual life, then it may have backfired.

Where is the evidence that Australia has grappled in its own way and in its own unique style with the great eternal questions of life, death and redemption? Where is the Australian imprint on our experience of the infinite? Nietzsche wrote that a people is worth only as much as it is able to "press upon its experiences the stamp of the eternal".[5] Placing some images of wattle or kookaburras in a few Christian hymns does not seem quite enough, and for too long this is all that some churches have contributed to the massive task of 'enculturation'. We require more than local decoration of universal religious images; rather, the universal must be made to appear local if we are to develop a truly indigenous spirituality.

The living spirit must be encountered and realised in this time and place; otherwise, our rituals are hollow, or at best allegorical, performed much better in the more impressive architectural structures of Europe.

In our mainstream secular life, we continue to be plagued by a chronic and ongoing identity crisis. At times, we panic about who and what we are, because we realise that our roots are superficial; we do not draw from the powerful forces deep within ourselves or within this landscape. Regularly, our state and federal governments, the tourism industry, media, film-makers, writers and others decide to conduct confidence-boosting drives to fill our psychological vacuum. During 'nation-building' events such as the 1988 Bicentennial Year or sporting festivals such as the Sydney 2000 Olympics, we set to work to tell ourselves who and what we are, what the Australian loves most of all and what constitutes Australian-ness. We decide to elevate this or that aspect of the Australian experience to iconographic status, and to focus on it with prayerful attention, whether it be the beach, the bush, the barbeque or the football. But when the hype is over and we wake up the next morning, we are left with the familiar emptiness and quiet despair. We have forgotten who we decided we were.

Our national self-images and identities are short term and ineffective precisely because they are merely secular and materialistic. Unless we forge an identity for ourselves at a much deeper level, this identity crisis will keep coming back to haunt us. I firmly believe that the question 'who are we?' or 'who am I?' is not just the ego's question — it is the soul's question. The soul in us, repressed by materialism, keeps disrupting the surface of life, asking us to tell it who we are. Understandably, we get sick of this emotional disruption, and Australians notoriously make fun of our own identity crisis. This is our intellectual defence against the calling of the soul, which continues to gnaw away at us from within.

Many people believe that turning ourselves into a republic will solve our identity crisis. The republic may represent a logical development of our political evolution, and it may provide sharper focus to our social and economic identity. But it will not automatically solve our deeper emotional and spiritual problems. Indeed, if we do not build a republic with vision and meaning, it could well represent the spread and triumph of the profane bureaucratic rationality that our spiritual development is seeking to displace. Only if the republican idea contains mystery, grandeur and a decolonised understanding of place could it provide dimension and life to the soul. Moreover, no colonised country can ever achieve spiritual integrity until the wrongs of colonialism have been addressed, so that a republic not based on racial reconciliation would represent a mere technical arrangement and would not educate the soul of the nation. As yet, we have no idea what the republic stands for or what its deeper message would be. As Dennis Altman has said, "republicans need to tell Australia exactly why we should change the present structures, and what symbols of nationhood are available to replace the monarchy".[6]

It might be too much to expect that a secular country will publicly enshrine a spirituality in its idea or model of a republic, but it is not too much to expect that our republic will be morally sound and imbued with a postcolonial ethic. Certainly, the republican idea itself can evolve into deeper and more profound realities, so that once the republic of politics is in place, we can then work towards the construction of a republic of the spirit. We must have symbolism of a cosmic or transpersonal kind, and we must add public depth and dimension to our lives. We must try for a new dreaming, a new cosmology, a new pact with the invisible forces that move through and beyond us. Australian society needs something more than common sense and rational economic goals to make it work.

Until we discover collective and effective modes of spirituality, the burden of this spirituality will fall to the individual level, and this can present real dangers to those sensitive individuals who absorb this archetypal imperative and feel compelled to live it out. Every so often, individual Australians lose their bearings. Sometimes we can't shake this madness off; it clings to us for the rest of our lives, destroying our normality and our social adaptation. Sometimes, if we find support from friends, books or intuitions, we can convert the madness into a spiritual journey and go in search of our true selves. Years ago, there was little public tolerance for this kind of activity, and it was frowned upon as an antisocial indulgence. Today, we still find some formal protest or resistance, but it is softened by curiosity and interest. So-and-so is doing their own thing, and if it doesn't infringe upon anyone else's freedom, let them go for it.

Often, people on personal journeys become involved in the arts, crafts and creative activities, because they wish to begin a dialogue with the non-rational side of life, for which they need to find some channel or expression. The spiritual or artistic quest may be long or short, protracted or brief, and during this experience, the person will be hunting around in new and unfamiliar territories, looking for clues, hunches and guiding images. Not all of these people end up in religious groups, whether old age or New Age, but most of them will experiment with some kind of community of faith.

But there are increasing numbers of Australians who do not voluntarily court depth but who involuntarily fall into it. Our soaring suicide figures indicate that significant numbers of lives are shattered by experiences that have not been integrated. Some people are dragged down, subdued into depth, often with no apparent cause or reason. In mythological language, we think of the innocent Persephone, who was picking flowers in a meadow when suddenly seized and abducted by Hades, god of the underworld. Sometimes, the ground beneath our feet appears to open up, exposing a terrible abyss. Often, the more we cling to surfaces and insist on our innocence, the more violently we are drawn into the strange, eternal realm that seems to underpin our own.

The surface of our lives can be punctured by the death of a relative or friend. Suddenly, our familiar world can be turned upside down and we have to make for ourselves a whole new world. An intimate relationship crumbles, the marriage falls apart, the kids get into dangerous activities, and chaos seems to break loose. Depression is nothing if not a call from the underworld. Also, chronic fatigue, *ennui*, burnout, neurosis, and various kinds of physical sickness — these are, as it were, the 'left-handed' path into depth and potential spiritual growth.

Medical science struggles valiantly to find 'real' causes, an organic basis for all our neurotic illnesses and maladies. The media like to announce the discovery of scientific bases for chronic fatigue syndrome or repetitive strain injury, for instance, claiming that "this illness is not merely mental, after all". I smile every time I hear this sort of announcement. 'Merely' mental? Our culture continues to arrogantly underestimate the value and importance of mental life, and no-one wants to be stigmatised with a mental illness. Such an illness does not 'really' exist. The patient is making it up. Continuing to deny the reality of the mental, psychological or spiritual dimension makes our science hopelessly inadequate, especially as the culture as a whole acknowledges its need to shift towards a more holistic, sacred orientation.

But the impact of tragic events and suffering forces us to become more aware of who and what we are; they force on us a deeper reflection and a kind of existential spirituality. The gifted artist Michael Leunig has explored this situational spirituality in his poem 'The Common Cold':

> *God bless those who suffer from the common cold.*
> *Nature has entered into them;*
> *Has led them aside and gently laid them low*
> *To contemplate life from the wayside;*
> *To consider human frailty;*
> *To receive the deep and dreamy messages of fever.*
> *We give thanks for the insights of this humble perspective.*
> *We give thanks for blessings in disguise. Amen.*[7]

This captures succinctly the prayerful moments of reflection that arise when we are felled by the experience of illness. And if we are wise, this spiritual feeling will last beyond the period of crisis or turmoil, so that we carry a sense of our deeper selves with us into the surface world when we are allowed to return to it. Life is fuller then, larger, and we walk around not just as skin-encased egos but as beings who participate in a great and mysterious cosmos.

Jung argued that, according to his own experience, no-one finds a lasting resolution to any neurotic condition or real suffering without achieving a new sense of personal and social identity, and this new identity invariably involves a profound readjustment towards the sacred, the divine and extrahuman reality. It is as if, until we find our true relationship with the sacred, we have no real bearings and no orientation that allows us to endure suffering or realise its spiritual value. We must not, of course, make a negative cult out of suffering, so that we come to indulge the condition of suffering and become neurotically fixated upon it. There is, in fact, a grave danger of romanticising our pathologies. For instance, I have heard people report their misfortunes — a broken leg, a nervous breakdown, chronic fatigue — with a good deal of personal pride, as if at last they have been visited by the gods.

The real challenge is to bring relevations from the depth dimension back up to the surface, using them to transform the habitual, the everyday. It is relatively easy to be 'deep' when afflicted, much more difficult when we are healthy. In other words, we have to learn to exchange painful and involuntary deepening for voluntary self-sacrifice, devotion and religious awareness. Mahatma Gandhi's wisdom remains sobering today: "Suffering is the one indispensable condition of our being. But the purer the suffering the greater the progress".

It is my firm belief that if Australian society as a whole can recover a sense of depth and forge some effective link with the sacred, fewer individuals will have to fall into, or be painfully sacrificed to, the depth dimension. There is an inverse relationship between the amount of superficiality and surface in a society and the number of those who will have to fall into the deep end and possibly drown. This is simply to say that the healthier the society, the healthier the individuals in it. However, change must necessarily affect individuals before it influences society at large, since society is, as Jung has said, "merely the sum total of individuals in need of redemption".[8] Only when enough genuinely contemporary individuals have made creative contact with the spirit of the time will Australian society be able to achieve a spiritual integrity and find its moral, social and religious direction.

FALLING IN THE MUD AT CASTLE HILL

Like many Australians, Patrick White could not readily digest the spiritual claims of the Church and felt ambivalent about any organised religion. By the time he was a teenager, he had dismissed religion as intellectually implausible and emotionally irrelevant. He felt this way until his own encounter with the sacred. This experience shattered his cocoon of reason and defiance, making him much more receptive to the claims of religion, though it did not necessarily reconcile him to the historical church.

White's encounter with the sacred has nothing conventional or sentimental about it. It is a genuine, direct, mystical encounter. This is the positive side to Australian spiritual experience, and something of which we can be justly proud. That is to say, when the sacred is finally contacted, there is nothing artificial, impure or pretentious about the encounter. The experience is not tainted by artifice or human design, and there is nothing fraudulent or showy. Mostly, the Australian who actually encounters the divine does not seek the experience. It happens, and all the individual can do is surrender to the greater power that has arisen. Our secular tastes and attitudes clear away all unnecessary encumbrances, paving the way for a direct and often shattering revelation of the divine. In this light, the Australian antireligious temperament can be viewed almost as a kind of radical Protestantism, an attack on religious orthodoxy, a resistance to authority, a clearing away of icons, not to get rid of God but to know God more directly. Australians have unwittingly set the scene for a dramatic incursion of the sacred into their lives.

Patrick White was forced to experience this personally: "One day when I fell on my back in the mud at Castle Hill, I started cursing a God I had convinced myself did not exist". "This was the turning point", White wrote in *Flaws in the Glass*. "My disbelief appeared as farcical as my fall. At that moment I was truly humbled".[9] After that event, White realised that he had to develop a religious framework for his life. He and his partner, Manoly Lascaris, attempted to return to the Church of England, Patrick's natal faith. However, this was 1950s Australia, and White was a homosexual who felt sorely rejected and judged by the church. He wrote that he "could not accept the sterility, the vulgarity, and in many cases the bigotry of the Christian churches in Australia".[10]

White believed he had been struck by the living spirit, whereas the church seemed to him to be preaching a simple gospel of faith that knew nothing of the power of the living God. White gradually withdrew from the church, and then found Jung, whose works had been given to him by another Australian artist, Lawrence Daws. Jung's thesis, which is ideally suited to Australian social conditions, is that the living spirit has fallen out of religious high culture and into the soul of the individual, where it has to be rediscovered and encountered anew. With Jung's support, and with eclectic interests in Jewish mysticism and Zen Buddhism, White conducted an internal, personal quest for the sacred. Manoly Lascaris, meanwhile, had returned to the Eastern Orthodox Church, dismissing White's individual spiritual quest as a "non-religious or mystic circus".[11]

White's personal experience may well prove to be paradigmatic for a future Australian culture. More Australians are falling on their backs in the mud, and cursing a God they had convinced themselves did not exist. And, like Patrick White, most do not know exactly what to do about it. Some are attempting to return to the churches they associate with childhood, slinking back into those ancient buildings like prodigal sons and daughters. Some are turning to Jung for psychological and spiritual guidance during periods of intense personal crisis. Some are developing Eastern meditation practices or esoteric spiritual disciplines. Some are turning gnostic or mystic, theosophist or Christian scientist, while others are going back to nature, celebrating the earth spirit and going wild. Some are joining fundamentalist churches, becoming involved in the charismatic movement, or following occultism, astrology, spiritual feminism, the mythopoetic men's movement, and a host of other philosophies, cults and beliefs. Manoly Lascaris is right: those of us who do not enjoy the security and solidity of an established church are engaged in a mystic circus, which encompasses much more than the so-called 'New Age'. What our contemporary experience reveals, if nothing else, is that the old tired notion of the 'typical Aussie' as a practical person who despises religion and practises a kind of bush scepticism has finally been laid to rest.

Nevertheless, the return of the sacred into our lives is a potentially disorienting experience that can actually unbalance society and throw us into temporary madness. My worry is that unless we work through this historical situation with care and concern, the specifically Australian nature of our religious experience will be lost. A religious spark has been rekindled in Australians, but how are we to tell the genuine spark from all the New Age fires currently burning in our towns and cities, fires kindled originally in California? The truth is, we are completely unprepared for the spiritual renaissance that is upon us. This is understandable, if somewhat lamentable. Who could have predicted fifty years ago, when White fell on his back in the mud, that his fellow Australians would soon be following him in exploring non-traditional forms of the sacred, embarking on a mystic circus? Why is there not more widespread concern about the spiritual health of the Australian nation? Where are the teams of committed researchers looking into this problem?

3

In Defiance of the Sacred

> *Practical. It is the word they use in Sydney when they wish to do something damaging to the spirit ... It is a word dull men use when they wish to hide the poverty of their imagination.*
>
> — PETER CAREY[1]

This chapter ponders national and cultural issues surrounding our relationship with the sacred. It asks whether Australia, as a nation or as a cultural identity, can become spiritually mature and responsible, or whether it must always shrug off the big spiritual questions, forcing its individual citizens to embark, often unaided and without support, on personal and existential journeys in search of meaning. Obviously, we need cultural and national solutions to our spiritual problems, but these solutions do not appear to be forthcoming. What forces or factors are blocking our spiritual growth, and why does Australia's public or official identity (despite what goes on beneath it) remain stubbornly secular and defiantly non-religious?[2]

In its social persona and outward political mask, Australia is brazenly secular, pragmatic, disbelieving. At this level, Australians live life as if material reality is all, forgetting both the meaning of religion and our responsibility towards the divine ground of our being. We Australians even boast about our secularity, our freedom from divine authority, our ability to live only from the conscious and deliberate human will. Our philosophy of life appears to be summed up in the popular saying: "Where there's a will, there's a way", a testimony to secular humanism. Our secular persona is much admired and ardently revered, perhaps virtually worshipped. Indeed, contemporary secularism makes a quasi-religion from its adherence to the values of the human ego and its concept of social progress.

The 'bottom line' economic policies adopted in Australia over recent years constitute a low-level form of religious fundamentalism. These policies, which have been called 'economic rationalism', are ardently supported, rarely questioned, and viewed as self-evidently and incontestably true. Many human values and community needs must be 'sacrificed' to them. Economic rationalism is a hungry and irrational god that demands more and more sacrifices from us. Even in the most secular and disbelieving of societies, the religious impulse can never be expunged; it keeps making an appearance in various political forms and social guises, often enslaving us to this or that ideology because we have been unable to find an official or acceptable outlet for our instinctual religious urge towards service and sacrifice. If we do not sacrifice to the sacred, we find ourselves involuntarily sacrificing to the false, idolatrous gods of modernity, of which 'economic rationalism' is a prime example. It thus becomes a form of social 'irrationalism' in that we can neither critique this system nor remove ourselves from its fascination.

But our secular persona requires constant grooming, maintenance and support lest it becomes obvious that, far from being free of the imperatives of the sacred, we in fact remain under the sway of powerful irrational forces. We must keep reminding ourselves that we are a free, liberal, democratic people, with power and authority vested in our own hands. When any visionary artist or profound thinker sees through this surface persona, armies of rationalists, bureaucrats and petty thinkers rush to shore up public defences against the holy. We need think only of the recent experiences of Manning Clark, Patrick White and Caroline Jones to see this defensive aggression in action (in very different ways) and to understand that breaking down our secularism is tantamount to breaking a national taboo. Those artists and visionaries who remind us that we are not masters of our own destiny, that greater forces are at work in our lives and in society, risk public persecution. Since all great art is informed by a sense of the sacred, this means that every time greatness appears in our society, it has a difficult time with those who attempt to define and enforce our secular national identity.

Where does this taboo against the sacred come from and what fuels it? Our resistance to the sacred derives from a number of factors, some of which are universal and non-local but some of which bear a decidedly regional stamp. Among these factors we would have to include modernity's fear of the sacred, as well as secularisation, the masculine protest against greater forces, and the youthful or adolescent passion for independence and self-control.

DENIAL OF THE SACRED AS MASCULINE PROTEST

The Australian national character is governed by a rationalistic, masculine and practical ethos. Central to this character are the notions of independence and heroic male virtue. Rationalism and modernity both lead inevitably to desacralisation, with the code of manly independence making reliance on any external or transpersonal authority a sign of personal weakness, even effeminacy. To admit any need for the sacred is a sign of defeat or loss. The sacred is felt to be an enemy or antagonist, something that would humiliate the ego by demonstrating the ego's reliance upon non-egoic and non-manly sources. This kind of ego does not know the true strength and per-sonal character that can be achieved, paradoxically, by renouncing egoic control and by consciously drawing on sources of mystery and spirituality.

In the 1950s, social historian Russel Ward, still working within the materialistic framework and bias of nineteenth-century Australian nationalism, defined the so-called 'typical Australian' as "a practical man, rough and ready in his manners and quick to decry any appearance of affectation in others". The typical Australian, he claimed, "is a 'hard case', sceptical about the value of religion and of intellectual and cultural pursuits generally".[3] The Australian secular persona is still tied up with prevailing gender stereotypes and is a product of a powerful, controlling masculinity. Alfred Adler's "masculine protest"[4] is alive in Australia, where a dictatorial masculinity has sought to repress feeling, promoting the ideal of 'stoicism', to banish mystery, in favour of the ideal of 'secularism' or science, and to suppress natural wonder, preferring 'rationality'. This same masculinity seeks to control women and the feminine, under the banner of patriarchy. My previous book pursued these issues, so I will not repeat here what I have said elsewhere.[5]

DENIAL OF THE SACRED AS AN EXPRESSION OF ANTI-AUTHORITARIANISM

The denial of the sacred is linked to Australians' well-known antipathy to external authorities and outside powers. According to many historians and commentators, the Australian cultural ethos derives largely from our convict heritage and from the pool of values, visions and principles guiding the new society of emancipist convicts, free settlers and immigrants. The new society emphasised freedom, self-rule and a strongly anti-authoritarian and democratic temper, as a direct resistance to the old authoritarian, hierarchical British system under which many Australians had suffered and, under colonial rule, continued to suffer. Hence, at the very heart of the idea of 'Australia', as Joseph Furphy and Henry Lawson proclaimed, was a passion for fairness and freedom.

The new society would resist and reject hierarchical and tyrannical authorities, especially those that threatened punishment or retribution. On this basis, a divine or otherworldly authority threatening punishment in hell and eternal torment for sins in life would be as prone to rejection by public opinion as the British legal system that deported the convicts in the first place. The convict background would work against any religious system that employed similar rhetoric, imagery or moral laws to the hated penal system that was about to be overthrown and discarded. There is, then, something deeply inevitable about the experience of God, or the experience of the old punishing image of God, coming to grief in the Australian context. One can hardly imagine that a national style would develop here that would extol subservience to a wrathful God, or subordinance to its laws, ethics and restrictions. The ideal of becoming a 'free' Australian would, presumably, not include the notion of becoming 'a prisoner for Christ', nor would it include the idea of being 'bound' by divinely revealed covenant.

If God was defiantly rejected in this way, then what chance did organised religion have in Australia, especially when this religion was virtually synonymous with, often an extension of, the colonial rule that had condemned the convicts in the first place? In their readiness to conform with the forces of the political state, the Anglican and Protestant churches made themselves dangerously vulnerable to rejection and condemnation by the newly developing Australian community. However, for Irish convicts who had fallen foul of British law, Roman Catholicism appears to have been enthusiastically endorsed in the early colonial period as a kind of 'oppositional' religion, a faith that pointed to a system of authority in contradiction to the British colonial and penal system.[6]

Very early in the days of Port Arthur and Botany Bay, some convicts eventually were allowed Catholic sacraments and worship, although not without enormous misgivings on the part of their captors. Clearly, the passion for Catholicism in this context had a mixture of political and religious motives, and the more the British jailers hated these practices, the more they were enthusiastically endorsed. Historians argue that Anglicanism in the Sydney area had to adopt a vigorously evangelical approach, to counter the lack of interest and the resistance in the local community. This stance appears to have left an indelible mark on the Anglican Church in Sydney, which still adopts a fiercely evangelical posture and which bases its mission on an oppositional and defensive code that seeks to 'convert' the pagan masses.

Of course, Australian anti-authoritarianism can be seen in quite a different light: not as completely irreligious, but simply as rejecting those images and concepts of God, such as the Lord God and Master, that take on a threatening or magisterial aspect. Australia would become a country where the Old Testament God would be viewed with amused contempt or scorn but where the New Testament image of God as loving, redemptive and forgiving might actually gain some credibility, especially for convicts in need of forgiveness and reacceptance into the community. Hence, a typically

Australian 'rejection' of religion might actually involve a more limited or circumscribed rejection of tyrannical images of God, and an openness and receptivity towards new and gentler images of the sacred.

An ideal instance of this process is found in the poem 'The Gentle Water Bird', by the Australian poet John Shaw Neilson. The poet announces that he was introduced as a child to wrathful and frightening images of the Lord God and that his adult development was synonymous with a rejection of this religious background. However, he makes it clear in his poem that his adult life could not be lived without a relationship with the sacred, and that the sacred had for him undergone a dramatic change of character. The poem documents this gradual but certain transformation, confidently announcing that the sacred is now to be identified with nature, grace and gentleness, which he finds personified in the image of the native Australian waterbird:

> *God was not terrible and thunder-blue:*
> *It was a gentle water bird I knew.*[7]

Another positive aspect that might emerge within the context of Australian anti-authoritarianism is an emphasis on democratic worship and egalitarian faith. The old clerical system, based on a firebrand priest who imagines himself a divine emissary and who orders people around with arrogant authority, would obviously fail in Australia, and has already done so, except for isolated pockets here and there. The people simply will not tolerate a clerical dictatorship, and to this extent, the episcopal hierarchical systems of both the Anglican and Roman churches are contrary to the egalitarian ethos of this country. However, there would be much hope and purpose in encouraging a democratic Church, in which lay people could make creative contributions to liturgy, prayer and worship. The Australian emotional climate would favour the displacement of the clerical system, and the empowerment and elevation of the laity, who would respond well to the recognition and development of their latent priestly capacities.

But at the very least, the church in Australia would have to listen to the people, not dictate to them, and make real attempts to integrate a democratic, perhaps even a humorous aspect into religious life. A church that communicated with its flock and did not look down upon it from a great height might fare better within this social context. A great many sensitive priests and ministers in this country have realised that if they are to maintain the respect of the people, they have to become 'of' the people, not lord it over them in an authoritarian manner. To survive in Australia, organised religion must be democratic — or give the appearance of being so.

A democratic church would need to institute democratic internal processes, not impose from above systems that infantilise or compromise its followers. I think that, in this regard, Australian churches have failed dramatically. For too long, they have presented a basically fundamentalist message that encouraged people to take the gospels literally and to believe the unbelievable. Religion has not appealed to adult taste. It has not become intellectually sophisticated, nor has it allowed itself to be influenced by the major philosophical trends of recent history. It has isolated itself from the development of the mind, instead preaching a simple gospel, based on miracles, wonders and supernatural events, that appeals more to the 'magical thinking' of children. With the spread of education, numbers dropped away suddenly, because the church was no longer able to speak to the national consciousness. It was requiring us to leave our minds at the door, bringing only our souls and spirits into the religious service. The majority of Australians have obviously grown beyond and away from a church that has remained at a magical level of thinking more appropriate to the Middle Ages than to the modern era.

Australian anti-authoritarianism might also give rise to a cultural emphasis on personal spirituality and inward faith, based on an entirely individual and original experience of the sacred. There might develop here a personal spirituality that called directly on the presence of the holy spirit rather than relying upon the mediations and ministrations of clergy or church. This has to be considered a real possibility, and would give rise to a popular mysticism or to an existential theology, much of which would not be recognised by the church or by any other social authority. Our famous refusal to toe the line in religious matters could be seen not as a sign of our dreadful materialism, paganism or disbelief but as a sign of our desire to accept personal responsibility for our spiritual lives. It could well be that our rugged individualism has been misinterpreted, especially by those who equate 'religion' with 'church', as an expression of an antispiritual national character. The lack of conformity or collectivity in our religious lives may have blurred our perception of our national character, causing some to designate us non-religious, when in fact we have simply been non-conformist.

THE SECULAR IDEALISATION OF YOUTH AND COLONIAL YOUTHFULNESS

Ironically, if the church has declined because it has remained a 'parental' authority dictating an infantilising religion, the secular state has thrived because it has institutionalised an image of youthfulness and held out to its citizens the prospect of eternal childhood. The church is rejected because it makes us feel like 'bad' children in need of repentance and redirection, but the state is condoned because it makes us feel like 'good' children in a 'lucky' country. The state has rejected religion as something belonging to 'old' nations, and has seductively invited us to live in the present, without concern about eternity and in denial of the reality of death. The official secular idealisation of youthfulness and young people keeps us removed from the sacred, which is associated with age, wisdom and maturity.

It could be that the secular nation of Australia is too young and headstrong to achieve a public spirituality, which is another reason why spirituality in this country has remained fundamentally personal and individualistic. One could almost say that our spirituality is 'adolescent', practised behind closed doors and kept away from the gaze of public scrutiny. We celebrate and extol our supposed 'youthfulness', not realising that this could be a very great burden, a barrier against spiritual maturity and an inhibiting factor against forging a relationship with the sacred. Any public spirituality or high culture requires maturity and wisdom, as fantasies of independence and adolescent notions of self-sufficiency have to be renounced in order to achieve the humility and serenity that must precede any communion with the sacred. The national ideal is to be young and free in life (as in our national anthem), or young and immortalised in death (as in the ANZAC legend). Everywhere we find youth being touted as the ideal condition, as if in denial of the inevitability of ageing, growth and decay. Youth is valued above all other states of being. But in the Australian historical, geographical, spiritual and cultural contexts, a national cult of youth denies too much and is flying in the face of too much human reality.

To start with the Aboriginal people: they are not young, and they are proud of it. As Aboriginal leader Galarrwuy Yunupingu told an assembled crowd in Sydney on Australia Day during the Bicentennial Year, 1988: "Australia's too old to celebrate birthdays".[8] Aboriginal people realise that depth of culture and spiritual integrity come with time and tradition. Aboriginal culture itself is passed on by the elders, invested in the elders, and held as the responsibility of elders. The state of youth is viewed with enormous suspicion, because in youth, the ego governs our choices and decisions; the desires of youth are generally personal and narcissistic, not cultural or spiritual. At the centre of Aboriginal culture is the initiation ceremony, designed to terminate the state of youth, and to help the individual make a transition to a new world, where he or she acts responsibly towards the community and acknowledges the role of the ancestor spirits at the centre of life and creation. A young, uninitiated person is not expected to have this sacred knowledge about ancestry or culture, and so it is that indigenous cultures everywhere, not just those in Australia, extol the virtues of age and promote the elder as the focus and centre of cultural attention.

But in white, youthful Australia, old people are forgotten about, locked up in retirement homes away from the public eye, and treated more as a burden of responsibility than as a cultural treasure. We do not look to the old for the wisdom they possess; we simply pity them for not being young. White Australia has no elders, only the elderly and the aged — and there is a big difference. Age in secular Australia simply means restriction, disadvantage and physical loss. Our public awareness is that in old age, the body slowly degenerates. Secularism cannot see that the whole point of age and maturity is to grow outside the personal ego and to develop a relationship with the forces beyond it. Old age is not just about losing youth but is also about gaining wisdom, gaining understanding of the sacred and entering into a full relationship with it.

This is why so many Aboriginal people consider white culture to be young, silly and 'uninitiated'. By using this latter term, they mean that white people have not initiated themselves out of the desirous and personal state of youth. What are our initiation ceremonies? How do we educate ourselves out of youth? These are questions I was often asked by Aboriginal people while growing up in central Australia, and I hardly knew how to answer them. In our society, we make little attempt to live beyond the ego or to move beyond the purely personal state. In fact, we try to cling to youth for as long as possible; the elderly are valued only if they have a 'twinkle in their eye' and are 'young at heart'. Hence we often come across to Aboriginal elders as stupid, pathetic or full of youthful illusions about life. We have made no reckoning with the sacred — at least, not publicly or officially — and remain blindly committed to worshipping and prolonging the state of youth.

Is Australia really so young and free? Aboriginal cultures have inhabited this continent for tens of thousands of years, an occupation that has been synonymous with an imaginative and religious possession of place. Remarkably, the Aboriginal religious tradition is probably the oldest continuous sacred tradition in the world, making even the Judeo-Christian European tradition seem very recent in comparison. How tragically ironic and blind, then, for European colonials to come to this land and imagine it to be virginal and new.

Fantasies of newness are also belied by the facts of geography and geological science. This country is one of the oldest land masses on earth, especially in its western and central desert regions. Even a casual, untutored glance at the country will reveal the enormous age of the landscape, which is everywhere worn down by time, eroded by wind, rain and ancient rivers, and shaped by elemental forces over countless millennia.

But the national obsession for youthfulness also denies the age, background and ethnicity of all non-Aboriginal Australians, including myself. Those of us who are migrants to this land have countless generations of ancestral linkages to other times and other places. Although we may not be consciously aware of this background, in our deeper psychic being we are very much the product and inheritors of cultural histories that continue to influence our existence and shape our identities. We did not just arrive here out of the blue, but came bearing the scars, wounds and spiritual inheritance of other cultures and national histories.

The fantasy of youthfulness has always been central to white Australian nationalism. In the late 1890s, nationalist writer Joseph Furphy, in his novel *Such is Life*, declared Australia to be a young, free and "recordless land", devoid of spirits, presences and the superstitions of the past, or as Furphy put it, "clogged by no fealty to shadowy idols".[9] Such nationalist sentiments always assume that this country had not been imaginatively possessed or shaped before the white Europeans, wilfully denying Aboriginal cultural and spiritual occupancy of place. The notion that Australia is a young country, devoid of the sacred, is thus directly linked to the colonialist-supremacist idea of Australia as *terra nullius*, empty land, which the colonials had every legal and moral right to appropriate.

Contemporary Australia is belatedly realising that the *terra nullius* view is a blatant lie with serious legal and constitutional consequences, especially with regard to land ownership and native land title. This is creating an enormous shock wave in our society, and we are having to readjust our laws, politics and attitudes as a result. But we will have to go through a similar reappraisal at the spiritual and cultural level when we learn to understand that the idea of the youthfulness of the country and the absence of the sacred is yet another colonialist-supremacist, egocentric delusion. Our poets have long been aware of this fallacy, as in A. D. Hope's poem *Australia*: "They call her [Australia] a young country, but they lie".[10] And Prime Minister Paul Keating announced: "The great myth about Australia is that we are young. We're not. Not only is this the oldest continent and

Aboriginal Australia the oldest society on earth, this multicultural Australia is also old."[11] Deconstructing and dissolving the lie of our youthfulness will one day create as much havoc and excitement as the contemporary readjustment relating to legal ownership of land, as we rediscover our own psychospiritual depth and age, and our inevitable involvement in, and responsibility towards, traditional Aboriginal sacrality.

DENIAL OF THE SACRED AS MODERNITY AND PROGRESS

Linked to the national ideal of eternal youthfulness is the much broader international ideal of modernity and permanent progress. For modern man and woman, the 'new' is highly valued, while the 'old' is frowned upon as irrelevant and out of date. The old, which so often includes the concept and image of the sacred, must be discarded and overcome in order that the new can take control. The nation of Australia has styled itself as a 'modern' country in the sense of being intellectually and morally advanced. For many nationalist Australians, spirituality is viewed as a fuzzy European import, something that once may have had a place but that is not relevant in 'progressive' society. As early as 1899, A. G. Stephens, the influential editor of the Sydney *Bulletin*, wrote: "the religious stage was one stage in human evolution, as natural as the irreligious stage which is superseding it".[12] And a few years later:

> *Our fathers brought with them the religious habit as they brought other habits of elder nations in older* lands. *And upon religion, as upon everything else, the spirit of Australia — that undefined, indefinable resultant of earth, and air, and conditions of climate and life — has seized; modifying, altering, increasing, or altogether destroying. In the case of religious belief the tendency is clearly to destruction — partly, no doubt, because with the spread of*

*mental enlightenment the tendency is everywhere to
decay in faith in outworn creeds.*[13]

The founders of Australian nationalism made the
fundamental error of assuming that the sacred was a
phase of human history, which would be outgrown by
social development and replaced by Enlightenment
principles. The sacred was somehow culturally specific to
and fused with 'ancientness', so that it was appropriately
contained within the precincts of so-called 'older lands'.
This discredited nationalist discourse failed to see the
hidden irony of its own terms, since the land of Australia
is itself older than these 'older lands', and thus, according
to this logic, spirituality has a legitimate place here. But
modernity and positivism attempted always to particu-
larise the religious instinct, to freeze it in time and place,
and hence to deny its continuing life of revelation and
mystery. In countering this falsely progressive argument,
Mircea Eliade writes: "It suffices to say that the 'sacred' is
an element in the structure of consciousness, not a stage
in the history of consciousness".[14]

One of the best descriptions of the modern Australian
condition is provided by Mircea Eliade in his classic
work *The Sacred and the Profane*. Eliade did not have
contemporary Australians in mind when he penned this
description of the so-called "non-religious man", but the
description reflects with remarkable accuracy our official
secular pose:

> *The non-religious man refuses transcendence [and]
> accepts the relativity of "reality" ... Modern non-
> religious man ... makes himself, and he only makes
> himself completely in proportion as he desacralizes
> himself and the world. The sacred is the prime
> obstacle to his freedom. He will become himself only
> when he is totally demysticized. He will not be truly
> free until he has killed the last god.*[15]

Australians have been hearty myth-busters, god-killers and levellers of the spirit. We are well known for our delight in lopping tall poppies, and the tallest poppy of all, God, has been lopped time and time again. In Patrick White's novel *The Vivisector*, we read: "God is dead, anyway — thank God — in Australia".[16] The ironic appeal to God's presence, even as God's absence is announced, is typical of Australian ambivalence in religious matters, and White's genius constantly exposes us to our habitual duplicity in the realm of the spirit. Our secular mask believes that by debunking the metaphysical, and by 'exposing' religion as a sham or fraud, an affront to common sense, we are thereby released from the tyranny of the irrational and the burden of primitive superstition. We consider ourselves at the forefront of enlightenment, a step ahead of those nations still bogged down in archaic notions about the sacred.

THE WHITE LIES OF COLONIALISM, AND THE POSTCOLONIAL SPIRIT

We are discovering today that secular Australia was founded on a series of white lies (pun intended), and a series of denials of a pre-existent Presence. First, there was the lie of the emptiness of the land, devoid of Aboriginal cultural presence (*terra nullius*); second, the lie of the newness and youthfulness of the country, devoid of spiritual presence (matter without spirit); third, the lie that the sacred is an anachronistic construct, lost to ancient history, with no validity in contemporary experience; fourth, the lie that the sacred impedes the independence and integrity of human striving; and fifth, the lie that a hegemonic masculinity can impose its own values and attitudes on society, denying everything that does not fit in with its own rationalistic prejudices. These are the white lies that constitute the 'creation mythology' of colonial Australia, many of which are rapidly being exposed and undermined by education, reflection, changes in national awareness, and historical research.

The passing of a colonial mentality is a gradual and complex process, with the most visible and apparent injustices being dealt with first. Hence, we have already witnessed legal, social and political attacks on the *terra nullius* concept, on oppressive colonial attitudes and on tyrannising masculinity. The Aboriginal land rights movement, women's liberation, and progressive attitudes in law, government and politics have combined to usher in the first wave of our 'postcolonial' consciousness. Even here, however, and especially in the area of Aboriginal land rights, the resistance of the old colonialist white regime to positive change and transformation is keenly felt. Progressives, intellectuals and Aboriginals fight what is often felt to be a losing battle against the conservative representatives of the old social order, and while much lip-service is paid to the cause of Aboriginal reconciliation, very little appears to have been done about it.

But beyond the political and social changes we will need to achieve if we are to believe in ourselves as a *post*colonial society are a new set of changes, with different challenges and opportunities for growth. The next wave of postcolonial protest will expose the metaphysical and spiritual injustices of colonialism: the tyrannies of secularism, the oppressiveness of irony, the vapid emptiness of materialism, and the desiccating impact of scientific literalism. So far, we know the postcolonial revolution only in terms of law, economics and politics (and even at this level, the revolution has already stalled), but there is still a long way to go before we 'decolonise the mind' and win back the spiritual life that colonialism has denied us.

As a postcolonial society, the United States has had to deal with a great amount of deconstructing and righting of moral and political wrongs, but spirituality was not one of the casualties of American colonialism. America was founded by passionate seventeenth-century religious puritans who wished to construct a New World in accordance with a glorious metaphysical vision, and this spiritual idealism has been central to the American project and can still be found and felt in American public life today. James Tulip has observed that:

> *To hear the speeches of American presidents — Kennedy, Johnson, Reagan, Bush and Clinton — is to hear a language impregnated with the Bible and almost four centuries of prophetic and cadenced rhetoric. The jousting and secularised invective from Canberra seems a world apart.*[17]

It is true that there are generally no echoes of transcendence, nor appeals to transcendental authority, in the secular political discourses of Australian public life. However, it also has to be said that the presence of a God discourse in American public life need not necessarily point to the presence of a living God, only to the presence of God language, much of which strikes many Australians, and many Americans, too, as habitual, glib and empty. But certainly, the cultural contexts of Australia and America are radically different with regard to the sacred: God is very much 'at home' in America (which is constructed as 'God's own' country), whereas in Australia, God is still viewed as a foreigner. We have no indigenous cosmology and, hence, no indigenous religious discourse. We are speechless, naked and empty before the sacred.

Colonial Australia was founded upon a passionate nineteenth-century materialism-cum-atheism that contrasts markedly with the religious idealism of seventeenth-century America. As Barbara Thiering has argued, "Australia was formed and developed at a time which saw the close of day for Christendom, following the upheavals of the Enlightenment and the subsequent critical movement of the nineteenth century".[18] Australia, the newest of the British colonial acquisitions, was to be the social *locus* for a new experiment in a postreligious mentality. Ironically, it was the Spanish Catholic explorer Pedro de Quiros, who had ventured forth upon the South Seas to discover the Great South Land long before the British expeditions, who named our island continent. He called it *Austrialia del Espiritu Santo*, the South Land dedicated to the Holy Spirit, in 1606,[19] a century and a half before Captain Cook. One wonders whether the sentiment underpinning that original naming will overcome the soulless British concept of *terra nullius* or *terra australis incognita*.

But certainly, the white, secular, colonial world view that has been wilfully imposed upon Australia from above has long been crumbling and is now beyond repair. Popular right-wing political movements such as One Nation, Australia First, the League of Rights, and other racist and conservative forces will always attempt to prop up the ailing colonialism, but these movements will have only momentary and sporadic life, because the psychic and spiritual life of this country is moving steadily away from these early colonial constructs and towards a new style of social integration. The progressive forces have the spirit of the time on their side, but ironically, the progressive forces are entirely unaware of the presence of 'spirit' in their activities, and there will be much confusion and disorientation among our progressive ranks when it finally becomes clear that the Australian cultural situation demands and requires a regional spirituality.

This spiritual reckoning belongs to the future of this country; we see only the earliest, almost inarticulate beginnings of this reorientation today. Progressive thinkers in Australia are still prone to dismiss the presence of spirit as some weird and strange phenomenon, not quite true-blue. Spirituality is either a New Age phenomenon — that is, viewed as fashionably cultic and anti-intellectual — or it is berated as an Old Age superstition — that is, considered to be a cultural back-lash against modernity. We have not yet realised that our shedding of colonialism and our movement towards a postcolonial consciousness will involve us in a direct encounter with the reality of spirit.

HAUNTED BY WHAT WE HAVE DENIED

Under the reign of secular materialism, the sacred does not disappear from our lives; it merely falls into the background and becomes subject to repression. We have grown accustomed over many decades to think about the 'repressed' in Freudian terms of sexuality, desire and libidinal instinct, but in a largely permissive culture in which everyone talks about sex and where desire is widely viewed as the primary human motivation, we can no longer examine the repressed in terms of Freud's largely Victorian assumptions. Freud remains influential and important, but I feel that the present time and the near future belong more to Jung. Jung believed that we have powerful symbolic and religious urges, which are just as strong as the sex instinct and which, when repressed or ignored, create just as much havoc.

In getting rid of the sacred and in making God appear un-Australian, we have unwittingly made psychological suffering and mental torment very Australian. A great amount of Australian art, especially modernist painting, music and literature, is concerned with the mental torment and spiritual anguish that is endured in a land where we are expected to be happy, democratic and free. While secular Australia set about to build a working man's paradise in which few would go hungry and all would be protected by the state, our major artists were showing that Australia was becoming an empty, fast and shallow society, in which traditional spiritual and moral values had been replaced by psychological suffering, meaninglessness and torment. In Sidney Nolan's Ned Kelly paintings, the Kelly figure inside the iron mask is revealed as haunted, isolated and afraid as he peers out through the slats in his metal helmet. In the classic novel *My Brother Jack*, George Johnston constructs a narrative based on the national legend of the heroic Aussie male, revealing that figure to be tyrannical, violent, and plagued by the problem of inner emptiness and despair.

Our secular society contented itself with the philistine explanation that our modernist artists were becoming fashionable, and were importing depression, *ennui*, and angst from Paris, Berlin and London. There has always been enormous resistance in Australian public life to anything dark, morose or morbid, and to any impulse that threatens the simple-minded positivism promoted by the concept of the lucky country (even if Donald Horne originally intended this title in an ironic sense). Secularism likes to imagine that man lives by fairness and democratic principles alone, and whenever any complex spiritual feeling enters the social fabric, we have generally looked for an outside cause for our rising anxiety (yellow peril, communism, modernism, Americanism). But as we built the working man's paradise, strange feelings invaded us from within, and we did not experience the freedom promised by the secular contract.

A remarkable expression of our predicament is found in White's novel *The Solid Mandala*:

> *After he retired, Dad would sometimes recall, in the spasmodic phrasing which came with the asthma, his escape by way of Intellectual Enlightenment, and the voyage to Australia, from what had threatened to become a permanence in black and brown, but in the telling, he would grow darker rather than enlightened, his breathing thicker, clogged with the recurring suspicion that he might be chained still.*[20]

The Intellectual Enlightenment and the journey to Australia are connected in this passage. Both are viewed by Australians as escapes from the burdens of the past and as ways of transcending oppressive tradition. And yet "in the telling" of this tale of liberation, the teller "grow[s] darker rather than enlightened", fearing "that he might be chained still". The denial of the sacred gives rise to a darker, more subtle and morose form of bondage, because it is an *unconscious* and unknowing bondage to unseen forces. This is detrimental to the ego's health, even life-threatening, as is evident in this description of George Brown, freed from the Old Country yet dumbly suffering from a spiritual malaise in the New. Mircea Eliade could have been speaking about George Brown, and the tragic Australian figure, when he wrote: "Modern nonreligious man forms himself by a series of denials and refusals, but he continues to be haunted by the realities that he has refused and denied".[21]

THE REPRESSED SACRED IN ART AND LITERATURE

It has always seemed remarkably ironic to me that this country's best artists, writers, musicians, architects and designers are, with a few exceptions, intensely visionary and spiritual, if not overtly religious. A country that boasts its secularism and rationality has bred generations of visionary artists: in poetry we have Charles Harpur, John Shaw Neilson, Judith Wright, Vincent Buckley, A. D. Hope, James McAuley, Gwen Harwood, Fay Zwicky, Les Murray, Kevin Hart, Phillip Hodgkins, to name only a few that come to mind. All of these poets shrink from the superficiality of the official persona, and attempt to discover imaginal depths and spaces in religion, nature, art, Aboriginality and language.

In fiction we have, among many others, Patrick White, Grant Watson, David Malouf, Tim Winton, Helen Garner, Rodney Hall and Richard Flanagan, each of whom creates a depth dimension in a society that constantly pushes us to the surface. In a range of other arts, we find such figures as Arthur Boyd, William Ricketts, Peter Sculthorpe, Ross Edwards, Michael Leunig and Greg Burgess, seeking mythological intensity and religious feeling in a variety of artistic languages. The roll-call goes on, and this listing is highly selective, provisional and idiosyncratic. Studies of the history of the arts in Australia will show how the neglected sacred in this country has expressed itself, often in indirect ways, in the creative arts.

The prophetic role of the arts in enabling us to track the sacred can hardly be underestimated. Our political and social leaders are rarely concerned with spiritual matters, and many secular intellectuals do not believe that there is any spirit to listen for, since their training has taught them that man made God, not the other way around. Church leaders are expected to listen to this divine voice, but the claims of the institutional church often do not permit receptivity to the voice of the new. The voice of the living spirit is always the voice of the new, and those within institutions often respond to the new with fear and loathing. Indeed, visionary figures within Australian churches, such as Paul Collins or Michael Morwood,[22] are sometimes scapegoated and marginalised, since they represent too great a threat to the stability and certainty of established structures.

But let us not underestimate the difficulty of tracking the sacred in a time that has witnessed the collapse of religious meaning. Mircea Eliade, perhaps our best guide in tracking the modern experience of the sacred (as Vincent Buckley also found), warned that: "In a period of religious crisis one cannot anticipate the creative, and, as such, probably unrecognizable, answers given to such a crisis. Moreover, one cannot predict the expressions of a potentially new experience of the sacred".[23] He intimated that this new experience of the sacred may, in fact, "not [be] recognizable as such from a Judeo-Christian perspective".

Artists generally are not beholden to any institution, and are able to follow the call of the spirit, no matter where it leads. Artists tap the hidden or repressed life of our culture, often looking beneath the present time to what will become conscious and collectively expressed at a later point in our development. They often point to what we do not want to admit, to patterns or processes that many of us would rather avoid. Art is subversive in its revelation of truth; it tells us things we are yet to know about ourselves, things that will become evident in time. I mean this quite literally: art shows us the side of ourselves that we usually do not see and often do not want to see. It is truly revolutionary, and in an oppressively secular society it will dish up a hearty meal of symbols, myths, rituals and religious images.

From my own experience, however, it would seem that those who teach and research Australian literature and culture are generally not on the same wavelength as the artists. In my undergraduate courses on Australian writing, I was repeatedly told that Australian culture was primarily secular and that our writers were a godless bunch, with a strong preference for irony, realism and practicality. In other words, the Australian secular persona was attempting to read Australian art according to its own image, rather than accepting the challenge — perhaps the embarrassment — that the arts deliver to our official persona.

To read the critical and introductory textbooks on Australian literature, one would assume that the entire canon of Australian writing belonged to the so-called bush tradition of naive realism, where mateship and the democratic ethos of the 'wide brown land' are celebrated. Books such as Arthur Phillips' *The Australian Tradition*, Russel Ward's *The Australian Legend* and Inglis Moore's *Social Patterns in Australian Literature* are written in a strongly secular, positivist key. Certainly, there is no room for metaphysics in these easy-going, self-assured, no-nonsense accounts of our national identity. With chapter headings such as 'Realism', 'The Creed of Mateship' and 'The Keynote of Irony', what chance does the religious impulse have? My teachers of literature assumed as axiomatic the 'sceptical and utilitarian spirit' of Australia (an oft-repeated phrase), and this same rugged, radical materialism was enshrined at national conferences on Australian literature.

This critical tradition either completely ignored the religious dimension of the books it studied or, more often, converted the visionary strain in the art to other purposes, usually political, to support different contexts. For instance, John Shaw Neilson, a deeply religious or mystical poet of nature, was constantly constructed as a democratic socialist rather than as the powerful visionary poet he is. Les Murray and Judith Wright were hailed as 'bush poets', rather than as religious writers who struggle in each poem to reveal the divine presence found just below the surface of all things natural. In a work of unconscious irony, the intellectuals and critics perpetuated in their interpretations the very social reality the poets were attempting to explode.

I realise that the bush-realist perspective once advanced as Australia's artistic reality has been debunked by new waves of intellectual activity, especially postmodernism, feminism, postcolonialism and new historicism. But these critical approaches, though interesting and sophisticated antidotes to the naivete of bush realism, are still singularly incapable of coming to terms with the primarily religious nature of Australian art. Our best writing and art cannot be understood within any materialist frame, whether modern, premodern or postmodern, and this country's students and readers are being short-changed, their horizons limited, by a series of inflexible secular ideologies that are incapable of seeing what is there. I can only support the observation of Veronica Brady that "many of the major works in the canon of Australian literature reject the premises of naturalism and move into areas of metaphysical and even theological concern". She considers it a travesty to "disregard what these writers have to say merely because it does not square with the image of ourselves which has by now become official".[24]

However, I am not especially convinced that conventional religious criticism can do justice to modern Australian art or letters either. Eliade indicates that the new experience of the sacred would probably not be recognisable as such from a Judeo-Christian perspective, and this point continues to echo in my ears, and to resonate with a great deal of Australian art. For instance, in what sense could Murray, White or Malouf be described as 'Christian' artists? We could ask the same question of Leunig, Sculthorpe, Burgess or Ricketts. These artists are intensely spiritual, but not religious in the narrow definition of that term. There is something else present in our midst that we are not quite seeing, and I will suggest what this could be in the next chapter. The new spirituality of White or Wright may account for the fact that conventional religious accounts of these writers and their works do not yield a very good harvest. Wright has not been impressed, on the whole, with the proffered religious interpretations of her poems, and we are more conscious of what religious interpretations of *The Tree of Man* leave out than of what they include. We are in the grips of a new *numen*, or revelation, and the theological ideas of the past are not much help. Thus, we would have to reluctantly conclude that all forms of existing criticism, whether secular or religious, fail to grasp the subtlety and spiritual uniqueness of our artists.

Meanwhile, our major artists have moved ahead of our ability to comprehend them. On the whole, they are remarkably patient, but they lose their patience when their spiritual visions are reductively interpreted as examples of secular mateship, folksy bush culture, agnosticism or even atheism. Wright and Murray, in particular, have made it clear that they do not appreciate being rendered spiritually impotent by a timid and shallow literary establishment. It is of great concern that our best artists are being so denied their visionary and transformative power.

This crisis in our cultural self-awareness came to a climax in the career of Patrick White. White wrote intensely mythological fictions, drawing his inspiration not from a cheery bush tradition but from the spiritual depths of his own imagination. Here was possibly our greatest writer, whose works were so deeply mystical that even school children could see he did not fit the official Australian ironic-sceptical or bush-realist mould. Yet critics were either prepared to pretend that he was essentially an ironic writer, not affirming religious life, or were willing to pronounce his works 'un-Australian' or 'antisocial'.

Leonie Kramer, first Professor of Australian Literature, continually wrote about White in terms of her own secular and rational world view. She wanted to turn White into a ironic modernist, which at the time was the best standard to which great writers could aspire. What would learned professors do with mystics and prophets? How could they argue that such people were 'great' unless the all-important irony was paramount? The presence of religious feeling in *The Tree of Man*, she argued, was misleading. Actually, White was presenting an "essay in scepticism".[25] In an astonishing essay, 'Patrick White's Gotterdammerung' ('death of the gods'), Kramer presented White's work as a whole, and even the intensely visionary *Riders in the Chariot*, as sceptical and debunking of religious life.[26] This is a serious and damaging misreading of the novels, and understandably, it angered Patrick White. White was outraged by the academic misrepresentation of his work, seeing it as designed to support the mainstream denial of the sacred that had become institutionalised in Australian high culture. White's attacks on academics in general and Leonie Kramer in particular are well known, and readily accessible in his essays, autobiographical works, letters and other writings.

A powerful collision between creative artists and rational intellectuals is perhaps unavoidable in a split culture such as ours. The critical mind wants to believe one thing, while the passionate heart and spirit know and live something else completely. To borrow some philosophical terms from Paul Ricouer, the hermeneutics of suspicion that govern the intellect have no way of adequately relating to the hermeneutics of affirmation that control the life of the heart. The problem is that the critical mind continues to set the agenda and hold sociopolitical power; it is still the rational mind that establishes what Veronica Brady calls the 'official image' of ourselves and our culture. Meanwhile, the creative arts are at odds with the people who attempt to speak for them and who try to teach them. This neurotic state of affairs is graphically exemplary of the deep structural rift in the national psyche.

4

Spirit and Place

An Aboriginal elder of the Ngarinyin people, David Mowaljarlai, told me in 1996 that "spirituality is coming back in Australia". "This is a spirit country", he said, "and we will all have to face the sacredness of the land". David Mowaljarlai's "all" included both white people and black people; unlike so many other voices in Australia at the time, voices supporting racial exclusivity and difference, his was extraordinarily generous and inclusive. For a moment I lost my bearings, hardly knowing how to receive the gift of his insight. We non-Aboriginals are so used to being told by secular authorities and liberation activists that a land-based spirituality in Australia is off-limits for white people, none of our business, that we have no framework for seeing ourselves as a people spiritually united by the sacredness of the land.

And yet, for all our self-created political, economic and racial barriers, there is a deeper level at which we are all united in the spirit. This experience of spiritual interconnectedness has much to do with the land, and appears to arise, as the Aboriginal elder intimates, quite spontaneously from the lived experience of this earth. When we experience this spirituality, some materialists claim that we are stealing indigenous property, since for them, 'spirituality' does not exist apart from the cultural forms in which it is expressed. But Mowaljarlai and indigenous elders like him believe that in sharing their vision with all Australians, they are strengthening the spiritual life of this country and its community. The suspicious see sharing as stealing, while the open-hearted see sharing in terms of generosity and abundance.

SACRED GROUND

How to conceptualise this 'spirit' is still beyond our imagining. In most European countries, spirit is felt to come from above, to descend from the sky like a dove, to shower upon the Earth like the flames of Pentecost. Spirit is linked to the heavens, and to a Father God perceived to be 'above' us. Yet in Australia, the country of reversals, the upside-down land, whose symbol is the tilted Southern Cross, the celestial realm appears to be 'below' us, in the earth itself, in the soil, rocks and plants of this ancient land. Here, the spirit has not departed the earth and retreated to its heavenly abode. The spirit is in the earth, under our feet and below our normal level of vision and understanding.

Western European cosmology is reversed in Australia, and this gives rise to a completely different spiritual phenomenology. Here, spiritual feeling enters us, as it were, from the feet, travels along the legs and through the trunk of the body and, if we are lucky, ignites a new life in the heart. But it rarely reaches our heads to be expressed through the voice or articulated by the educated intellect. It operates below the level of normal ratiocination, which is why so few people in this country can intellectually express their spiritual experience. We don't 'have' spiritual experiences in Australia; rather, they 'have' us, and hold us in their grip.

In Western cultures, religion has become a remarkably heady experience. It is a way of the mind and a way of moral understanding. If we are very fortunate, it reaches down into the heart as well, igniting a life of true faith. In the West, religion is intimately tied up with language, words, verbal expressions, sermons, creeds, catechism, theology. As Veronica Brady has said, there is a lot of chattering about religion, a great deal of God language, but not always much God presence. In Australia, I would contend, this pattern is reversed, so that we have a strong sense of God presence but not much God language. Many Australians feel the presence of God in silence, not in words. An enormous amount of Australian literature extols a "philosophy of silence", as Leonie Kramer has argued,[1] and is quite suspicious of words, doubting their ability to express spiritual feeling.

Aboriginal culture has emerged from the silence of the land, and this human culture has not represented an attempt to obliterate that silence; rather, it celebrates and honours it. As a spokesperson from the Ngangikurungkurr people explains: "My people are not threatened by silence. They are completely at home in it. They have lived for thousands of years with Nature's quietness. My people today recognise and experience in this quietness the great Life-Giving Spirit."[2]

The Australian experience of spirit is direct, existential, non-ecclesiastical and almost preverbal. Our society does not *appear* to be very religious, because hardly any of our religion is articulated or on show. The country appears to be anti-intellectual, because the vital energy of the nation is 'down below', in the heart, not 'up in the head'. When I become too articulate and wordy about spirituality, people suspect me of not being very spiritual at all, just caught up in my intellectualism. I can see their point, and then I tend to shut up, but there is also a great beauty and revelatory power in words used in the right way, words which honour the silence at the core of our being. This philosophy of silence can become, for natural intellectuals, a new kind of social tyranny, but we do have to respect the fact that the Australian experience is 'down to earth', and that this is the price to be paid for living in a country where the earth archetype has such a powerful, almost gravitational, hold upon human consciousness.[3]

THE LANGUAGE OF THE EARTH

The main language in Australia is earth language: walking over the body of the earth, touching nature, feeling its presence and its other life, and attuning ourselves to its sensual reality. Aboriginal culture is of the land, and Aboriginal religion is a spirituality of place. The sacred songs and chants are sung to gigantic and ancient rock formations and to vast expanses of red earth. The sacred dances are earth dances, where the celebrants gather to 'sing up' and sustain the spirits of the earth. Significantly, Aboriginal dance and celebration is concentrated upon the movements of the feet. Mowaljarlai says that when he is engaged in attunement in the bush, he performs movements with the feet to create greater spiritual intimacy with the earth: "You feel you want to get deeper, so you start moving around and stamp your feet — to come closer and to recognise what you are seeing".[4] Stamping the feet gives connection to the land, spiritual quickening, and focus to the mind.

In traditional dance, the feet of the dancer are at first gently raised, then strike the earth with much energy and vigour. At the climax of the dance, the feet hit the ground with great force, as if to raise fire out of rock, to cause the spirit to flame up from below. Often the arms are limp or immobile; the feet do the communicating, as in Irish Celtic dancing. Aboriginal visual art, as well, is governed by the feet. The so-called abstract paintings are not abstract at all, but are experiences of the land as seen from above and as felt through the feet. The feet register the contours of place — the proportions, lines, dots and rhythms of the landscape.

In contemporary, postcolonial Australia, spirituality is entering our lives from below, and the feet play a more important role than the intellect, which struggles to recognise what is taking place. Barbara Blackman once said in a lecture that if we want to "under-stand" spirituality in this country we have to "stand-under" our habitual logic and our usual perceptions, since that is the vantage point from which the spirit is found. Understanding calls us away from our conscious conventions. Insight arises from a deeper intuition, from a level of mind and matter below consciousness. Writing of the experience of divine presence in Australia, poet Les Murray has said that this presence is:

> *Almost beneath notice, as attainable as gravity, it is*
> *a continuous recovering moment. Pity the high madness*
> *that misses it continually ...* [5]

That is what Western European high culture can seem like from the perspective of the Australian spirit: a field of "high madness" that "continually" "misses" the experience of the sacred. Or, as A. D. Hope put it, the spirit of Australia is a:

> *... spirit which escapes*
> *The learned doubt, the chatter of cultured apes*
> *Which is called civilization over there.* [6]

Even this country's greatest intellects, such as Hope and Murray, can in certain lights appear antisophisticated, because they are deeply suspicious of the routine chatter and madness that passes for civilisation. But they are suspicious of the chatter only because they can *feel* something more, something greater. A reality larger than ourselves beckons us in this country, a reality born of silence and not readily translated into concepts or language. The analytical left brain may not perceive it at all, but the poetical right brain, which governs the intuitive dimension of experience, must sing in praise of this larger and greater world:

> *After the tree falls, there will reign the same silence*
> *as stuns and spurs us, enraptures and defeats us,*
> *as seems to some a challenge, and seems to others*
> *to be waiting here for something beyond imagining.*[7]

How we conceptualise spirit in Australia is still beyond our imagining. And this spirit appears to be "waiting" for something to happen, waiting for some transformation or transfiguration. But of what? And of whom? Perhaps this is what the early sailors meant by *Austrialia del Espiritu Santo*, a land dedicated to the holy spirit.[8]

It may be that Australian spirit is presently beyond our imagining because it is non-dualistic, non-other-worldly, and deeply linked to physical reality. As such, it could be "unrecognizable" (Eliade) from the point of view of the old Judeo-Christian dispensation, with its transcendentalist and dualistic character. This is perhaps why the churches have not been able to identify the spiritual renaissance in Australia, nor offer leadership in this spiritual discovery. In Western cultures, 'spirit' is almost a synonym for that which is abstract, remote, and detached from matter and nature. In contemporary Australia, people can feel spirit in this place, but it is the opposite of transcendental and remote. Leading the new development have been those artists, writers and visionary poets who have been close to the earth and its poetic wisdom. Murray, Wright and Neilson, for instance, were born on the land, from which they gained their insights and intuitions.

Intellectual poets have rarely been able to access or affirm the special spirit of the country. Often, the intellectual poet is aware only of what has died in Australia, what has been lost from European origins, what has faded through time and distance, not what has been reborn. Chris Wallace-Crabbe, an ironic urban poet, writes of the city of Melbourne: "Though much has died here, little has been born".[9]

In the work of urban poets, Australia is seen as a colonial graveyard, a place no longer spiritually sustained by the strained umbilical cord from Western Europe. But the poets of the earth have a vastly different message to impart. According to our earthy artists, Australia is the exciting birthplace for a new kind of consciousness. The new cultural spirituality to emerge here will be embodied, physical and incarnational. This Australian spirit may even look 'pagan' to the old dispensation, because it will be unashamed of the body and unafraid to find the sacred in the ordinary and everyday.

Aboriginal spirituality, although seemingly esoteric to the casual observer, is the opposite of otherworldly. It is intensely of this world, linked to the practical experience of being in the world. The newly emerging sense of spirit in postcolonial Australia is in many ways similar to the early Aboriginal religious experience. The difficult task of theorising the cultural dynamics that produce this return of an ancient spiritual apprehension of the world will be taken up more fully in the following chapter, 'Aboriginal Reconciliation as a Spiritual Experience'. But after two hundred years of white colonial arrogance, where we believed that we 'conquered' the land and imposed European images and practices upon it, this land is now conquering us. We are experiencing a 'colonisation in reverse', where the land we thought dull and inert, an empty field (*terra nullius*) upon which we would stamp our own authority, is proving to have a spiritual authority far greater than our own.

THE SPIRITUALITY OF EMBODIMENT, EROS AND NATURE

Whatever is "waiting here for something beyond imagining" is drawing us all, black and white, into its power. We are witnessing the rebirth of an ancient experience of the spirit. This spirit is holistic, embodied, mystical, and immanental rather than transcendental. And while the process has only just begun, and will take a great deal more time to be realised, Australia could provide important spiritual leadership to the Western world, because what we are undergoing here is a transformation that all Western nations will eventually have to undergo if civilisation is to recover a creative relationship with the earth.

With the inevitable demise of our former supremacist concept of spirit, the West will have to develop humbler, more holistic concepts of religion and spirit. The popular Celtic revival in Ireland, France and the United Kingdom is a positive sign that an earth-based, celebrative spirituality is already growing in parts of the West. The cure for our modernist woes and our 'death of God' alienation is active involvement in the spirituality of the earth and immersion in the revitalising capacities of the body, physicality and nature. By virtue of our geography, history, and necessary racial atonement with Aboriginal people, Jewish-Christian Australia is already going through this spiritual revolution and is developing new and healing concepts of spirit.

We have come a long way from the early colonial days, in which some Christian missionaries attempted to 'save' Aboriginal people by replacing traditional beliefs with recognisably Western European religious practices. Some missionaries taught Aboriginal people that their religion was evil, heathen, and that only the Christian West could offer truth and salvation. But Christianity is no longer able to adopt this arrogant, supremacist position. Our own understandings have broadened and deepened, so that clergy today are more interested in finding the presence of the spirit in this ancient culture than in destroying its religion to promote our own. We have been reminded that the ways of the spirit are many and diverse, and this has forced a relativisation of our own spirituality, an attitude of humility rather than arrogance, and a radically ecumenical inclusiveness in place of the destructive imposition of a single model of absolute truth.

Christianity today is languishing and dying partly because it has lost touch with the immediacies of everyday living, including our erotic and embodied lives — sexuality, eros and physical animation. The celibate clergy are ageing and dying, and some priests are in disgrace because they have fallen prey to aberrant expressions of eros. Everywhere we turn, we find eros demanding readmission into the sanctity of life, wanting to re-establish its essential kinship with the spirit. For the Church to respond to this crisis by placing even tighter restraints upon eros is a deeply regrettable move. The majority of educated people feel that Christianity has lost relevance to our lives because it continues to preach an otherworldly message, failing to keep pace with the social revolutions in sexuality and behaviour that have characterised the last hundred years and more. These social revolutions have led to new ways of relating to embodied, physical reality, and because religion has not been a part of these movements, it has become dangerously irrelevant to the incarnational thrust of recent history.

Westerners are also looking for a religious vision that is able to again make sacred the physical world and the natural environment, as our need to direct positive attention to the environmental emergency becomes more apparent. Here is where Aboriginal religion can contribute major insights. Aboriginal cosmology does not subscribe to the myth of the atomised individual, instead expanding the sense of self to include the extended family, the tribe, the nation, the Dreaming trails, the wider landscape and the cosmos. The individual is linked to these larger realities through the active presence of sacred forces, and through these forces, he or she is taught to honour the world at large, because the forces that run through our individual being are the same forces that animate the land. This understanding is essential to Westerners if we are to halt the ongoing desacralisation of the world. We need to draw again a series of sacred lines that connect us outwards to the world, and horizontally to the creation, and not focus on a single vertical line upwards to our personal God or individual redemption. I will review this important theme again in the chapter on ecospirituality.

RENEWAL THROUGH THE FEMININE

Aboriginal spirituality is a spirituality of the body, movement, animal life and the land, with an Earth Mother as its central focus. Judeo-Christianity is of the sky, the mind, the word or *logos*, and has as its central deity a Heavenly Father. According to Western high culture, our Sky God is dead, or has fallen into some ineffectual stupor, so that we can no longer look to Him for our redemption. However, my own view is that our Heavenly Father is not dead, but requires grounding, 'incarnation', and reinvigoration through passionate involvement in the mysteries of the feminine and in natural creation. This is exactly what Aboriginal spirituality can inspire in us, since it is steeped in the mysteries of the natural world. By recovering a deep sense of wonder and astonishment in creation, we can build again a cultural ladder, an *axis mundi*, linking heaven and Earth, so that the Earth can be redeemed by the transcendent while the transcendent, in turn, is invigorated by its new contact with the Earth. As soon as a new cosmology is constructed that allows the spirit to come down to earth and earthly life to reach upwards to transcendence, Australia will give birth to a new religious high culture.

Paradoxically, I predict, it will be by recovering the feminine face of the divine or by recalling to our cultural memory the image of God as Mother that God the Father will be revived. God the Father will not be revived directly; all the vital energy of our time and place is with the feminine spirit, and we must accept its cultural and religious leadership. Although I am not a feminist, it is here that my own project for an Australian spirituality is in full accord with the feminist theological mission. Both the Australian experience and the feminist theological movement recognise that the West's experience of God is exhausted and historically anachronistic. Revival is needed, and revival can come about only by sacrificing some of our time-honoured images of God. I believe that we have mistakenly confined God's incarnation to the literal-historical person of Jesus, failing to see how Jesus is symbolic of an infinitely larger pattern of recurring incarnation more wondrous than anything conventional Christianity has so far allowed.

TWO-WAY DIALOGUE AND CULTURAL EXCHANGE

For civilisations, exchange is oxygen.

— *AIME CESAIRE*[10]

It is by rediscovering the presence of the spirit in creation with the help of indigenous religions that Christianity can recover the expansive dimension of the sacred, and reinstate the horizontal link with the world that has been attacked by individualism and modernity. Christianity can no longer behave in a superior manner towards Aboriginal religion, but must see how its own spiritual essence, the Holy Spirit, is discovered in this 'wholly other', non-European religion. It will not judge and denigrate this other religion, but realise its fundamental kinship with it. The need to convert (evangelism) will give way to a need to discover a deep religious mystery common to both traditions (mysticism). Western religion can look upon Aboriginal religion as if witnessing the lost dimensions of its own religious heritage. It will look into the mirror, darkly aware that what is reflected is the image of its own alter-ego, with whom it needs to make a pact for the sake of transformation.

Creation theologian Matthew Fox believes that:

> *Eight thousand years ago, in the Fertile Crescent, we set aside the Mother Goddess tradition but we can locate it again and creatively refine it in ... Australia.*[11]

He included North America in this statement, and it is true that when Old Europe meets the New World, it actually discovers its own lost or repressed unconscious life in the new-old landscape. That is why it is mainly the oldest traditions within the Christian West — namely, the Catholic traditions — that can respond theologically and imaginatively to the challenge of the new cultural situation. The antiquity of these Christian traditions is a kind of two-edged sword, for while their great age brings depth, remnants of paganism, and adoration of the feminine (even if in limited form), all of which grant us the capacity to relate to indigenous peoples, the very ancientness of these religions is also a burden, in the sense of being politically and institutionally antiquated. But even if ancient Christianity groans under its own weight, we must be deeply thankful that the Protestant Reformation did not completely obliterate the deeply mystical and feminine elements that we need so desperately today.

Of course, as well as gaining new energy, depth and femininity from its encounters with indigenous cultures, Christianity also gives new life and dimension to indigenous people. Although there has been much hardship and tragedy as Christianity was inappropriately imposed from above, indigenous lives have been profoundly transformed by the spiritual richness of Christianity, a fact I could not recognise for many years. But it has become clear to me recently, especially from conversations with Aboriginal elders and the published testimonials of Aboriginal clergy and theologians,[12] that Christianity has been as much a gift to Aboriginality as the indigenous spirit has been a gift to us.[13]

Western religion cannot be revived by stealing the sacred contents of Aboriginal religions or by filling our appalling emptiness with their fullness. This is the disastrous error of the New Age spiritual movement, and it misunderstands the challenge that lies before Western societies. Our task is not to engage in spiritual appropriations, but to learn from the indigenous example how to discover new and meaningful forms of religious life, forms that can bind us to our environment and reconnect us to the mystery of creation. In my experience, Aboriginal elders are keen to support us in the creation of such a new spiritual covenant. But as yet, Western religion is dragging its heels on this necessary spiritual project, despite the encouragement of Pope John Paul II, who told Aboriginal people in Alice Springs in 1985:

> *You are part of Australia and Australia is part of you. And the Church herself in Australia will not be fully the Church that Jesus wants her to be until you have made your contribution to her life and until that contribution has been joyfully received by others.*[14]

I agree wholeheartedly with this visionary decree, and urge religious authorities in Australia to pursue this goal through cross-cultural exchange and interfaith dialogue.

Many political thinkers cry foul as soon as we set foot upon Aboriginal sacred ground, but we are already on Aboriginal sacred soil, so this protest seems rather late in the day. Since Aboriginal people are keen to participate in the creation of a new Australian spirituality, the objections from the political left, which I will explore in the next chapter, are drily academic, even if intended to protect the interests of an oppressed people.

The important point here is that no religious tradition can be locked up in static and isolated space. As soon as religion becomes static, it begins to die. This is true for any religion, whether Aboriginal or Christian. The Aboriginal people long for religious transformation as much as we do, and they will not achieve this renewal by shutting themselves off from white people. The radical left idea that isolation from and resistance to white Australia will bring new strength to Aboriginal culture is an illusion. Many Aboriginal elders have expressed the desire to establish a new sacred dispensation, and contrary to leftist ideology, they would like to do this in cooperation with non-Aboriginal Australians. In 1991, the Institute of Criminology hosted a conference in Alice Springs entitled 'Healing Our People', at which an elder from the Kowanyama Community in Queensland said:

> We can't go back. The old law was for the old problems. Now we got this new law, this Whiteman's way. And we got these new problems. This law doesn't fix them either. It's no good. What we got to do is put them together, the old and the new. Mix them up. And they'll be hard and strong like cement.[15]

The old ways need to incorporate the new experiences if religion is to be relevant and powerful.

This call for change within Aboriginal sacred traditions is not being heard by contemporary mainstream Australia, which likes to think of Aboriginal spirituality as something contained in an hermetically sealed vessel, a remote, eternal 'sacredness' within a static Aboriginal culture. The cry within Aboriginal culture is for spiritual transformation, and Aboriginal people are, I believe, far more prepared than we are to take risks with culture and the sacred. Because we are further removed from the sacred, we are less understanding of its needs.

RED SPIRIT: THE WARM GLOW OF THE EARTH GODS

In his monumental 1939 poem 'Australia', A. D. Hope imagined that a new 'spirit' would arise from Australian soil, a spirit unlike that which has emerged from European cultures. The Australian spirit would be "savage and scarlet as no green hills dare".[16] Fifty years later, novelist Peter Carey expressed similar insights in *Oscar and Lucinda*; Oscar Hopkins "could not imagine ... what this countryside was like. He used soft words like brook and lane and copse. He could not imagine its raw-toothed savagery".[17] Even artists who are not expressly religious, such as Peter Carey and others, nevertheless cannot resist speaking metaphorically about the rise of a new kind of spirit in Australia.

Artists appear to agree that what will emerge here will be qualitatively different from our former European spirituality. Australian spirit will be 'savage' in the sense of being untamed, primordial, definitely not Wordsworthian; it will be challenging rather than consoling. And Hope's word 'scarlet' suggests not only the red earth and pink mountain ranges but also red blood, instinct and passion. One of the great themes of Hope's poetic career is the profound continuity between spirituality and sexuality, between religion and the body. We will not have any 'disembodied' spirit here, no spirituality which is embarrassed by the body or sexuality.

The cultural 'mixing' of Aboriginal spirituality and Christian revelation will give rise to an embodied religious sense, an awareness of the sanctity and sacramentality of nature. Judith Wright has worked for decades to express this embodied religious sense, a celebration of the sacred that is at once sensual and passionate. Yet, in struggling to articulate this intuition of cosmic interconnectedness, Wright has had to put aside a good deal of her European heritage, especially the dualism of Hellenic sources and Pauline Christianity. We cannot arrive at a non-dualistic state just by thinking about it; rather, the sensitive poet has to suffer enormously to dissolve the rigid dualistic framework most of us have inherited. In achieving a vision of non-duality, Wright's teachers have been the land and the Aboriginal people, since in Australia, as she says in 'At Cooloolah', the conventional dualisms cannot be replicated because "earth is spirit".[18] The earth is animated, and saturated with the spiritual life of our indigenous people.

In Australia, Hope suggests, we might emerge with an earthy, passionate spirituality such as the green hills of Europe would not 'dare'. The rising spirituality will not be 'more of the same', another expression of dualistic-patriarchal religion, but will be immanental and non-triumphalist, that is, a 'truer' version of Christianity in its original, radical meaning. Australia's future contribution to world religious experience will be profound, and many Aboriginal people, who appear to know this already, are waiting for the new to be consciously embraced by this country. This development will put an end to the colonial phase and allow the postcolonial spirit to be born.

Upon returning to Australia from Oxford, and after viewing an exhibition of Australian art entitled 'Spirit and Place' at the Sydney Museum of Contemporary Art in January 1997,[19] expatriate critic Peter Conrad said: "The whole curse of the modern world just doesn't seem to have imposed itself here. When the sky-god expired, the earth gods were re-animated."[20] There is poetic truth in this statement, although it is an exaggeration. As I explained in the previous chapter, there is a great deal of modernist feeling in Australian art, although this (quite deliberately) was not in evidence at this important exhibition. But running alongside or parallel with angst-ridden modern art, and sometimes found together with it in the same artist or writer, is a tradition that we can only call romantic, spiritual and celebrative. In the literary arts, we need only mention the names of Patrick White, Judith Wright, Les Murray and John Shaw Neilson to demonstrate the prominence of this tradition and its national importance. The special character of the Australian arts is not to be found in the way it repeats the existential angst of the modern European arts, but in how it posits a new kind of spirituality based in earthly experience and everyday sacrality. This was the spirituality that so confounded the modernist sensibilities of our urbane visitor from Oxford as he viewed the 'Spirit and Place' exhibition.

It is not that we have bred a nation of naive artists. Our artists are naturally influenced by modernism, and by the so-called postmodernist style as well. But beyond the modern cry for meaning, or the postmodern disregard for or deferral of meaning, we find a deep spiritual sureness and conviction, a new basis for living, which our artists draw from their experience of the land or from Aboriginal culture or from a mixture of both. Our best art expresses a vitality of feeling and a primordial experience of nature that cuts across the modernist sensibility and replaces it with a new earth-romanticism or earth-mysticism.

In the literary works of White, Wright, Murray and Neilson, modernist alienation has been experienced and overcome. They have walked through and beyond T. S. Eliot's arid and sickening Waste Land and crossed to the other horizon, entering a new world of dynamic colour and energy, akin perhaps to the red desert in full bloom. This is the "savage and scarlet" spirit that Hope saw, and that has to be rendered meaningful and coherent in the future. Certainly, it is a serious mistake to suggest that Australian experience is backward or has not yet 'caught up with' the leading centres of world civilisation. This would be to read the red spirit regressively in terms of the old 'cultural cringe', which reduces everything Australian to second-rate status.

It is as Peter Conrad suggests: when the sky god expired, the earth gods were reanimated. Our culture has gone through the 'death of God', the loss of meaning, the absence of cosmic orientation, along with every other Western nation. We have not sidestepped modernity to discover a new romanticism or mysticism, but have found earthly vitality and meaning after the collapse of the sky god. This has had, let us say, a modifying impact upon our experience of modernism, which was cut short by the reawakening of a warm, earthly presence. Even Kenneth Slessor, our nearest approximation to full-blown modernism in poetry, stopped short of nihilism and futility, and wrote about landscape and the natural world in such a way as to modulate the modernist tone.[21] Slessor cut short his poetic career, partly, I believe, because his mystical sources of inspiration conflicted strongly with his consciously modernist programme.

But throughout the twentieth century, most of our artists have felt compelled to break ranks with their northern hemisphere models and guides, and with fashionable existential philosophies, in order to respond creatively to the ancient call of a primordial land. Creative artists cannot afford to follow fashion or trend for its own sake, but must move to where creative life is to be found. In Australia, our artists are called to put down solid roots into the soil, and as soon as they do this, their work takes on new energy and conviction, and they celebrate the deep links that connect us to place. Witness the difference, for instance, between Patrick White's drab novel *The Living and the Dead*, set in London in the 1940s, and the passionately religious and sonorous tones of *The Tree of Man*, written after the recovery of his childhood connection with the Australian earth. White's masterpieces of the 1950s and 1960s all draw their strength and spiritual vitality from the land.

Literary and art critics may choose to read this negatively, calling us rustic or folksy or backward or naive, but there is something very profound in the dedication with which Australian artists pursue their connections with landscape and with soil. This downward or underworld connection has led to a renaissance of spiritual feeling, even as the churches and the official religious culture appear to have lost authority and vitality. The earth gods have indeed been reanimated here, and this insight helps us to understand what is actually behind the flourishing of the arts in contemporary Australia.

ORDINARILY SACRED: EVERYDAY REALITY AND DIVINE PRESENCE

My next and related argument is that Australian spirituality is, and will continue to be, grounded in the ordinary events and experiences of daily existence. The sacred here will be ordinarily sacred; we will receive what Les Murray calls the "ordinary mail of the other world, wholly common, not postmarked divine".[22] This may give us an important clue as to why some regard Australia as a secular and godless country. If we are looking for the God who produces otherworldly miracles and wonders, He will not necessarily be found in Australia. If we fix our gaze through a conventional metaphysical lens, we may not be seeing what is really here. The sacred may be, paradoxically, beneath official religious notice. This would not be for the first time. We think, for instance, of the lowly stable in Bethlehem, a divine presence in the midst of excrement and straw. A typical feature of scripture is that the sacred is to be found where we least expect it and where 'official' consciousness least suspects it.

In Australian society, we find a certain preoccupation with the ordinary and the everyday, a down-to-earth sensibility which, in spite of its name, often reaches mystical intensity in its focus on the depth and goodness of ordinary things. We sometimes find, especially in outback settlements and country areas, a reverence for objects, places, landmarks that exceeds the bounds of materiality and becomes a kind of spiritual reverence. Again, we do not necessarily have the words or terms to describe this phenomenon, but in *The Tree of Man* White points to what he calls a "mysticism of objects" in Australian experience.[23] Les Murray speaks, semi-humorously, about what he calls "Strine Shinto", an Australian religiousness of the ordinary.[24] In Strine Shinto, or the mysticism of objects, things become more than things; they become emblems or icons invested with symbolic significance. Things stand for themselves, but they also stand for things as yet unknown. This is not necessarily paganism, a worship of idols, but rather *panentheism*, the presence of the divine in the manifest world.

Les Murray writes that what originally led him to poetry as a vocation was a desire to give voice to this hidden religious life of Australians:

> *From earliest childhood, I was almost always conscious of a strong, sometimes frightening, sometimes deeply reassuring current of sheer* meaning *in things and people, a pressure of significance that only rarely carried over into what people commonly said. The world was* resonant *and* radiant *with meanings and, knowing this, how could I speak as if none of it mattered, or leave it out the way people seemed to do?'*[25]

This "spiritual inarticulacy", as he calls it, is as prevalent today as it was in Murray's boyhood, perhaps more so now that religious discourse is rapidly disappearing from our common vocabulary, seen as antiquated and irrelevant to our workaday lives. In a society where religion is being eroded, the revelatory and sacred role of the artist is even more vital than ever before.

Like Les Murray, the artist Michael Leunig sees more than is commonly seen, and feels more than is commonly felt. This, perhaps, is the key feature of the visionary artist in any country at any time: he or she 'sees' the sacred, when apparently the habitual consciousness of the day does not. The creative artist is a *seer*.

> *I think from the time I could open my eyes I was aware that there seemed to be something else going on amongst those around me which was not talked about. There was another truth. It's as if I want to run up to people on the street and say, 'Look, I feel this; do you feel this, too?'*[26]

The task of the artist is to remind people that they do in fact have spiritual lives, that they do feel and sense a level of being that is beckoning them to new awareness and self-identity. This task is both psychotherapeutic and spiritually redemptive: the more we can feel and know these radiant meanings, the less we will be bound to compulsively act out the desire for more things and more experiences. Once we break through to a deeper level of reality and find the religious source that sustains us, the more we will be freed of fake, parodic or symptomatic questing for human fulfilment.

ABORIGINAL SPIRITUAL RECEPTIVITY TO ORDINARY THINGS

The ordinariness of the sacred is, I think, a further aspect of the Aboriginal gift. The Aboriginal Dreaming is a cosmology of the natural and the given. A creek or rocky outcrop is explained in terms of the primaeval workings of the creator spirit. The divine spirit did not perform miracles that transformed the Australian geography into some stupendous metaphysical wonderland. The spirit created things in their ordinariness and in the particularity of their physical embodiment.

The wonder or miracle is in seeing the divine hand within this ordinariness; the miracle of revelation is an act of perception, an act of imagination, and that is why it is best called the 'Dreaming'. The sacred here is shy, low-key, and must be 'sung up' by means of various ceremonies. The sacred has to be constantly renewed by human ritual, giving ceremony a divine, not merely a social, imperative. The sacred does not announce itself in boastful statements, but is a lowly and parallel reality within this reality. Importantly, the sacred is not confined to so-called sacred sites; these sites simply intensify and focus what is found everywhere.

It is instructive to listen to an Aboriginal view of the enchantment of the everyday and the natural world. David Mowaljarlai, a Ngarinyin elder, is the author of the important work *Yorro Yorro: Spirit of the Kimberley.* 'Yorro Yorro', a key term from the Ngarinyin, Worora and Wunumbal peoples in the Kimberley region, is defined by Mowaljarlai as, "ongoing divine Creation, in holistic terms, or 'everything standing up alive, brand new'".[27] We recognise from Christianity and also from Western mysticism the idea of everything being 'made new' by the spirit. Aboriginal sacred traditions are concerned with the art of reaching beyond the external appearances of things to connect with the animating spirit within the world. The act of attunement to the spirit of Yorro Yorro has a two-fold effect: it replenishes and rejuvenates the spirit in its work of ongoing creation, while simultaneously reviving and revitalising the person engaging in this attunement, in the act of renewing the spirit. Moreover, through the celebrant's efforts, the family, tribe and wider community are also made new in the presence of the spirit.

This process of spiritual attunement with the land and the everyday world resembles the shamanistic activity of North America. Firstly, it necessitates a highly receptive, even passive state of consciousness, one that is able to respond deeply and profoundly to the forces of the natural world. Mowaljarlai explains this beautifully to his co-writer, Jutta Malnic:

You know, Jutta, when daylight starts, it wakes me up. I can't sleep any more. It wakes the whole body. So I turn round and have a look. There is brightness. Piccaninny daylight makes you feel like a different person. Morning gives you the flow of a new day— aah![28]

Mowaljarlai allows himself to feel called by the promise of a new day, where the dawn, of course, symbolises new life through contact with the spirit:

With this beautiful colour inside, the sun is coming up, with that glow that comes straight away in the morning. The colour comes towards me and the day is waiting.

Then he explains how he receives new knowledge and deeper vision as this intuitive 'flow' with the world leads to mystical participation with the things of the world:

You have a feeling in your heart that you're going to feed your body this day, get more knowledge. You go out now, see animals moving, see trees, a river. You are looking at nature and giving it your full attention, seeing all its beauty. Your vision has opened and you start learning now.

In this heightened — or, perhaps more accurately, deepened — state of awareness, nothing in the world is without its inner life. Everything has a story to tell, and the celebrant is duly astonished by what the world has to say about itself:

When you touch them, all things talk to you, give you their story. It makes you really surprised. You feel you want to get deeper, so you start moving around and stamp your feet — to come closer and to recognise what you are seeing. You understand that your mind has been opened to all those things because you are seeing them; because your presence and their presence meet together and you recognise each other.

*These things recognise you. They give their wisdom
and their understanding to you when you come close
to them.*[29]

Finally in this extraordinary passage, Mowaljarlai records
the feelings of celebration and renewal that attend this
kind of experience:

*In the distance, you feel: 'Aaahh — I am going to go
there and have a closer look!' You know it is pulling
you. When you recognise it, it gives strength — a new
flow. You have life now.*

*Then you put it in your storeroom, in the little
room in your brains here. You taped him, you got 'im
in there! You are going off now, to see what the day
will hold. You feel a different person. One more day is
added to your life, you will be one day richer.*

For Mowaljarlai, it is not enough to have this ecstatic
experience and gain momentary delight. For him, the
idea of 'storing' it in one's awareness is crucial, because
this is the celebrant's bank of spiritual wisdom, a fund of
knowledge to be drawn upon in the future and that can
protect us in moments when enchantment deserts us and
we feel desolate. This perception is not a common one,
even for the celebrants of sacred law, and all of us have
to deal with the reappearance of the 'separate self', the
interference of the personal will, which will always limit
our experience of unity and harmony with the world
around us.

Mowarljarlai indicates that this spiritual experience
involves a kind of phenomenological paradox. One is
both present and not present as one moves through the
world. One is present with an attentive consciousness
but not with the ordinary ego. This involves not so
much looking *at* nature (the perennial gaze of the
Westerner, the tourist), but allowing the objective life
of the world to penetrate our barriers. This is diffuse,

indirect awareness, akin to what Sufism calls 'walking through the world with soft eyes':

> You got country as far as the eye can see, and it's yours. But because of this consciousness, you are going through it reverently, quietly — through the middle of all this nature. What will happen? Well, every contact you make with the eye — perhaps you don't bother to look at it — but everything is present for you to see.

So he is not necessarily looking at everything, in the sense of examining things in camera-like detail, but he is dissolving the hard forms of the world, the forms of separateness. In this act, profane time and space is abolished, and he walks through the soul of the world, the *anima mundi*. In this state, there is no alienation, only recognition as the things of the world speak to him and he communes with them.

Aboriginal spirituality, then, is a spirituality of deep seeing and deep listening. Miriam-Rose Ungunmerr describes this using a word from Ngangikurungkurr language, *dadirri*, and says this "is something like what you [white people] call 'contemplation'".[30] The celebrant has to conjure up the right mood, so that the separate self will not create a barrier between the celebrant and the spirit of the land. This kind of receptive spirituality is very hard for us Westerners to achieve, because we come from a 'conquering' consciousness, which forever strives to impose our own mental and psychological life upon the reality of the world. Aboriginal spirituality does not impose a metaphysical machinery upon the landscape; it sees through the landscape to the mythic forms and spirits behind it.

ANGLO-CELTIC SPIRITUALITY OF PRESENCE AND EMBODIMENT

Now let us see how another Australian poet, Les Murray, expresses a parallel kind of awareness. Les Murray is of Scots-Celtic background, but we see throughout his work that, like Mowaljarlai, he is not interested in staring blankly at landscape like an outsider or tourist, but instead longs to reveal the divine dimension of the ordinary world. This, of course, is the sacred task of all great art — not to reflect the profane features of the world, but to release and record the divine authority that is at the very heart of creation itself. This gives authority to the artist or poet, in so far as he or she becomes the instrument through which the divine is made apparent. Murray is fully aware of this awesome responsibility, and this recognition, together with his awareness of the source of his inspiration, is perhaps why most of his books of poetry are dedicated "To the greater glory of God". It is vital that inspired artists maintain this religious sensibility; otherwise, if the separate self identifies with this creativity and considers itself its source, the power of what is revealed can overwhelm and destroy the artist.

The artist's role is not representation but revelation. However, the irony is that the artist, like Mowaljarlai, reveals what is already present. This is not some super-galactic cosmic invention, but a simple act of restoring to our vision a dimension of the real from which we are habitually excluded, but only by our own making.

I have quoted from the poem 'Equanimity' before, but I would like to revisit it. Murray indicates that the first task in the act of sacred revelation is to peel back the profane layers of perception, so that the divine reality can be made apparent. This is a very humble act, since we walk over or cut across this sacredness all the time, without knowing it:

> *Almost beneath notice, as attainable as gravity, it is*
> *a continuous recovering moment. Pity the high*
> *madness that misses it continually . . .*
> *Through the peace beneath effort*

> *(even within effort: quiet air between the bars of our*
> *attention)*
> *comes unpurchased lifelong plenishment;*
> *Christ spoke to people most often on this level*
> *especially when they chattered about kingship and the*
> *Romans;*
> *all holiness speaks from it.*[31]

This is a remarkable insight, and a clever reversal of
religious expectations. The divine in our lives, typically felt
to be 'too high' for us to grasp, is actually below the
surface of our normal attention. And even if we are so
observant and receptive as to be able to participate in this
realm, it is beyond our capacity to articulate; it falls
"between the bars of our attention". The next line posits
Murray's antidote to the frantic pace and obsessional
longings of the consumer society: if we could break
through to this deeper level, we would discover, or
uncover, "unpurchased lifelong plenishment". The rewards
promised by the gospels are true, but we do not know
how to access them, how to draw them out so that we are
freed from our consumer compulsions. Traditionally, this
process of atonement is expressed through religious ritual
and sacrament, but secularism has declared these rituals
meaningless and unnecessary. Pathetically, the consumer
society busts itself to reach a fulfilment and a satisfaction
that it has actually turned away from.

> *From the otherworld of action and media, this*
> *interleaved continuing plane is hard to focus:*
> *we are looking into the light —*
> *it makes some smile, some grimace.*

The divine presence is an "interleaved continuing plane",
an extension in space, but Murray has also described
the divine as "a continuous recovering moment", an
extension in time. It is always present — in everything
we do, between the things we say, "between the bars of

our attention" — a partly obscured realm that will always give us support, offer to redeem us, if we allow it. Our hectic frazzle is not entirely mad while this offer of redemption is still held out to us.

We drift in and out of the divine plane, unable to stand its radiance, which can actually disintegrate our consciousness if we become immersed in it too deeply. There is God's presence in every tree and stone, in every detail of matter, and yet, strangely, we report that God is dead, not because God is dead but because we are dead to God's presence. Hence, Murray often advocates that we become less human and more like nature, so that we can live more in the divine radiance that emanates from the natural. In this poem, Murray ends with the image of birds, whose tiny lives, geared like ours to self-preservation and gratification, are nevertheless permeated by a sense of grace:

> More natural to look at the birds about the street,
> their life
> that is greedy, pinched, courageous and prudential
> as any on these bricked tree-mingled miles of
> settlement,
> to watch the unceasing on-off
> grace that attends their nearly every movement,
> the crimson parrot has it, alighting, tips, and recovers it,
> the game grace moveless in the shapes of trees
> and complex in our selves and fellow walkers; we see
> it's indivisible
> and scarcely willed. That it lights us from the
> incommensurable
> we sometimes glimpse, from being trapped in the point
> (bird minds and ours are so pointedly visual);
> a field all foreground, and equally all background,
> like a painting of equality. Of infinite detailed extent
> like God's attention. Where nothing is diminshed by
> perspective.

This triumphant end of the poem reminds us of the mediaeval saying that 'God is a circle whose centre is everywhere and whose circumference nowhere'. There is nowhere, nothing that is not embraced and lifted up by the divine grace of the creator, and this recognition leads us to a revolutionary understanding of religious experience. We do not just walk through the world; we also walk through the soul of the world, and at every point in our journey, it is possible to catch something of this original divine spark, often in the most unexpected way. For Murray, the crimson parrot serves as a symbol for creation, for while it strives to meet its own needs and desires, it nevertheless cannot help but reveal the greater peace and mystery of its creator. The parrot has grace, loses it, teeters, then regains its balance. This redemptive dimension radically modifies the earlier theological understanding that we live in a corrupt and fallen world; we do not live 'in' God, but we do not live outside or away from God either.

An important phrase here is that "bird minds and ours are so pointedly visual". This emphasises the visual, perceptual, wordless dimension of sacred experience in this country. Australian cinema is internationally renowned for its attention to visual detail, to natural setting. A number of our poets and essayists have made this point, including Fay Zwicky and Rodney Hall. Australian art wants to elevate the natural, the physical to greater focus and intensity. It wants to allow the visual to speak, because, as Murray says, our relationship to details contains a lot of religious energy and sacred intensity; therefore, the expression of this intensity could well be a major site of our religious and cultural renewal. What will be released by this revelation is a radically democratic God, a God revealed in the ordinary.

This is the sacred in a new key, the God within creation who works with us and who participates lovingly in the world of time and space. This God is of "infinite detailed extent", at once foreground and background, non-hierarchical, mystical and revealed through wonder. Australian spirituality, guided by the power of the elemental Earth and the endowment of the Aboriginal heritage, is destined to be a spirituality of immanence, a 'creation spirituality'. The disintegration of our transcendentalist, patriarchal, otherworldly religion may preface the birth of the new, which has already been mapped extensively by artists and other visionaries.

5

Aboriginal Reconciliation as a Spiritual Experience

The dreamworld is a frequent and natural place for white and Aboriginal Australians to meet.

— *LES MURRAY*[1]

OUT OF THE TOO-HARD BASKET

There is a missing side to much of our public discussion about Aboriginal reconciliation, and this side involves spirituality and religion. In some ways, the spiritual aspect is far more complex than the political and economic issues of reconciliation, which is why it is so often neglected or repressed. Perhaps Australian public life places the spiritual element of Aboriginal reconciliation in the too-hard basket, hoping for some future light on this difficult problem or, perhaps, hoping it will go away altogether. One way of avoiding the deeper moral and spiritual dimensions of reconciliation is by losing our focus in the quicksand of legalistic minutiae and technical jargon. It is a cynical ploy of governments and officials to deliberately subvert the debate about race and land by making it a debate that only a few experts, equipped with technical knowledge and skill, dare to enter. This is yet another way in which the letter of the law killeth, whereas the recovery of spirit would give us life. Aboriginal reconciliation involves every Australian man, woman and child, regardless of race or creed, and it is a travesty of social justice if each of us is not able to contribute to the debate.

It is often assumed that when we speak of spirituality in connection with Aboriginal cultures, we are advocating the appropriation of Aboriginal spirituality, and that white people such as myself have no business in that domain. Even if I protest that my own involvement in Aboriginal spirituality is non-exploitative and anti-colonialist, my critics will argue that I am just playing word games and would be better advised to leave this taboo area alone. But the censoring or suppression of the spiritual dimension of this debate does not serve Aboriginal people at all, nor help to protect them from neocolonial exploitation, but merely defends and protects the materialistic empire of Western intellectual discourse, which is threatened by the sacred and has no way to engage in a dialogue with it. The taboo silence and extreme sensitivity around this area is largely self-imposed, a very precious work of white political contrivance. It certainly does not arise from Aboriginal people, who are constantly encouraging us to extend the debate about reconciliation into the spiritual domain. I am convinced that the stone rejected by the builders of our official discussion about reconciliation can become the cornerstone of a truly authentic racial and cultural reconciliation.

But despite our secular prejudices and official attitude, spirituality is going to be impossible to avoid. For non-Aboriginals to grasp the depth of the Aboriginal claim to traditional ownership of land requires an act of spiritual perception. It is impossible for an economic rationalist to understand what Aboriginal people mean when they say that the land is their ancestral mother or that the country is a field of creator spirits, without a leap beyond materialist senses of reality. The Aboriginal view of the world is a deeply spiritual and religious one, and if we lack soul or spirit ourselves, how are we ever to respect the cultural and historical importance of this animated land to its indigenous people?

Aboriginal reconciliation will demand more from us than we have so far imagined. If land rights and indigenous custodianship is going to mean more than clichés and slogans, we will have to abandon our patronising pretence at empathy and instead make a genuine attempt to view the world the way our indigenous people do. The land rights platform in Australia needs a spiritual basis, not so that white people can pretend to be Aboriginals, but so that we can approach the land in a psychologically more complete way. Non-Aboriginal Australians need to engage in a leap of understanding, and strive to perceive what living in an animated cosmos would be like. Reconciliation might then be imbued with transformative power. When our hearts have changed, we will be in a position to change our minds, and our social and political policies as well.

THE GAIN OF LOSS AND THE ART OF SACRIFICE

Only spirituality can teach us the value of sacrifice. Many non-Aboriginal Australians do not see what they would gain, what they would 'get out of' the land rights movement. They cannot see why we should concede land to its indigenous caretakers or give some of our moral and legal authority over the land to Aboriginals. As the erstwhile 'winners', they see no point in returning to the vanquished some of what has been falsely acquired.

Such a focus leaves little room for real reconciliation, which requires a morality unknown to those motivated by greed or ego gratification. This deeper morality, I would contend, inevitably involves a sense of the spirit. It cannot be legislated by government, but is brought into being only through the activation of the human spirit. From the spiritual point of view, loss, concession or sacrifice can be a gain. Indeed, this is the whole paradox upon which religious experience is based and which the rational ego finds so puzzlingly irrational. To the spirit, which has a larger sense of history than the ego, Aboriginal land rights is not a loss, simply justice.

The Australian poet James McAuley closes his religious poem 'An Art of Poetry' with this magnificent last stanza:

We know, where Christ has set his hand
Only the real remains:
I am impatient for that loss
By which the spirit gains.[2]

This is simple, profound and true, and I believe that more ordinary Australians are longing for precisely this kind of experience. Many of us are growing impatient for that loss of greed by which the Australian spirit can gain. Most of our political leaders are out of step with this process. They still campaign on behalf of the greedy, consumerist ego, whose cry is for more property, more wealth, more exploitation of natural resources. In 1998, the conservative politician Tim Fischer thought he was doing Australians a great favour by opposing indigenous land rights, and by delivering morally corrupt legislation that brings what he called "bucketloads of extinguishment [of native title]". However, the cry of this nation's spirit is for Less rather than More, for justice rather than further exploitation. The human spirit finds the greedy ego's More to be heavy, burdensome, profane. It is more concerned with the quality of life than with its quantity, and Australians today are looking for meaning, purpose and justice rather than 'more of the same'.

So this is the real dilemma that we Australians face. We have not factored spirituality, or the deeper morality that spirituality brings, into our secular institutions. The people are moving in a different direction to the institutions that pretend to serve them. What kind of scenario does this produce? It creates a very stressful and dangerous social situation, as expressed, for instance, in the epidemic wave of public disillusionment in our political system and in the widespread distrust of all figures of authority, including politicians, doctors, lawyers and academics. If our public figures and institutions work only on behalf of the greedy ego, itself such a tiny portion of the human experience, then in what sense do they have any authority at all? And if they have so little moral authority, why can we not divest them of their power? Reform and dissent are in the air, because the Australian people are growing tired of the mean little public ego and its tyrannical control over our lives.

There is, I would suggest, a kind of grassroots spiritual movement among non-Aboriginals about this political process. Reconciliation is, above all, a religious term: it is a word often used by the Apostle Paul in his letters and epistles. Reconciliation with the sacred, Paul reminds us, involves sacrifice. The very word 'sacrifice' comes from the same etymological root as the word 'sacred', and the notion of sacrifice connotes 'making sacred'. The return of significant amounts of land and the granting of expanded legal rights to Aboriginal people would certainly restore the traditional sacredness of the land to those who have been dispossessed of it. But in addition to this, this same act will restore a sense of sacredness and justice to non-Aboriginal culture as well.

These spiritual gains cannot be underestimated. The gnawing emptiness that many white Australians feel at the centre of their lives is spiritual in nature. Many try to fill this emptiness with compulsive economic consumption, absorption in the mass media, faddism, cults, ideologies, substance abuse and various other kinds of escapism. Our symptomatic behaviour gives us no sense of enduring meaning and the inner emptiness always returns. The so-called 'identity crisis' of white Australians is itself a spiritual crisis; it is a sense of disconnection from ourselves, from the land, from history and from the world. Australians instinctively search for connection, for a sense of belonging that continues to elude us even in our 'own' country. Only by way of reconciliation with the land and its indigenous people can we achieve that belonging, connectedness, identity, purpose we seem to lack. These are the spiritual values driving a grassroots movement that will transform this country.

THE RECOGNITION AND INTEGRATION OF EVIL

I don't think we need to feel guilty or shameful about pursuing these values. Some highly educated white people believe that whatever brings white society a sense of moral or spiritual redemption must be bad, because we are inherently evil and in need of punishment. A kind of old-world puritanism and punitiveness has arisen from our progressive intellectual movements, creating inflexibility, intolerance and a lack of forgiveness. We have no business being in this country, the argument goes, and any attempt to change the existential condition of our lives or to reduce our fundamental anxiety is seen as a product of colonialist exploitation and self-justification. I meet this attitude often in the universities, where rigid versions of postcolonialism become synonymous with self-flagellation and 'racism in reverse'. This indulgence in white guilt furthers the interests of no-one, least of all Aboriginal people, who cannot be expected to feel that justice has been done merely because white intellectual elites are afloat in an ocean of guilt.

I do not consider non-Aboriginal Australians to be inherently evil, although we have certainly created evil in the past, for which we have an urgent need to atone. The problem with the radical view is that in completely identifying white Australians with this evil, it pins us to the wall and leaves us unable to move. At least some Aboriginal elders do not feel this way, believing in the human capacity for self-transformation and holding out hope for our moral redemption, as will be discussed at the end of this chapter, in the section on Ned Kelly Dreaming. The fashionable cult of guilt is out of touch with the complexity and flux of life, fixing us in an unregenerate pose from which there is no progress or movement. What postcolonial awareness does achieve, however, is a dramatic raising of the shadowy and evil side that has been systematically refused by the dominant mainstream consciousness. According to our national persona and our official story (what we tell ourselves about ourselves), we are still an heroic and blameless people, descended from pioneers who tamed a wild and dangerous land. We are, in this forgetful discourse, adorable Aussie battlers who fashioned a new society in a difficult, unfamiliar environment.

Hence, politicians such as Prime Minister John Howard reject the presence of evil in our national story. He believes this great country has an unsullied great and noble history. He will not subscribe to what he calls the "black armband view of history", because he reads our history only through the perspective of the conquering ego and will not tolerate any divergence from this view. The get-ahead white ego suffers from an 'inability to mourn', because it is fixated on the surface of life. Any mourning for past wrongs could drag it below the surface, where it fears it would drown in unassimilable darkness. This ego cannot afford to remember the past or apologise to the Aboriginal people, because it lacks the depth of soul that would carry it beyond mourning and through a process of deepening. In Jungian language, this national ego refuses its own individuation, and therefore, according to Jung, it renounces its claims to authenticity and growth.

Our superficial, semi-blind public ego sees no serpent in the Garden of its Eden and has no awareness of its own sin. Prime Minister John Howard has a profane and secular vision, a vision without a sense of the sacred and, hence, without any regard for the reality of evil, or the need to atone for our evil. Atoning for evil is a religious process, requiring an understanding of religious reconciliation. It is little wonder that a society unable to understand religious reconciliation cannot get Aboriginal reconciliation right either. Both require an awareness of evil, both the reality and inevitability of evil and our constant need to be redeemed from its burden. We may all be suffering from the continued fallout from the separation of religion and state, because although the secular state gets on with the business of political process, our secular institutions are faced at almost every turn with decisions that demand the deeper morality that can arise only from a profound spiritual awareness. A country without this awareness is a country without a soul, and who among us truly imagines that our present institutional system can deliver the soul we all so desperately require?

The secular political institutions seem unable to realise how important morale and spiritual integrity are to the nation. If we want to put it in economic terms, we could say that purpose, meaning, harmonious race relations and a reduction in the burden of guilt have incalculable social value, and constitute 'social capital' recognisable to any political leader with sense. The impact of such a lack of morale upon young people is considerable, since they are the ones who feel and suffer the nation's lack of integrity particularly acutely, often internalising that lack of integrity as poor self-esteem and low motivation. Suicidal impulses can arise from such a perceived sense of worthlessness. Acknowledging past evils and atrocities may seem a small price to pay if it means that fewer of our contemporary youth, black and white, lack that sense of spiritual integrity that makes life worth living.

It must be admitted, however, that the secular state when guided by progressive social attitudes and high moral principles is able to perceive the reality of evil, and thus achieves a kind of 'secular spirituality' in which the deepest truths of history and the human condition are realised. In the High Court's 1992 Mabo decision, Justices Deane and Gaudron described Aboriginal dispossession as "the darkest aspect of the history of this nation". Australia must "remain diminished" until its "national legacy of unutterable shame" is acknowledged. In response to this High Court finding, Prime Minister Paul Keating delivered his famous Redfern speech, in which he frankly admitted a history of "dispossession" and "national shame". But these profound sentiments were to be stifled when the Keating Government was ousted from office by a general population that did not give such considerations the same priority. When we leave crucial moral issues in the secular domain, we place them at the mercy of popular whim, and justice glimpsed by a progressive government can be quickly reversed if the fickle collective ego decides to withdraw its interest in or sympathy for issues relating to a higher order of truth. The political state separated from religion is a state separated from the very foundations of truth and justice, and relying on 'good' governments to institute 'enlightened' policies is a hazardous and disappointing business. I cannot put my trust in our political process as it stands today, because it represents the claims of the ego rather than the truths of the spirit.

I am aware that the burden of our necessary sacrifice falls heavily upon pastoralists, graziers, and men and women of the land. Often, city-based people do not realise what land-based settler Australians are having to endure, and I believe the burden of sacrifice will have to be balanced so that all Australians, not just farmers, contribute to the sacrifice as native title and racial justice claims are met. This sacrifice is best expressed not only in money, land and legal rights, but also in personal gestures of generosity: in time, voluntary service and working holidays on Aboriginal lands, in ecumenical and non-sectarian religious ceremonies, and in public rituals of forgiveness and reconciliation.

Since some of the clergy have recently begun to speak out in strong support of Aboriginal land rights, this has set some churches at odds with their flock, especially in the rural areas. Some people in the bush are saying that the churches have betrayed them. This throws up many pressing problems, not the least of which is the church's historical complicity with white imperialism and colonial rule. Whose side is the church on? Theologically, it is supposed to support the outcast and the dispossessed. But the church in Australia has tended to reinforce, not oppose, mainstream social values, and in that sense it has not always been true to its radical mission, instead becoming a kind of civic religion in support of the status quo. The loss of the church's oppositional role has meant that as soon as it recovers its original vision, it is felt to be suddenly 'political', so that the more conventional among its followers protest that the church is failing them.

There have been many reports of graziers, farmers and their families boycotting church services and refusing to contribute monies to churches, which they see as apparently working against white prosperity. This situation represents an enormous challenge to the churches, but it also affords them a great opportunity to explain the full meaning of sacrifice and to explain the spiritual gain that can come with material loss. The churches must not speak on behalf of the ego's material security; rather, they must appeal to a deeper security, where the needs of the spirit are met.

One of the gains of reconciliation could be that the idea of single ownership of land is revealed as an egotistical fantasy. Land may have to be shared, or subject to multiple ownership, which would genuinely displace the concept of ego as lord and master of its property. Such a move towards plural ownership and land use could also awaken us to the complexity of our relationships with each other. In outback Australia, for example, it has often impressed me that numerous Aboriginal Dreamings overlap, or intersect at the same geographical site, but that these multiple overlappings do not cancel out the integrity of any of the Dreamings. In Alice Springs, we find that the Pitjantjatjara and the Arrente have overlapping Dreaming sites, and the same geophysical site can be sacred to different tribal nations. Perhaps this geophysical fluidity will be returned to our contemporary understanding of place, and one of the mysterious features of this ancient land will be restored, thus ensuring that the land triumphs over white concepts of ownership.

BEYOND LEFT AND RIGHT: THE NEED FOR A RADICAL CENTRE

In their contribution to the land rights debate, the churches may have recovered something of their original spiritual fire, and this is largely due to the great work of social justice campaigners such as Father Frank Brennan, Sister Veronica Brady, Father Eugene Stockton and others. In the grassroots spiritual movement that will restore moral integrity to the nation, they will be joined by artists and independent thinkers who have the courage to dream new and better dreams.

The political scene, however, largely remains dreary and depressing. Many of our politicians are too unimaginative or petty to notice the spirit of justice that is emerging from the nation's soul, while most academic political thinkers seem unable to factor a transformative spiritual dimension into their calculations. The left-wing avant-garde appear to have too much hatred for themselves and for society to work towards the redemption of either. On the other hand, the political right is constitutionally opposed to social change and wedded to a sense of class pride and race privilege, believing in the rightness of the questing ego, and therefore is unable to perceive its own satanic aspect. Pleased with the way things are, those of the right do not want any social or political revolution.

On the left, there is revolutionary impetus, but no redemptive vision to bring any revolution to birth. The left is choked with guilt and sees evil everywhere, but has no way of transforming this evil because spirit is denied and berated as an illusion, "opium for the masses". Although the left correctly perceives corruption, it is incapable of offering a solution, since only spirit can provide the circuit-breaker. What we need is a new cultural and political position, a radical centre that respects the value of tradition, but that also recognises the necessity of reforming our institutions according to spiritual and moral precepts.

THE INDIGENISING PROCESS AND THE POWER OF THE LAND

As anticipated in the chapter 'Spirit and Place', there is another process, more hidden and less easy to identify, which has a significant impact on the psychology of the nation: the *indigenisation* of the non-Aboriginal psyche. Despite the fact that we sometimes continue to feel disconnected from this land, at another level we are putting down roots in the soil and are being transformed by it. I began to open up this area of debate in my book

Edge of the Sacred, and again I find myself reflecting on this phenomenon, because it is deserving of our continued attention. I return to this theme in the hope that I am able now to express these thoughts in plainer language, since it is perilously easy to lock up insights in this or that system of knowledge (in my case, psychoanalytic), where they then remain inaccessible to all those who have not been inducted into the specialised discourse.

I am intrigued by the process of 'colonisation in reverse', which is primarily spiritual, psychic or subtle. As we deepen our connection with place, the place slowly conquers us. "Man can be assimilated by a country", writes Jung.[3] He also wrote that:

> *Certain Australian Aboriginals assert that one cannot conquer foreign soil, because in it there dwell strange ancestor-spirits who reincarnate themselves in the new-born.*[4]

I have personally heard this view put several times by Aboriginal people in the Alice Springs area. I find that it haunts my mind constantly, although I am unable to properly understand it. This ancient wisdom speaks in an animistic language that we moderns do not comprehend. In the past, I have tried to psychologise this statement, but it loses a little in the translation. The Aboriginal idea of the transmigration of ancestral souls posits a full-blown 'assimilation' of white people to the reality of the Aboriginal sacred. For Aboriginal religion, this indicates a kind of poetic justice, where the indigenous victims of colonisation triumph over the invading people by converting the souls of their children into Aboriginal spirits. Or as Jung puts it: "The conqueror overcomes the old inhabitants in the body, but succumbs to his spirit".[5] My reading would be that the archetypal field of Australia constellates in all who come to live in this country the indigenous archetype within the deep unconscious. With the stirring of this archetype, often deeply repressed by sophistication, it looks as if the newcomer has been taken over by an ancestor spirit or Dreaming figure.

Although the Christian West believes in neither reincarnation nor ancestral spirits, many sensitive Australians have felt profoundly at home in Aboriginal Australia, although only a few brave souls, such as William Ricketts, have made these feelings public, at the risk of persecution and scorn. Many of us feel drawn into the mystery and poetry of this place, almost as if we were indigenous to it. Both sets of contradictory feelings — indigenous belonging and colonial alienation — can be found, for instance, in the poetry of Judith Wright (witness the poem 'Double Tree') or the fiction of Patrick White (as in *The Tree of Man*).

In my own experience, Aboriginal people sometimes announce to surprised and astonished Euro-Australians that 'we are your soul', partly to taunt our rationality and partly to invite us into a deeper mystery in which our rationality dissolves. But this remark is also intended to awaken in us a more powerful sense of social responsibility, establishing a spiritual foundation upon which right action and reformed sociopolitical behaviour can be based. Whenever it is expressed, I find that it calls me beyond my familiar self, away from modernist anxiety and self-concern, to spiritual interconnectedness. This, in turn, leads me not to cosmic speculation but, rather, to a strong sense of political responsibility, which draws me back to earth, increases my social awareness and mobilises my energy. The best way for Aboriginal Australians to bring about a social revolution is not to shout "Europeans, go home", but to cry "we are your soul", then observe the changes.

The first stage in colonisation is visible and always tragic, involving a clash of cultures and the super-imposition of a foreign society upon the body of the land. In this first stage, no-one asks about the spirituality of the land, or wonders what the land might teach us, because colonisation is a one-way street in which all cultural traffic moves outwards from an aggressive colonising force towards what is regarded as an inert and passive landscape. The colonial spaces are manipulated to suit the desires of the colonising ego. Indeed, the slogan of colonisation could well be Freud's regrettable motto: "Where there was id, there shall ego be".

But eventually this process is reversed, as we become more sensitive to place and as psychospiritual traffic starts to move from the land towards us. The colonial-ising project is subverted by an indigenising project. This second stage is not especially visible. It takes place underground, and is discerned mainly by artists and prophets. Formerly perceived as inert and passive, the land assumes an entirely different character. No longer merely property and real estate, it becomes spiritual landscape, drawing us into itself. The colonising ego looks small in the face of the hugeness of this land. The presumptions of the colonisers seem almost absurd, as history begins to be undone and as the land acts on us in a new way. In her work *Survival*, Margaret Atwood provides a powerfully lucid account of this spiritual process in the Canadian context, while her work *The Journals of Susannah Moodie* expresses the same sentiments in the language of poetry, which remains the language of the spirit.

As this process unfolds, settler Australians begin to acquire some of the characteristics of indigenous Australians. This process is spontaneous, and I am not suggesting that it is achieved through conscious theft or appropriation. It is simply that as settler Australians relate more fully and organically to the land, we find ourselves *aboriginalised*, since both white and black races are now being fed and nurtured by the same geo-spiritual source. The earth becomes not only the spiritual mother of Aboriginal life, but also the poetic and visionary matrix on which non-Aboriginals also rely for their spiritual sustenance. Visionary poet Les Murray gets it right when he asserts:

> *In Australian civilisation, I would contend, convergence between white and black is a fact, a subtle process, hard to discern often, and hard to produce evidence for. Just now, too, it lacks the force of fashion to drive it; the fashion is all for divisiveness now.*[6]

I will come back to the "fashion for divisiveness". This subtle, 'inside' story has intrigued me for many years. I became alert to it while growing up in central Australia in the 1960s, where the external persona of white society continued to be supremacist but where the inside life seemed profoundly indigenous. It often appeared ironic to see settler Australians prejudiced against Aboriginals on the basis of racial difference, yet the settlers themselves were becoming increasingly like Aboriginals even as they indulged their xenophobia.

As a youth, I was fascinated by the phenomenon of white Australians 'going native' in the bush, renouncing their European manners, mores and training and acquiring a basically Aboriginal attitude to life and land. I met several of these people, some of whom were articulate about the process. I also observed the numerous small, yet distinctive ways in which the dominant white culture had 'taken on' certain attributes of indigenous people: love of the land; a delight in cooking and eating under the open sky; a shy, often self-deprecating sense of humour; our inexplicable urge to 'go bush' or 'walkabout'; our love of travel across enormous desert expanses; and our strong attachment to very specific kinds of landscape or favourite geo-graphical locations. It has probably never occurred to most Euro-Australians that their favourite national activity — the social barbeque in the bush, park or backyard — recreates in essence the lifestyle and ritual activity of

Aboriginal people. Although a large number of white Australians would vehemently reject the notion that they are being 'aboriginalised' by the powerful spirit of place, poets such as Murray and Wright see it, and increasingly, they are not alone in this understanding.

INDIGENISATION AND DEEP CULTURAL MEMORY

Jung writes that "the foreign country somehow gets under the skin of those born in it". I admit that the word 'somehow' sounds extremely vague, but then, we have no rational or scientific explanation for this indigenising process. It must be emphasised that Euro-Australians are not turning into white or de facto Aboriginals. The power of the land and the influence of Aboriginal culture are activating primordial levels of the Euro-Australian psyche, stirring its deeper layers, layers that have been overlaid by civilisation, to new activity. The indigenous archetype within non-Aboriginals is not synonymous with Aboriginals, but is related to our own deep cultural memory, what Yeats called the *spiritus mundi*.

In this context, for instance, a descendant of the Celtic world is likely to discover that a version of ancient Celtic spirituality is awakened and stirred to new life in this country. One can see this in many different ways in Australian folk culture, where the attempt to 'grow down' into Australian soil has the effect of revitalising Celtic roots, giving rise to a kind of Celtic revival. It is as if the psyche, automatically realising that a bridge must be constructed between the colonising consciousness and the primal landscape, reaches back into cultural memory to find an answering image to Aboriginality. In her travel book *People Under the Skin*, Clare Dunne writes:

> *The more Aboriginal people I meet now, the more I seem to be talking to them about my Irish background and finding it a bridge to them.*[7]

The psychospiritual response to Aboriginality and land has to be authentic. However, although it must come from within the self and from within one's own culture, it is not necessarily a product of recent personal experience of our culture. We can 'remember' lives we have never actually lived, by virtue of Yeats's *Spiritus Mundi* and Jung's collective unconscious.

The psychologist Gebser has another mythic concept of this nature: the "ever-present origin". [8] This is an idea to be put alongside those of Yeats and Jung. At the heart of our lives, according to Gebser, is a psychocultural source that always remains with us, even though our lives may depart radically from it and even though our awareness cannot grasp it. At deep levels, we do not forget this ever-present origin, which we carry with us and which reveals itself to us at points of spiritual clarity, emotional crisis and personal transition. The awakening of the ever-present origin in Euro-Australians is a decidedly mystical and atavistic experience, giving a nation of practical realists an inner glow of mystic vitality. Suddenly, in this distant southern land, an ancient heritage, not necessarily lived in one's own lifetime, can come back to haunt us. This theme, as it relates to a Celtic ancestry, has been stunningly portrayed by Rodney Hall in his work *A Dream More Luminous than Love.*[9]

It is time we paid more attention to this atavistic process, because it is part of the spiritual destiny of Australian cultural life. If we do not become conscious of this process, we could readily fall foul of this urge in at least two ways. One unconscious response to indigenisation is to remain sheltered in our colonial mentality while we find ourselves drawn to Aboriginal art, literature, ceremony and religion. We feel an urge to acquire Aboriginal cultural property and the trappings of primordial desert life, but remain snugly ensconced in our suburban world view, unwilling to risk any personal or cultural change. I feel ambivalent about so many of our houses, offices, bank buildings and governmental premises displaying wall-to-wall Aboriginal art, Papunya-Tula dot paintings, and indigenous souvenirs and arte-facts. This dangerously symptomatic behaviour denotes an acting-out in which we surround ourselves with the symbols of a primordial consciousness that we continue to deny ourselves in our own lives. We give the impression that we have been moved by Aboriginality, but our response to it, in reality, is merely decorative, externalist and literal.

The second unconscious response to atavistic revival is found in those who live so-called New Age and feral lifestyles. Sometimes, it is the sons and daughters of the middle-class collectors of Aboriginal art who are escaping to the bush, converts to ecospirituality and the values of the Age of Aquarius. In northern New South Wales and various other idyllic rural locations around the country live ferals who see themselves as 'white Aborigines'. Some, in an echo of the Aboriginal belief in the transmigration of souls, consider themselves to be reincarnated tribespeople. Ironically, according to recent studies, many members of Australian feral communities imagine themselves to be reincarnated from the Indian tribes of North America, partly because the New Age industry serving up the images and stereotypes that these people find so compelling derives from California, with its characteristic idealisation of North American indigenous people.

But the point is that if a culture fails to realise what is happening to it, or refuses self-knowledge out of laziness or fear, some of its members will be driven to 'act out' in a variety of literal ways the spiritual process being ignored by the society as a whole. Whether our obsession is with consuming Aboriginal cultural property to fill our homes, or living in the bush and pretending to be Aboriginals in hippy communes, we are engaged in an acting out of our desire to identify with the indigenous, but without a firm understanding of how this might be achieved in authentic ways. According to cultural theorist William Irwin Thompson, at the start of any cultural transformation we usually find a wave of activity that could be viewed as eccentric or marginal. The 'crazies' in society demonstrate first of all, often in silly ways, what the culture as a whole will later be forced to come to terms with in more integrated and mature ways. But the real danger of any first wave of cultural activity is that the emerging content is taken out of context, and behaviours can be compromising and socially disruptive.

We are being called upon to find within ourselves an answering image to Aboriginal spirituality, some kind of corollary to the Aboriginal experience and perception of the natural world. The Celtic background of many Euro-Australians is, in this context, a real source of spiritual possibility, a way of crossing the yawning gap that currently separates us from Aboriginality. The poet Vincent Buckley has written extensively in this area. The work of Tim Winton, Les Murray, John Shaw Neilson, Rodney Hall and others offers insights for our development and models for growth along these lines.

Traditionally, non-Aboriginal Australians have travelled overseas in their attempt to find hints, resonances or clues about themselves, which they can then deepen when they return to Australia. This characteristic of white Australian life has often been criticised by a rigidly 'nationalistic' consciousness that wanted us to locate ourselves in Australia. I often feel drawn to ancestral family places in Ireland, England and France, and these connections, far from diminishing my status as an Australian give me a sense of broader context and larger belonging. One Aboriginal elder told me that it is important to go on these international Dreaming trails, to "see where you belong" and to "see all the forces that make up who you are". He did not see it as un-Australian or as diversionary to explore one's roots in this way. He understood that I could be more fully present in Australia, and more receptive to Aboriginal indigeneity, if my own indigeneity were honoured and understood.

The view that all non-Aboriginal Australians draw on a tradition that is 'merely' two hundred years old is a convenient secular fiction, designed partly to keep us at the surface of life and away from the dangerous religious depths. All of us have ancestral roots and deep connections with the ancient past. These roots and connections need to be explored for whatever spiritual meaning that can be made out of them. The point is not to become fanatically identified with these overseas ancestral places or to become a major shareholder in Qantas Airways to support this expensive habit, but to draw imaginative strength from our ancestral origins, to add substance, meaning and historical context to our own claims to 'indigeneity'.

BLOOD-LINE ANCESTORS, HOAXES AND IMPOSTORS

A great number of white Australians may actually have biological and blood-line connections with Aboriginal cultures, which adds a new and surprising dimension to our search for indigenous roots. There have been many legal marriages between white and black Australians, but in the past, there was also a good deal of casual sexual exploitation of Aboriginal women by white males, which has produced many children of mixed racial background. There are perhaps more among us with Aboriginal ancestry than we have previously imagined, our backgrounds hidden because of shame, or residual racial prejudice. However, with recent shifts in public attitudes, themselves expressions of a newly arising indigenous archetype, it is now a propitious time to discover and affirm Aboriginal ancestry, where it exists. As John Morton has suggested,[10] a sense of kinship between white and black Australians is what accounts for the popularity of works such as Sally Morgan's *My Place*, Jimmy Chi's musical *Bran Nue Dae*, and the television series *Heartland*, portraying a love affair between a white woman and a black man. Marcia Langton has speculated that the popularity of the best-selling *My Place*, in which Sally Morgan traces the discovery of her Aboriginal roots, may well lie in the fact that it "raises the possibility that the reader might also find, with a little sleuthing in the family tree, an Aboriginal ancestor".[11]

This expectation also opens the door to a recent kind of exploitation: white people fraudulently claiming an Aboriginal heritage. We find numerous examples of non-Aboriginal artists posing as Aboriginal in order to gain ancestral integrity and commercial advantage, and we discover all manner of deceit, cunning, duplicity and fraud being employed to 'cash in' on the new fashion for indigeneity. As with New Age 'reincarnated' Aboriginals, or the exploitation of Aboriginal culture by art dealers, such fraudulent activities are symptomatic actings out of the need of all rootless, colonial or migratory peoples to discover the indigenous archetype. When the indigenous archetype first emerges, it does so unconsciously, which is why there is so much pathology and distortion attending the 'rebirth' of primordiality in our time.

However, we should not allow these shadowy dimensions to cloud our appreciation of the positive aspects arising at the same time. As Jung argued, when a new archetype emerges, both its positive and negative sides will appear simultaneously. In our case, it is the *literalisation* of this archetype that gives rise to most of the negativity we find around us: the pretending to be Aboriginal, the fraud, the imposture. Psychologically, we are already 'other' than we appear, we already have different faces, other sides, secret ancestral heritages, but we need to access this awareness and express this internal plurality in new and clearer ways. To allow our indigenous archetype to enter our lives requires a dislodgement of the conventional ego as the ruling power of personality and society. There can be no space for our indigeneity without a sacrifice of our conventionality, and the comfort zone that supports it. These are the psychodynamics that replicate precisely what must happen in society and politics: displacement of white power and a re-empowerment of indigenous black culture. The alchemists used to say, "As within, so without", and it is true that no social revolution will take place in Australia unless we attend to both levels of reality simultaneously.

The reawakening of the indigenous archetype will lead us to a new experience of primordiality and to a new kind of cosmic religious awareness. The key features of this transformation will be the dramatic expansion of our horizons by the breakdown of the typical Western, dualistic division between self and natural world, which will be discussed in later chapters. The archaic layers of the psyche, still dormant but soon to be reawakened, do not know about the modern condition of alienation, our imprisonment within the cocoon of self. The primal person within us is celebratory and affirmative, cosmic and relational, and this is the ecstatic experience that anyone who spends significant time in the outback inevitably comes to recognise. We may enter the outback cynical, atheistic and narcissistic, but mostly, we come out of it as converts to cosmic religion.

In a future Australia, it is to be hoped, this will create a more celebratory and disinhibited way of life, a culture in which the spirit is experienced in sensuous matter and nature and in which the elemental earth becomes spiritual and enchanted. It will be the task of our future culture to invest this newly activated archetype with shape, colour, content and direction. This will require creative dialogue with Aboriginal culture, but cannot involve mere appropriation.

> *The Franco-American totalitarian style we call political correctness could be swept away by a single strong law, or convention, against deploying fashion against any individual or group, and I live to see it vanish.*
>
> — *Les Murray*[12]

A certain kind of reductive political mind will never grasp the argument about indigenisation and spirit of place, because it is already convinced that white society is guilt-ridden, spiritually worthless, and imprisoned within its own profane spaces. In materialistic writing, we constantly run into the taboo that says: white people shall not enter sacred space, because it is not 'ours' to enter. In an essay designed to attack the search for a settler Australian spirituality, Julie Marcus argues that:

> *Settler Australian mysticism [claims to] understand the eternal truths of Aboriginal religion. The universalising and egalitarian sentiments of mystical doctrine are used to deny the specificity of Aboriginal belief ... and to insert settler Australians into the very heart of that secret Aboriginal knowledge on which their only recognised claim to land rests.*[13]

This view sees settler Australian spirituality as a theft of Aboriginal sacred space, a subversion of the cultural basis of the land rights argument. While this outrage may be justified in relation to a vulgar, exploitative mysticism, in which aspects of Aboriginal culture are taken out of context and misused, I cannot see its general applicability to a sensible and intelligent pursuit of settler spirituality. If settler spirituality is politically astute and guided by traditional religious precepts, it can avoid the fatal series of conjunctions and equivalences that equates settler land-based spirituality with the 'devouring' of Aboriginal spirituality, with cultural appropriation, and with the erosion of the basis of Aboriginal land rights, leading ultimately to the destruction of the Aboriginal race.

It is disturbing that this analysis is rarely critiqued or disassembled. Writers calling themselves 'discourse analysts' do not seem to have the ability to analyse their own discourse. Instead, such thinking is presented as logical and self-evident, possessing an internal coherence that most educated people are expected to accept. In this way, the ruling materialist ideology becomes an unchallenged hegemonic authority. In questioning these false assumptions, one runs the risk of being branded a backlash thinker, a defender of the colonialist establishment, and so on. We are indoctrinated by an extreme materialist view in which white spirituality is deemed to be out of bounds and dangerous, in which secularism has acquired intolerant traits, and in which a kind of racism in reverse has become fashionably entrenched.

Since all of my own work calls into question the value of this ideological fashion, it is hardly surprising that I have been subject to vigorous attack by cultural materialists. Writings by Mitchell Rolls, Paul Brennan, Ken Gelder, Jane Jacobs, Denise Cuthbert and Michele Grossman, among others, have been targeting my work in recent times. The accusation is the same in every case: I am charged with stealing Aboriginal cultural property and plundering the indigenous secret-sacred. Apparently, the idea that there is a deep source of spirituality in the Euro-Australian psyche is some kind of trick that allows me to justify the theft of indigenous religion. White people are seen as entirely secular, so that any "yearnings for a spiritualised Australian domain"[14] are viewed with enormous suspicion.

I am also astonished that any longing for spirituality is immediately construed as a sign of 'New Age' activity, which must be rejected by any thinking Australian. The 'normal' Australian is, apparently, secular, profane and non-religious, and any attempt to change this identity is frowned upon as escapism. Since Anglo-Celtic and Jewish-Christian religions have been largely eradicated in the materialist discourse, any spiritual feeling in a white Australian is interpreted as a 'New Age' indulgence, and this term is used frequently by these critics specifically because it has acquired a pejorative meaning. I consider it sadly ironic that any expression of our Christian, Jewish, Celtic, Nordic or Islamic inheritance risks immediate classification as 'New Age'.

I am interested in pursuing spirituality as a more stable and profound basis for reconciliation. Appeals to morality and fairness have not been effective in the past; had they been heeded, we would by now have fully recognised Aboriginal entitlement to land. Spiritual experiences will not only provide a stable basis for genuine morality and right action but might also serve to heal the internal wounds in the Anglo-Celtic psyche, by reconnecting us with our spiritual inheritance and its ancient cosmology. Grossman and Cuthbert correctly, if ironically, grasp my meaning when they characterise this as "a process construed not as one of taking but instead of quarrying and retrieval".[15] True morality and social justice will be achieved once we activate the lost spiritual side of personal and political experience. Morality, unaided by a spiritual dynamic, is weak, flawed, subject to the whims of governments and social pressures, and very likely to fail us entirely.

According to Grossman and Cuthbert, my "narcissistic solo dreaming" takes me far away from political reality; my conceptualisation of the "Aboriginal within" makes me forget the Aboriginal without, and my writings result in "indigenous deterritorialisation".[16] In attending to my argument, they assert, we "Forget Redfern" (Paul Keating's pledge to Aboriginal Australia). Here, we see how a typical intellectual dualism insinuates itself: if we are having any spiritual feeling, we cannot also be thinking about social justice. On the contrary, to my mind: spiritual feeling makes us remember Redfern all the more vividly, since a spiritual feeling for land should make us recognise more intensely the rights of those who have internalised this landscape before us.

Political analyst Mitchell Rolls argues that my work is deceptive, engaged in what he calls an "intellectual sleight of hand".[17] "Behind the rhetoric aimed at establishing Tacey's disapproval of appropriation, he actively encourages the process".[18] My work "advocates the need to prospect for our salvation in Aboriginal cultural property and identity". "Rather than facilitating reconciliation", my work "frustrates that goal" and proves "deleterious to Aboriginal interests".[19] "The people Tacey is locating in the non-Aboriginal psyche are the Aborigines, not merely some hidden aspect of ourselves". "Surely this is nothing less than the psychological consumption of the Other".[20] This critic has me discovering 'real Aborigines' within the white soul. Materialists can make outrageous claims in their attempts to interpret spiritual ideas.

Paul Brennan argues that my work boils down to a "tourist-eats-native" philosophy, because he cannot see how we might get spiritual substance into our white psyches other than by stealing it.[21] In *Uncanny Australia*, Ken Gelder and Jane Jacobs conclude that my pursuit of a settler spirituality leads to an "effacing" of Aboriginal identity and a desire to "cut Aboriginal people out of the political".[22] It is clear that the myth of white profanity is taken on by all of these writers as literal fact. For Gelder and Jacobs, there is in Australia only "the Aboriginal Sacred",[23] everything else is a hoax. Spirituality in Australia, it would seem, has become identified with race, which is an extremely dangerous state of affairs.

Ironically, it is materialists themselves who depoliticise the Aboriginals, by immersing their identity in the sacred.

When the sacred becomes synonymous with indigeneity, we inflate and idealise indigenous people, but we also fail to grasp their essential humanity. We see indigenous people not as real human beings in real time and space but as disincarnate spirits in the no-place of myth. Separating this dangerous conflation of spirit and race requires white Australians to own their own spiritual impulses. If we no longer had to keep projecting all this mystical life upon Aboriginals, we might set about meeting their real social, economic and political needs. By owning our own spirituality, we defeat the false idealisations, allowing Aboriginal people to shrink back to human proportions, saving them from that fatal process by which we are pushing them further into the eternal realm of dream and death.

But of equally great danger to Aboriginal people is the nominalist philosophy that underpins much contemporary intellectual discussion. According to nominalism and its appearance in postmodernism, abstract terms such as spirit, Earth Mother, ancestral soul, sacred site and so on are merely objects of social convenience; they have no reality in themselves. For cultural materialists, the sacred is not part of the real. It has no existence outside the language systems that pretend to point to it. By this logic, any discourse about the sacred, including my own, is seen as a work of obfuscation and escapism, but so, too, is any other discourse about the sacred, including Aboriginal discourse. Reductive thinkers seem to ignore the fact that this argument about the unreality of the sacred radically undermines Aboriginal claims about the sacredness of the land, upon which traditional entitlements are based.

I argue that spiritual recognitions provide a true basis for right action and social justice, and that these materialists are actually playing a game with Aboriginal sacredness. In effect, they are saying that no sensible person would believe in the sacredness of anything, but that for political purposes and for legal reasons, we had better pretend that Aboriginal claims about sacred sites are true. These theorists are still operating from a patronising, white-supremacist position. They are too highly sophisticated to believe in the sacred, but because the indigenous people do believe, we had better politely indulge their beliefs. The cynical 'support' these materialists provide for Aboriginal culture is symptomatic of the consciousness that undermines their world view, culture and ancestral traditions.

Sacredness cannot be identified with any one culture, and no single tradition has a monopoly on the sacred. The world is already infused with the glory of the sacred; sacredness does not have to be imparted by a spiritual race or a metaphysical language. The task of any culture, whether tribal or postcolonial, is merely to elucidate and frame the cosmic sacredness that is already present as that culture's animating and primal creative source. But for some intellectuals, there is no sense in which a modern white culture might find the sources of spiritual renewal within itself, or through a deeper contact with the natural world, since spirituality is felt to reside only with preliterate tribal societies. Any non-indigenous claim upon the sacred is viewed as a Promethean act, involving transgression, guilt, and the need for punishment and retribution.

One is made aware, finally, that one is not engaged in real intellectual debate, but that one is transgressing a cultural taboo, and rage is a consequence of this transgression. The taboo is: thou shalt not enter sacred space, unless you happen to be Aboriginal. The key issue is fear.[24] The secular mind is terrified of the sacred, and a political justification for avoiding its challenge is as good as any other. This taboo has been constructed by us, not by Aboriginal people, to protect us from having to make any contact with the sacred, whether in the land, in Aboriginal culture or in the still largely unexplored depths within ourselves. The only way to break this deadlock is to withdraw our spiritual projections upon indigenous people and to collapse the ego boundaries that block or repress our own natural experience of the sacredness of reality.

SURVIVAL THROUGH INTEGRATION AND ACCOMMODATION

At this point, I want to question the logic upon which much intellectual discussion about Aboriginality is based. As Les Murray has said, the current intellectual fashion is "all for divisiveness", and contemporary theorising is based on the idea of political resistance — namely, the belief that Aboriginality can remain intact and hopeful of a future only if it resists the intrusions of non-Aboriginals into its cultural domains, especially its spiritual domains. Contrary to this thesis, I want to argue that the way ahead is not in racial separation or apartheid but in cultural dialogue and spiritual engagement. Moreover, traditional Aboriginal cultural practice has always been relational, open and receptive to change, so that the resistance theorists are actually running counter to indigenous wisdom, supplanting it with the received Western ideas of Marx, Foucault and the radical left.

For thousands of years, Aboriginal tribal nations have related to each other and to different language groups primarily through negotiation and accommodation, not overt resistance. Anthropologist David Turner defines "accommodation" between groups as "part of the one embedded in the other and vice versa without affecting the integrity of either". Turner argues that Aboriginal Australians have never sought apartness or exclusivity but, rather, integration and change. Similarly, Peter Willis writes that Aboriginal religion has never been static but has always been involved in evolutionary process:

> There is provision within Aboriginal traditional
> culture for religious change on three counts. The first

is by Dreaming, when a ritual leader creates or dreams a new ceremonial. The second is by religious exchange, when new rituals are taken into the group's repertoire. The third is an adjunct to social and political exchange, when new ceremonies are the ritual part of new relationships and alliances.[25]

He concludes that "Aboriginal religious style allows for the exchange of ceremonial", and asserts that "It is culturally appropriate for Aboriginal leaders to seek to increase their access to, participation in and ownership of ceremonial."[26]

The aim of Aboriginal cultures has never been spiritual purity or cultural fixity through the establishment of strong boundaries based on elaborate defence mechanisms or the ethics of exclusion. This is entirely a Western fantasy, based archetypally on the idea of the warrior nation that dominates other nations and that conquers through subordination and power. The Aboriginal way is deeply concerned with human and tribal survival, but this way appears to be non-heroic or even counter-heroic. Ethnologist Deborah Bird Rose warns that we must "clear our minds of expectations" and not impose our own rigid notions of identity or purity upon this different people. She reaches the surprising conclusion that:

Whereas Europeans conquer with guns and economic manipulation, ... Aborigines, in contrast, accommodate through reciprocal sharing within and through a cosmic order.[27]

To the rationalist outsider who sits in university libraries studying theories of society and cultural liberation, this sounds like an unreal romanticising or distortion of Aboriginality. But to those who know Aboriginal cultures from the inside and who have first-hand experience of tribal interactions, this is, in fact, an accurate account of their sense of 'being in the world'.

This same sense of relating to the other through ritual inclusivity and integration was to be applied to the European invaders. This is probably one of the untold stories of racial interaction in the Australian historical context. It is untold partly because our methods of seeing and interpreting cultural dynamics have not allowed us to see it. Deborah Bird Rose argues that the Aboriginal response to invasion and colonialism was frequently so sophisticated and complex that Western observers have been unable to identify it. Scholars, she says, have been mystified and also frustrated by the apparent absence of the typical responses to invasion, which would include "overt resistance, abuse, or emulation [of the oppressor]". She points out that cargo cults, so common in native groups in the Pacific region and so deeply based in envious identification with the oppressor's material wealth, have never developed in indigenous Australian cultures. "I suggest that at least some Aboriginal responses have gone unnoticed because they offer us what, from a position of power, is virtually unthinkable".[28] Basically, she argues, Aboriginals seek to redeem Europeans of their own evil by ritually inducting them into the Aboriginal cosmic order. Far from judging themselves inferior to the intruders, Aboriginals "found Europeans to be ignorant, at best, and grossly immoral at worst".[29] Through a spiritual accommodation of the intruder, ritual acts would be performed that would reduce the power of evil and enable the different parties to share land, resources and religious culture.

Deborah Bird Rose argues that Aboriginals ·adopted their time-honoured practice of survival through accommodation with the intruder, and sought reciprocal arrangements with the Europeans through offers of marriage, exchanges of knowledge and access to resources. The Aboriginals were baffled and confounded by the Europeans' failure to respond to these gifts. Why would they not engage in mutually beneficial exchange?

To the Aboriginal elders, the Europeans seemed distinctly uncivilised and immoral. The intruders were obsessed with their own childish desire and brutish greed; they wanted to steal land, destroy culture and extinguish indigenous lives, in a desperate bid to contradict natural and cosmic law. The Europeans cut across the ethic of integration and the cultural strategies of accommodation. Ironically, as Europeans judged Aboriginals to be uncivilised and barbarous, due to their scant clothing and absence of technology or building, Aboriginals were observing an appalling lack of civilization and morality in the technologically advanced intruders.

NED KELLY DREAMING: STRIVING TO REDEEM THE INVADERS

The "unthinkable" response of Aboriginal cultures has been to seek the moral and spiritual redemption of the invading Europeans. In her ground-breaking essay 'Ned Kelly Died for Our Sins', Deborah Bird Rose shows how Aboriginal cultures have incorporated European symbols and figures into their ceremonial practices, in an attempt to cleanse the evil element through ritual acts of transformation. Rose analyses two sets of mythological stories: one set based around the figure of Captain Cook, who becomes a symbol of invasion, human evil and rapacious greed, and another set centred around Ned Kelly, who is constructed as a figure of goodness and truth, in that he resists the 'false law' of the established colonial society.

Aboriginal elders and ritual custodians have not been concerned about whether they are 'appropriating' cultural property into their own religious cultures. They perform these acts spontaneously and in pursuit of the common good.

Ned Kelly is Dreaming; and more than that he is allocated a creative position in Dreaming. No matter how many Captain Cooks, police, and settlers came later, it is unmistakably the case that Ned was here first, actively making the Australian continent. Furthermore, Ned Kelly encountered Aborigines, and his encounters did not result in death, dispossession, or dispersal.[30]

Aboriginal Dreaming stories convert the historical figures of Cook and Kelly into mythic beings, and these beings engage in epic battles and conflicts reminiscent of the universal clash between the forces of Good and Evil. Kelly emerges as the 'moral European', because he opposed the power of the ruling classes and aligned himself with the moral position of those being dispossessed. In this sense, the Irish and the Aboriginals share a common moral and symbolic heritage, and it is no accident that the Irish Kelly emerges as a symbol of good in the Aboriginal imagination. In the ethnological material assembled, it is fascinating to see Cook and Kelly transposed into mythic time and space, with no importance placed on real geographical boundaries or chronological time. Kelly becomes an original creator being or an Ancestor Spirit, by virtue of his creative and ceremonial fusion with the archetype of the common good.

Rose argues that Aboriginal groups as far removed from Kelly country as the Northern Territory recognised in the figure of Ned Kelly a spiritual opportunity to contain and delimit the forces of evil unleashed by colonialism and invasion. Absorbed into the Aboriginal Dreamings, Kelly ritually performs good works (such as feeding damper and tea to desert Aboriginals), in opposition to the evil works of Captain Cook. In Arnhem Land, however, it is told that there was an earlier Cook, "The first and true Captain Cook [who] did not destroy". Through conjuring a 'true' Cook prior to the historical Cook, there is a bid to limit European evil by appealing to a pre-existent European archetype of justice and morality. The 'true' Cook tends to fuse at times with the figure of Ned Kelly himself.

In the stories, the evil figure of Cook is often made to die as sacred law returns to the country and order is restored. As one Aboriginal custodian of ritual reports: "Captain Cook is dead now; he is dead, and his immoral law ought to have died with him. In contrast, Ned Kelly was opposed to what Captain Cook and his mob were doing to Australia."[31]

Kelly frequently triumphs in ritual ceremony, though not necessarily by remaining alive — sometimes, it is by rising again after death in glorious resurrection. Kelly's spiritual fate, ritual destiny and miraculous deeds overlap those of the archetypal figure of Jesus Christ. In some stories, the figures of Jesus and Ned Kelly appear to coalesce into a single figure, as in the Yarralin Dreaming story, in which Ned Kelly visits "Wave Hill station long before any whitefellows had come into the Victoria River District. There he taught people how to make tea and cook damper. Although there was only one billy of tea, and one little damper, everybody got fed".[32]

The moral, cultural and spiritual implications of these contemporary Dreamings are far-reaching, and in a real sense, we have to rewrite the history of race relations because of them. The marvellously redemptive feature of these stories is that they strive to defeat European evil with European good — that is, they do not engage in a simple-minded splitting of the archetypes of good and evil along racial lines, in which case Aboriginality would equal good and colonialism evil. This kind of splitting is found in extreme radicalism and in left-wing liberational thinking, but not in Aboriginal religious culture itself. Aboriginal people extend enormous moral and spiritual generosity towards the invaders, assuming that they cannot all be evil and must harbour within themselves the cosmic forces of goodness and justice. In other words, Aboriginal culture is asking us to seek and find our own moral redemption in this land. We are to discover the Christ-like aspect of our collective nature and allow that aspect to triumph over our wrongdoing.

Again, it is easy to see a further ironic reversal here. Just as the early missionaries worked to 'save' Aboriginals from their pagan ways and to give them new life in the spirit of Jesus Christ, so the Aboriginals themselves, working from a sense of cosmic law in which the spirit of Christ was already present, sought to reveal to the un-Christian invaders the Christ-like capacity in their own souls. In a profoundly religious reversal of fate, the vanquished were actually calling the invaders to a higher order of being and a deeper morality. In the Australian scene, the redemptive power of Christ reveals itself more fully in the conquered than in the 'Christian' conqueror. This awareness is enshrined in the national folksong 'Waltzing Matilda', and it is found wherever the underdog or loser is championed as the bearer of the moral standard. This is also the burden of Deborah Bird Rose's work, and the sense of intellectual surprise and shock that attends her ethnological research. She is effectively saying that political action and social justice are profoundly spiritual, and that our reconciliation with Aboriginal culture can bring spiritual transformation to all Australians.

A remarkably hopeful feature of this Aboriginal material is that while Captain Cook is always regarded as European or, more precisely, English, Ned Kelly is mostly imagined as genuinely 'Australian'. This means that the 'good' in the Euro-Australian psyche has been deeply integrated into Australian geographical space and into Aboriginal sacred law. The good, so to speak, has a real foothold here, and is organically part of the postcolonial experience. As Rose so eloquently puts it: "Ned Kelly is indigenous; he is resistance against invasion and injustice". "And in indigenising him, they have declared him to be not truly other, but truly us".[33]

There is hope for justice in Australia, but this hope is unknown to the cultural materialists who know nothing of grace or redemption and who are unable to bestow the capacity for spiritual transformation upon white people.

SPIRITUALITY, LOVE AND RECONCILIATION

In my own experience, Aboriginal people are longing, perhaps even desperate, for a new kind of spiritual interaction with mainstream Australia, one that will bring healing, reconciliation and redemption. Miriam-Rose Ungunmerr puts it this way:

> *Even today, many of my people are dying inside. Yet, as a people, we still survive. Survival is something that has become part of us from centuries of struggle and endurance. Culture keeps on growing. With education and interaction with other people, I hope our culture will grow strong again. I hope that with this education and interaction, we will all become better people.*[34]

This is what Aboriginal people are saying over and over; they have enormous love and generosity, and spirituality, and with this great endowment, they are able to go on, in spite of appalling adversities. Their deep spirituality makes it possible for them to forgive us, even if we cannot, officially, say we are sorry. And even beyond forgiveness, as Deborah Bird Rose discovered, they want to redeem us of our sins as well. But how can this spiritual reconciliation take place, if our culture has not the spiritual wisdom to understand what is being offered?

Aboriginals do not relate to the fashionable 'resistance theory' being promoted by the universities, and in fact they look forward, as Miriam-Rose says here, to increased "interaction with other people". As in Nelson Mandela's new South Africa, the Aboriginal people place great hope in education, which they see as the centrepiece of cultural interaction. It is an appalling irony that, in tertiary education at least, Aboriginals will not discover an environment in which their spiritual culture can be shared and their gifts received. In 'cultural studies' programmes, they will meet a radical, elitist, subversive culture based on Marx and Foucault that will want to turn them into radicals and victims. The studies will be based on power, resistance and revolution, not accommodation or growth through love. They will meet a hardened materialist culture that regards sacredness as "cultural property", and such property, they will be told, ought to be withheld and protected, not shared. The Aboriginal way, however, works in reverse: to withhold spiritual knowledge is to destroy it; only in sharing it is it strengthened and renewed.

Our university educators would do well to make themselves students of this indigenous wisdom rather than expecting Aboriginals to sit in our classrooms and take degrees in our mean-spirited materialism. David Mowaljarlai once said that we should have a bush university, where teachers in the Western education system can learn Aboriginal ways. Unfortunately, Mowaljarlai died before this vision could be realised, although there are already the beginnings of such a university in the Broome-Derby area. In the years before his death, Mowaljarlai was desperate to communicate the spiritual basis of Aboriginal culture, because, "There is no time; time is running out". He was astonished that white educators did not want to receive his vision. They would insist that his spirituality was a private and secret matter, which cultural sensitivities forbade them receiving. But given that they were speaking to a fully initiated lawman and tribal elder, just whose 'sensitivities' were being disturbed? Mowaljarlai got to the root of the problem when he told me that white people were scared of him. "They are afraid of me", he said, "and don't want to look into my eyes". This filled me with sudden emotion, but I knew that what he said was true.

Under the disguise of cultural sensitivity, political correctness or whatever we like to call it, Australians are missing out on opportunities for reconciliation and new life. Miriam-Rose Ungunmerr said that *dadirri*, the ability to listen deeply to the spirit in things, is the Aboriginal people's "most unique gift". "It is perhaps the greatest gift we can give to our fellow Australians".[35] Yet, with eyes downcast, wallowing in guilt and lack of faith in our own ability to change, convinced that we have no spiritual capacity of our own, how can Australians receive this gift? We currently lack the spiritual courage to engage it. Says Deborah Bird Rose: 'The last thing one would expect, or be prepared to hear, from a position of power, is that the dispossessed claim to have indeed understood. That they have accepted. And that they are offering us redemption'.[36] Discussions held "from a position of power" make it impossible to receive the gift of reconciliation, because that gift is bestowed by love, not power, and can be received only in the spirit of love.

6

Ecospirituality and Environmental Awareness

The seat of the soul is where the inner world and the outer world meet. It is where they overlap, and it is in every point of the overlap.

— NOVALIS[1]

SACREDNESS AS THE KEY TO ENVIRONMENTAL INTEGRITY

The environmental crisis is not just a moral problem or an economic issue relating to how we manage our natural resources; fundamentally, it is a spiritual problem about how we experience ourselves in the world. The environmental crisis is about our lack of a binding relationship to what we persist in calling the 'external' or 'physical' world. When we stop referring to the world as external or outside, or as 'merely' physical, I dare say the environmental crisis will be faced and solved, because its existence points to a limitation in our human love, an inability to extend love and concern to that which lies beyond the immediate realm of our personal lives. Ecological common sense resides in an all-encompassing inclusiveness, a refusal to designate the world as a reality apart from the self or beyond the self's care or concern.

Our lack of relationship to the so-called external world and to our fellow humanity is a religious issue. Myth, religion and cosmology have traditionally regulated our relationship to what lies beyond the self. Religion (from the Latin *religio*, to 'bind back to') binds us to that which is Other than ourselves, and enables us to make a pact with the Other. Myth and religion make us respect the world beyond the ego, enabling us to see it as a matrix of story and legend, involving the interplay of transcendent forces. While it is true that patriarchal religion is concerned with binding us to a heavenly reality rather than to nature, the fact remains that all religions build bridges between ourselves and larger realities, whether these realities are transcendent or immanent. Through myth, we are shown that the Other, in whichever form it appears, is intimately connected with our own inward life. Myth makes the cosmos friendly and intelligible in the act of making it sacred.

Today's society shows scant regard for the environment and little commitment to nature. Secular materialism and egotistical desires govern our relations with the land, we have no cosmology to link us spiritually with the world, and our official religious tradition is concerned more with heaven than with earth. It is hardly surprising, in view of this, that we face the prospect of ecological disaster. The disenchantment and desacralisation of nature resulted first in the 'death' of the nature spirits and the overthrow of Gaia, Mother Nature. We experienced the spiritual death of nature at the dawn of the Intellectual Enlightenment, and it was just a matter of time before the physical and material body of nature also suffered breakdown at our own hands. When the 'spirit' goes out of a living thing, the integrity is lost as well, and eventually, the physical embodiment gives up the ghost. It is not that nature is withdrawing its love or support, but that we are doing our level best to destroy its support and its capacity for self-healing and renewal. The responsibility now rests with us: it is we who must change our attitude and our relationship with the natural world. We urgently need to be bound emotionally and spiritually to the natural world, as this appears to be the only way to protect nature against human destructiveness and against a pervasive narcissism that, unchecked, must eventually destroy us along with the ecosystem in which we live.

Myth and cosmology invite us to extend our subjectivity, and to abolish the 'alien' character of the world by experiencing it as a living subjectivity. Then, as Thomas Berry argues, the world is seen as a community of living subjects rather than as a collection of objects. This is the transformative process at the heart of the mythic imagination, and the epistemological 'magic' performed by ancient or tribal cosmologies. We are not expected to terminate our subjective life to encounter an outside world; rather, we are encouraged to dream our dreams outwards into the world, so that our imaginative life is broadened to encompass wider fields of reality. The mythic imagination invites us to expand the circles of our identity to include first our family, then the tribe or extended family, and ultimately the trees, rivers and entire natural environment, even the stars and the galaxies beyond. Myth is wondrous and inclusive, and in tribal cultures it teaches that the physical surrounds are peopled by creator beings and ancestral spirits and that these same forces animate and control our own lives.

In Aboriginal Australia, it is often said that 'family is not just people'. There is a profound sense of spiritual kinship with the environment, because the things of the land are made 'kin' or 'family' by virtue of their connectedness with the deep sources of human experience. Spiritual identity with the land precedes any moral concepts of right or proper conduct towards the land. Because the land is our spiritual 'relation', we are in spiritual and moral relationship with it. The land is the Mother, a living mythic expanse that connects us with the ancient past, not simply an external or exploitable natural resource, as it is for those settler Australians who view the land in terms of property, real estate and material acquisition. For Aboriginal people, the 'natural' way to live involves also a supernatural, mythological or imaginal dimension, and yet this supernatural dimension is eminently realistic, since it commands respect for the land, restrains human brutality, and urges us to relate to the environment with love, reverence and awe.

MODERNITY'S DISENCHANTED UNIVERSE

Until comparatively recent times, such a cosmic or expanded experience of the world has been the normal way to live. But modern science treats such experience as a cultural oddity, although postmodern science has completely reversed this prejudice, about which more in a moment. Modernity treats indigenous relations with the world as exotic mysticism, and designates it variously as animistic, dreamtime or totemistic religion. The partic ipatory subjectivity of tribal peoples, in which the inter-connectedness of all things is honoured and in which the human propensity toward brutality is checked or constrained, is ironically construed by modern awareness as barbaric or unenlightened.

Modern psychiatry goes further than this, regarding it as a form of madness. Classical psychiatry's discourse about 'mental health' and psychological hygiene, based as it is upon the contracted life of the ego, considers a cosmic experience of land or environment a symptom of mental illness. It is seen either as an indication of paranoia, where the (supposedly dead) world 'speaks' to the self, or a symptom of psychosis, in which the habitual boundaries of the ego have been dissolved, causing human subjectivity to be invested in inanimate matter. In other words, modernity bases its investigations and judgements on the (now faulty) premise that the world is dead, with only the individual person containing spiritual life. In an ego-based culture, visionary experience is treated as insanity, because 'sanity' is defined as the habitual experience of ego separation and alienation.

Tribal and indigenous societies have acknowledged the worldly or universal dimensions of the soul, so that health to them involves a much broader cosmological perspective of our relationship to the environment, human society and the cosmos. The modern West, in its obsession with the individual, has an incredibly limited concept of health, and our medicine operates in a shrunken universe preoccupied with microscopic bacteria and diseases invading the bodily system. In the medical model, no patient would ever be prescribed more contact with the trees and woods, more gazing at the stars, more contact with community and neighbours. We do not believe such activities impact upon our health, because we have such a disastrously limited concept of the soul. Modern consciousness has destroyed the cosmic sense of the world soul, or *anima mundi*, and has given us instead an interior, private, narrow sense of soul. It was the philosopher Descartes who located the soul within human beings and who announced that the outside reality is spiritually barren, unalive. However, the great error of Western society has been its *privatisation of the soul*, so that the only 'spirituality' we can now imagine is a dialogue between ourselves and our conscience, a wrestling match with our individual demon or angel. In the Western world, the realm of meaning has been privatised and taken out of the public sphere, where it has also become depoliticised and disempowered.

If our shared public space is devoid of meaning, emptied of the sacred, untouched by transpersonal value, then we open up the frightening prospect of it being completely appropriated by commercial interests and materialistic concerns. The cold, banal, even sinister quality of so many of our public urban spaces is a direct consequence of the fact that the sacred has been drained away from the face of the world, locked into the deepest recesses of the human psyche or hidden in ancient religious dogmas and buildings. Since the sacred has been enclosed in this way, developers and commercial groups have been allowed a materialistic and exploitative field day. They believed they could do what they liked because the spaces they were filling or developing had nothing to do with the sacred. Nothing they did to the body of the world mattered, because matter did not matter. In the recent past, we felt no ethical, much less spiritual, responsibility towards the use of land and public space, and the consequence of this is the ugliness of many physical aspects of our contemporary world.

Our task now is to reverse this fatal process, to allow the sacred to flood back into the world, to become sensitive again to the mysterious presence or numinosity of the physical environment.[2] We need to develop — not merely for spiritual entertainment but for spiritual and physical survival — a postmodern animism, a heartfelt response to landscape, a *tao* of architecture, a *zen* of design, a *mysticism* of the ordinary. Our joy and love must be redirected towards the external world, by becoming receptive to the mystery of the world and by rediscovering our essential kinship with it.

THE CULTURAL AND SCIENTIFIC RECOVERY OF OUR SPIRITUAL BOND WITH NATURE

In many of us today, there is a sense of growing urgency about the need to recover our connection with nature. Not only are we seeing the destructive impact of our attitudes upon the physical environment, we are also noticing that we have become alienated from the deeper sources of our own lives. 'Nature' is not only outside us but also within, and ultimately, what we do to nature we do also to ourselves. In killing off the spiritual essence of the Earth, we end up killing ourselves, for this essence nourishes our own biological and spiritual life. The inner ecology of the soul and the outer ecology of the world are inextricably linked. As the artist Michael Leunig has said:

> *We are in the midst of the pillaging and rape of the psychological ecosystem, the ecology of the soul. There's a great, delicate, interconnected ecology that goes on in people's lives. We're defiling it, plundering it, exploiting it, and this will have tremendous consequences for the emotional health of society'.[3]*

It would seem that the soulful and living dimension of human beings is dependent, in turn, upon the greater soul or energic vitality of the world. The human soul cannot be expected to be healthy if it is not connected to the world soul or *anima mundi*, which is ultimately its own source of life and renewal.

In tribal and shamanic cultures, healing and traditional medicine involves bringing the 'sick' self into realignment with living nature, because alienation from the universal, animating forces at work in nature and in ourselves brings disease and disorientation. In a sense, contemporary 'deep ecology' is a version of shamanic medicine, since it shows us that we cannot live fully or creatively without careful and passionate attention to that which lies beyond the shallow world of the ego and its enclosed consciousness. Only something truly mythic or spiritual, such as an expansive Gaia hypothesis or the notion that the world is the living body of the Cosmic Christ, is large or effective enough to bridge the gap currently separating human identity from the natural world. No amount of moral proselytising or ethical preaching to our conscience will bring into existence this vital animating bond. It may be that humanity cannot survive without myth and religion. The original, cosmogonic creation myths not only explain the physical universe to the human mind but are, perhaps, largely responsible for continuing the work of creation through the act of *binding* creation together. Religion (*religio*) binds creator and creation into a living unity that allows the integrity of the universe to be sustained.

The interconnectedness of all things is a phenomenon that contemporary, postmodern science is discovering all over again. Researchers in the biological sciences (Sheldrake's "morphic resonance"), new physics (David Bohm's "implicate order"), mathematics, and field theory are all finding that the unity of the world is central to its very integrity and being and that only if that unity is maintained can the wondrous spectacle of the world continue. Aboriginal Australians understand this fact most profoundly in their insistence on re-enacting the dances and rituals of the Dreaming, which ensure that the world is revitalised, and singing the traditional songs, to ensures that the Songlines are renewed. Today, in view of the findings of the new sciences, we can no longer berate this cosmic experience of the world as primitive or unrelated to actuality. Rather, we must honour the spiritual unity of the world through ritual and art.

The problem today is that our postmodern science can recognise this fact but is unable to do anything about it. It can simply observe helplessly the deepening of our psychospiritual crisis. Science can (re)discover the crucial fact of interconnectedness, but it cannot actually compel us to emotionally experience it. Science needs art and religion just as contemporary ecological studies needs the wisdom of indigenous and tribal cultures. We can make this ecological unity happen only by feeling it in our own emotional and spiritual depths; only myth and religion can call the unity of the world into being.

Postmodern science can explain this unity and tell us why it is important to respect it, but science, like governments and environmental agencies, can only make its appeals to our ethical conscience. It is the role of myth, religion and art to actually transform our consciousness, to introduce us into the sacred experience of the greater world to which science and all rational discourse can only point.

How can we recover the sacred interconnectedness of all things? In her book *Teaching a Stone to Talk*, Annie Dillard writes of our contemporary spiritual and ecological dilemma: "It is difficult to undo our own damage, and to recall to our presence that which we have asked to leave. It is hard to desecrate a sacred grove and change your mind ... We doused the burning bush and cannot rekindle it; we are lighting matches in vain under every green tree."[4] It is indeed difficult to reverse our cultural attitudes and directions, to change our minds. But we *must* change our minds — probably first by changing our hearts — and bear witness to the ecological devastation wrought by our conquistadorial consciousness. We have to remythologise the physical world so that the primal unity of creation can be recovered.

We cannot simply invent a new religion or myth to suit this situation, nor can we appropriate an 'ecologically sound' religion from indigenous peoples, although the so-called New Age popular movement appears to condone such cultural theft. David Suzuki argues that we need to listen to the perennial wisdom of indigenous elders, and this is an important idea, particularly in view of the tragic impact of global 'development' on the survival of those tribal elders.[5] Clearly, we must engage in a legitimate soul-search, rediscovering our *own* historical roots and reanimating some of the religious attitudes and values we thought we had outgrown. But above all, we must start from where we are. We cannot 'graft on' new ideas or steal from exotic cultures. We have to build upon our own cultural heritage, and develop in ways that are directly linked to our history, lest our 'solutions' leave us more psychologically rootless and confused than ever before. We need to understand the cultural forces that have led to our disenchantment, then work towards reversing these forces, if enchantment or binding is to be found again.

A BRIEF OVERVIEW OF THE DESPIRITUALISATION OF NATURE

Western culture has been engaged in a long battle against the spirits of the green world and the hidden presences of the physical environment. This battle has operated variously under such banners as 'progress', 'science', 'rationality' and 'religion'. Mythologically, the onslaught has been directed against the 'goddess of many names' — Demeter, Gaia, Cybele or Aphrodite — or the Great Goddess who rules over the animal and vegetable worlds and whose life-producing spirit, which comes in the Spring, is personified in her phallic consort and son-lover, Pan, Dionysus, Attis, Adonis, the Green Man. The earthly spirituality that enlivens the natural world and that creates passional bonds between ourselves and the physical realities of place has always been conceived as a matriarchal spirituality, a spirituality emanating from a feminine deity or a primal world mother. This is true whether we speak of the early religions of Old Europe, or the present-day religions of Aboriginal Australians, who celebrate the sacred earth as the *Kunapipi*, 'earth mother'. Such earthly spiritualities have long been characterised, especially by Judeo-Christian and Islamic traditions, as heathen. Patriarchal religious traditions have launched persistent and relentless attacks upon earthly spiritualities, projecting upon these spiritualities the patriarchal fear of the feminine and of female sexuality. For patriarchal religions, such earthly spiritualities are impure and unclean, too close to the 'contaminating' and 'seductive' world of matter and physicality.

The patriarchal religions are characterised essentially by their designation of a transcendental spiritual source beyond the created world. If matriarchal religions designate an earth mother who rules over nature, the patriarchal religions construct a sky father, who lives in an otherworldly, heavenly abode, looking down in judgement upon the earth. Patriarchal religion declares the pagan worship of nature to be evil and sometimes even of the devil. Taking fright at the pagan delight in the material body, it calls into being an exalted Holy Spirit which is free from the bonds of matter and the flesh. The very word 'matter' derives from the Latin *mater* (mother), and the relationship with matter is as fraught and problematical for men as is their relationship with the opposite sex. St Paul declares, in the First Epistle to the Corinthians: "the natural man receiveth not the things of the Spirit of God". Western religion is based on the claim that an absolute reality, something transcendent and profoundly otherworldly, intersects with this world and transforms it into its own divine and magisterial likeness. The patriarchal spirit is *other* than nature, an *opus contra naturam*; it is apart from matter and the body of the earth mother. The aim is to shake free from the mother and to announce the triumph of a conquistadorial patriarchal spirituality, which we refer to as 'redemption', ie. redemption from the 'merely natural' condition.

All this will have to change if the world is to survive ecologically. Our transcendentalist spirituality may have lifted our culture out of a former dependence on natural urges and instinctual mechanisms, but unless we arrest and reverse this tendency, our lives will simply lift off from the earth altogether, leaving devastation and disaster in our wake. Our inherited antipathy towards the natural will have to be overcome, and in particular, the strong dualism, almost genetically implanted within us, regarding spirit versus nature, will have to be deconstructed, critiqued and transformed. The origins of our all-pervasive dualism are ancient and deep, and are intimately connected both with the historical rivalry between Christianity and Paganism and with Greek philosophy's rivalry between spirit and matter. The consideration of these enormous problems takes us away from our immediate concern, which is the disenchantment and re-enchantment of the natural world. I will refer the reader to the significant and burgeoning literature on this topic for further analysis of these issues.[6] Here, I simply wish to establish the detrimental role that a transcendentalist cosmology has played in the devaluation of nature and the despiritualisation of the physical world.

With this theological background, the Intellectual Enlightenment merely had to carry forward the negative view of nature and the despiritualisation of the green world that had begun with patriarchal religion. Although mutually contradictory in many other respects, the secular enlightenment and patriarchal religion share the common enterprise of seeking to debunk natural religion and to expunge all minor deities, fertility goddesses and phallic consorts from the green world. The aim in both cases is to create an hygienic environment, to rid the forests and streams of undesirable presences, in the one case to prepare nature for the transformative encounter with the one true God and in the other case to sub-ordinate nature to the demands and claims of the rational intellect and humanistic science. Christianity and scientific humanism were of one mind in renouncing the pagan view of nature and in presenting nature as a compliant, virginal field of reality awaiting the firm impress of the spirit of patriarchy. Any presences or spiritual realities found in nature itself were quickly exposed as fraudulent.

To this day, our secular humanist tradition has a host of handy concepts at its disposal by which anything spiritual in nature can be explained away. We have such elaborate concepts as 'projection', 'personification', 'anthropomorphism', and even, in art criticism, the 'pathetic fallacy'. If we imagine something alive and powerful in nature itself, this is explained as a perceptual fallacy, or a projection of our own internal life into the external field of reality. The West is keen to argue, both in its secular and sacred traditions, that the world is empty, *terra nullius*, virginal, unlived in. It is all waiting for the directive hand of patriarchal guidance, either politically, in terms of the conquest of social patriarchy over so-called virgin territory, or spiritually, in terms of the conquering penetration of the otherworldy Father God. Any life perceived in nature is either an error of intellectual judgement, or a devilish atavistic reversion to the paganism that Christendom imagined it had defeated long ago.

At the beginning of the third millennium, we now face the terrible prospect of patriarchy's complete triumph over nature and its utter desecration of the earth mother and her green son. There is a shocking irony in the fact that a scorched-earth apocalypse now looms ahead of us, not because the world has wilfully departed from the patriarchal law, but because the world has obeyed too fully the Western patriarchal commands and imperatives at both secular and spiritual levels. We have to revive our pagan roots, and rescue what we can of whatever 'natural religion' remains alive within us and within the indigenous cultures of the world, even if we have to dig down a long way to find it. It is certainly no accident that the environmentalism of the New Age coincides with a range of cultural activities related to the so-called return of the goddess, including the Gaia hypothesis, ecofeminism, feminist spirituality, and pagan earth worship practised by urban wicca circles and the so-called 'feral' communities who inhabit forests and mountain places. We have to find new respect for the pagan forces that we arrogantly imagined we could do without.

Or, to put it in terms perhaps less threatening to Western culture, Judeo-Christianity has to (re)discover the feminine and maternal dimensions of its own concept of God, whether as Sophia, the principle of wisdom, or Lilith, the woman of the night and Adam's original consort, or Shekinah, the Jewish female symbol of God's presence in the world. Only the feminine dimension of the Godhead is supportive of the Earth, protective of its creatures, and unwilling to engage its ransom for the sake of patriarchal spiritual purity and perfection. Goethe wrote that "the Eternal Feminine leads us on", and in times of environmental disaster, it is the eternal feminine in men and women alike that acts as the visionary and guiding force, an intuitive survival instinct within us that refuses to endanger the world for the sake of patriarchal power and glory.

MORAL AND SPIRITUAL DIMENSIONS OF THE POPULAR ECOLOGICAL REVOLUTION

A great social change or peaceful revolution is already upon us at the popular level. We are seeing the moral or ethical phase of this change first. We are reminding ourselves and each other that we have to *care more* about the human and social worlds, and be more responsive to our use and development of urban space, to landscape and the natural world. Virtually everyone is now in on this act, with governments, social planners, academics, scientific industries, and even developers and commercial interests mouthing the ecologically sound statements that have become a key part of contemporary experience. At last, the environment is firmly on the public agenda. The phenomenal success of the international green agencies and political parties in recent times demonstrates just how important the lived environment has become to contemporary consciousness.

But how much of this popular ecological discourse is heartfelt and real? Many people have become aware that it is relatively easy for us to mouth cliches about the environment without even realising what we are saying. The public may well become cynical when the perpetrators of environmental abuse are often in the front line of the slick new discourse, every company having a public relations officer well trained in the art of 'greenspeak' and able to use the emotionally charged language of environmentalism to persuasive effect. The fact is that we must not only stir our public conscience about environmental abuse, we also must change our consciousness about self and world. Threats about environmental damage and apocalyptic scenarios are generating the desired moral response, but moral forces alone will not change the root cause of the problem, which is our psychospiritual alienation from the environment.

The second phase of this universal change is just on the horizon of our cultural experience. We can simply call this the spiritual phase, which must follow the moral and ethical revolution we are currently undergoing. The point is that we cannot have a moral revolution without also having a spiritual revolution. We cannot urge each other to care more about the environment unless we have, at our deepest levels, experienced a fundamental redefinition of our human identity, unless we have achieved a sense of our primal at-one-ment with the created world. Through sacrament and ritual, we are able to collapse old boundaries between self and world, and experience the world as an extension of self or, in reverse, the self as an extension of the world. Only by resacralising the world will we become better citizens, responding to the world with love.

Spiritual understanding will allow us to see the hidden unity behind creation, to view the world as part of ourselves and our life as belonging to its life. We must agree with the Australian scientist Grant Watson, that "man's mental health and his very humanity depend on a sacramental and symbolic relation to the larger world".[7] The truly ecological task is to repair not just our damage in the outer world but also the deep splits in our psychological make-up and dualistic world view. We must work towards a *rapprochement* between the human and the non-human. We have to turn the soul inside out, to return meaning and interiority to the outer world, to reanimate the environment and rediscover soul in the world.

Many ecologically minded scientists today point to the Aboriginal culture as one that honoured and respected the Earth and maintained a sensitive relationship with it. But do these same scientists actually realise the full implications of their exemplary indigenous model? The Australian Aboriginal people have long been ecologically committed, not because they laboured, like us today, under moral constraints about what we *should* do or feel about the environment, but because they spontaneously felt the environment to be part of themselves, intrinsically related to their inmost human and emotional reality. The land was, and still is, felt to be an extension of themselves. It represented their primal origin and source, as well as framing and defining their present social existence. This spiritual bond civilises and restrains our behaviour towards the world, since the tribal person recognises his or her own expanded identity in the natural realm. The ecological benefits of an ecospirituality are virtually incalculable, and purely on practical and survival grounds, there are many arguments to be put for why we alienated moderns must strive towards a recovery of mythic imagination, expanded subjectivity and a cosmic identity.

THE NEW AGE AS A PARODY OF OUR SPIRITUAL RENEWAL

Because we are so profoundly out of touch with our sense of cosmic identity, we are bound to make many mistakes as we move in search of this lost dimension.

It is of great concern to many of us that the popular New Age spirituality should be offering a kind of parody of the spiritual changes that need to occur in our society. The New Age responds to the need for reanimation of the universe by adopting a consumerist approach to the problem. Ancient tribal cultures, in particular those of the North American Indian and Aboriginal groups, are seen to possess the desired spiritual ideas and cosmologies, and desperate white people in search of a new consciousness simply plunder these cultures for their spiritual booty.

This is a serious cultural problem, since this attitude does considerable damage to indigenous cultures. Politically, this can be seen as the final insult in a long history of European colonial appropriation of Aboriginal cultural reality: first land, natural resources, people, language, and now, finally, 'spirituality'. Moreover, on a psychospiritual level, this cultural theft does nothing to effect real change in white colonial consciousness. The whole point of our present cultural crisis is to awaken our *internal* psychospiritual resources, not appropriate those of others. As Jung so often argued, just below the surface of our alienated consciousness is the vast world of our ancient past. We do not explore this lost archetypal resource through the plundering of spiritual ideas from another culture. Indeed, such cultural consumerism would allow our alienated consciousness to continue as before, unchallenged and untransformed by deeper levels of our being.

Above all, we must find the courage to risk a descent into the deep unconscious, to see what treasure might be buried there. The way ahead is certainly back and down. Jung argued that we are more than we seem, and I see no reason to disbelieve him. At deeper levels, we still have within us the 'psychic inheritance' of our ancestral background, and this includes the historical development of the 'ten thousand-year-old man' within us. At this level, even the most rootless and alienated modern contains vestiges of an older indigeneity long since outgrown. A part of our psyche still views the world through the eyes of expanded or subjective identity, but unfortunately, this part can express itself only in symptomatic or neurotic ways. In our dreams, fantasies and psychotic episodes, we can still find evidence of that ancient background. In such expressions, our directed modern thinking is eclipsed by a more primal and symbolic vision, which knows no boundaries between self and other, psyche and world, or subject and object. We are so out of touch with this latent reality that we deem it to be senseless and absurd, unless we turn to psychotherapy to have our ancient knowing deciphered by a specialist.

For many Australians, including myself, this deep heritage involves an encounter with Celtic spirituality and ancestral inheritance. In the previous chapter, I tried to show why this is so and how such atavistic reactivation comes about. For Anglo-Celtic Australians, the experience of Aboriginality serves to awaken our forgotten Celtic heritage, a renewal which is profoundly explored in Rodney Hall's trilogy *A Dream More Luminous than Love*. In this great work, Hall shows that our necessary contact with Aboriginal Dreaming is for some of us a home-coming to our lost or overlaid 'aboriginal' nature. Some will say that this renewal is fanciful, escapist, but the fact is that the 'collective unconscious' is just an empty term, a vain idea, unless it can be fleshed out and imagined in historical, ancestral terms. Our existential and psycho-logical proximity to Aboriginal animism calls forth from us an 'answering image' to this country's very strong tradition of mythological vision and earth-based spiritu-ality. Reimagining our own ancestral past, even for people who are, like me, third- or fourth-generation Australian, may be our only guarantee against the dangers of appropriating Aboriginal spirituality.

ELIADE: THE MODERN LONGING FOR RE-ENCHANTMENT

Mircea Eliade, the historian of religions, presents an interesting case in point here. Like many of his contemporaries, Mircea Eliade held an essentially negative image of Christianity. He could not look to his natal Christian faith for religious identity, much less for any ecospiritual understanding. In his autobiographical memoir, *Ordeal by Labyrinth,* he tells how institutional Christianity had, for him, degenerated into what he calls an "acquired custom":

> *I wasn't satisfied. I simply felt that the essential something I really needed to find and understand had to be looked for elsewhere, not in my own tradition. I hadn't grasped the religious value of our Sunday services in my early days.*[8]

He points out that the Christian message was a transcendentalist message, and that he was hungering for a "cosmic religious feeling" that was in direct opposition to transcendentalist Christianity. He did not want to be instructed in the life of a divinity far away, but wanted to share in the experience of the sacred as a present and immanental reality. Intellectually, however, he recognised the uniqueness and historical importance of Christian revelation:

> *The manifestation of the sacred in objects [and in the natural world] is precisely what the biblical prophets were fighting against. And quite rightly, since Israel was the vessel of another religious revelation. Mosaic monotheism entails personal knowledge of a God who intervenes in history and who, unlike the gods of the polytheistic religions, makes his power manifest in ways not solely confined to the rhythms of nature.*[9]

Eliade could follow with his intellect the importance and uniqueness of Christianity, but still his heart longed for something more sensuous, lived and incarnational. He tells how he became alert to the mystical depths of existence by living and working in India:

> In India I discovered what I later came to refer to as 'cosmic religious feeling'. That is to say, the manifestation of the sacred in objects or in cosmic rhythms; in a spring of water, in a tree, in the springtime of the year ... I had lived among people who were able to participate in the sacred through the mediation of their gods, and those gods were figurations or expressions of the mystery of the universe, of that inexhaustible source of creation, of life, and of sacred joy.[10]

Eliade reports that he was fortunate enough:

> to spend a few weeks in central India — the occasion being a sort of crocodile hunt — among the Santali aborigines; in other words, among pre-Aryans. And I was struck by the realisation that India still has roots going down very deep, not just into its Aryan and Dravidian cultures, but also into the very subsoil of Asian culture, into aboriginal culture. It was a neolithic civilization, based on the religion that accompanied the discovery of agriculture, particularly the vision of the world as an unbroken cycle of life, death, and rebirth.[11]

Some might criticise Eliade, however, on the grounds that, although he has nothing other than enthusiastic admiration for this tribal culture, that hunger is consumerist, and therefore dangerous to the foreign culture. In particular, he is idealising an indigenous Indian culture ravaged and exploited by the West, and it could be argued that his acquisitive taste for this exotic spirituality is the final insult in a long history of cultural appropriation.

However, an interesting twist in his narrative reveals that Eliade is not merely engaged in exoticism or consumerism. His encounter with archaic vision in India alerted him to the primal roots of his native Romanian and Balkan folk culture: "Like that of India, it was a folk culture, based on the mystery of agriculture". But in Eastern Europe, such primal mysticism had been Christianised and overlaid with doctrinal belief: "for example, wheat was thought to have originated from drops of Christ's blood". However, despite the Christian overlay, he contends, "all such symbols have a very archaic, Neolithic foundation".

> *This cultural unity was, to me, a revelation. I discovered that even here, in Europe, our roots go far deeper than we had hitherto supposed, deeper than the Greek or Roman or even Mediterranean worlds, deeper than the world of the ancient Near East. And those roots reveal to us the fundamental oneness not merely of Europe but of the entire ecumene that stretches from Portugal to China ... As I grasped the profound oneness that underlies and unites aboriginal Indian culture and Balkan culture — and the peasant culture of western Europe, too — I felt I had come home.*[12]

Like Jung, Eliade imagines that civilisation does not completely destroy our primordial roots but simply overlays them, so that we have to dig deep in order to regain access to them. Eliade came "home" to himself, or to his primal experience of himself in relation to the wider cosmos, in India. This European/American scholar had to make a geographical journey in order to have his primal vision, his "cosmic religious feeling", reawakened into consciousness. This, surely, is a testimony to the importance of travel in the modern world: the over-civilised, spiritually damaged Europeans may have life-changing experiences in countries where the religious unity of all creation is still intact.

But travel to foreign parts, immersion in foreign religious cultures, is merely parasitic tourism *unless* some response is awakened in the depths of the pilgrim. If we have the courage to deepen our foreign experience so that we touch and awaken 'foreign' parts of our psychological being or lost dimensions of our spiritual ancestry, then a process develops that transforms our experience and quickens our perceptions. We are no longer trampling upon somebody else's sacred ground; we are becoming part of, and therefore responsible to, the sacred space we are temporarily occupying. This is the perspective that is frequently lacking in contemporary ecotourism and cultural encounter programmes. There is both a moral and a spiritual responsibility attaching to these experiences of foreign cultures, and if nothing awakens in our own soul, making claims and demands upon us, calling us to change the way we live, then we have been merely parasites and intruders. The alacrity with which many New Age travellers seek and absorb exotic religions is cause for concern, and for some, the addictive/repetitive nature of these experiences suggests that no personal deepening is taking place.

THE CIRCLES OF IDENTITY

To conclude this chapter, I would like to set aside issues of ethnicity and ancestral background to concentrate on the simple art of befriending the universe through psychological expansion.

For modernity and the Intellectual Enlightenment, progress involved withdrawing from the wider circles of expanded identity. The modern person decided that he or she did not belong to the stars, did not participate mystically with nature, was not profoundly connected to extended family, tribe or community. Progress was a centripetal movement towards the self, in which the wider circles of mystery and enchantment were dissolved, a kind of inverted spiral converging on the self.

Our circles of identity became narrower, converging at last on the tiny atomic self to which this movement always pointed. Modernity could be defined as a kind of psychological pirouetting around ourselves. We divorce ourselves from nature, family and friends, spiritual and cultural roots, all in a bid to find out who we really are. We set forth on 'personal journeys' to discover meaning, perpetuating the myth of the atomised individual, separate from others.

But if we continue our quest for spiritual meaning, one of the first things we discover is that our 'individuality' is largely illusory, even something of a hoax. We are spiritually, emotionally and psychologically the products of our families, our communities and our society. As we see through the illusion of individuality, the ancient circles of expanded identity begin to reappear. We restore our ties with previously alienated members of the family. We find that our connection to land and place is more meaningful than we had noticed before. We also link up with rejected or despised parts of ourselves, with forgotten or repressed experiences from our past, and as we move ahead into spiritual awareness, all our former certainties and boundaries become blurred and indistinct. We are no longer the person we thought we were.

The centripetal movement of modernity comes to a halt and an expansive movement takes over. We are overcoming boundaries, transgressing taboos, and this can be very disorienting, since our education has not prepared us for this process. The conventional walls of the modern self have to be broken down if we are to reach beyond the confines of modernity. There is a dark night of the soul, a period of dread and disintegration, that precedes the journey into spiritual experience. In a modern and desacralised society, which has no formal knowledge of the journey towards the expanded self, our experiences of expansion necessarily involve pain and suffering as we break down socially sanctioned limits and psychological barricades.

The consumerist society reinforces our shrunken, empty status. It is vitally important for capitalism that we continue to experience ourselves as empty and small, since this provides us with the desire to expand and grow, and this desire is what consumerism is based on. Consumerism assumes that we are empty but permanently unable to fulfil our spiritual urge to expand. It steps into the vacuum and offers its own version of expansion and belonging. As the circles of modern identity become ever-smaller, consumerism becomes ever-larger, to compensate for the loss of integrity and meaning. If we stopped believing in the myth of our shrunken identity, the monster of consumerism would die, because it would no longer be nourished by our unrealised spiritual urges.

Therefore, true spirituality, which punctures the bubble of the ego and leads us to the larger circles of our human and transhuman identity, is extremely subversive of the status quo. This is why consumer society is keen to debunk or ridicule true spirituality, but anxious to promote all manner of substitutes. Established commercial interests and the intellectual forces of modernity have reasons to keep the myth of the alienated self alive, and that is why the true spiritual quest is at once a protest against consumerism and a rebellion against the logic of modernity and the precepts of rationality.

7

Youth Spirituality and Old Religion

The wind blows wherever it pleases;
you hear its sound,
but you cannot tell where it comes from or where it
is going,
That is how it is with all who are born of the Spirit.

— *JOHN 3:8*[1]

SPIRITUALITY IN YOUTH CULTURE: OPEN, URGENT, AND POLITICAL

Young Australians today feel increasingly free to announce that they are searching for spirituality. What they mean by 'spirituality' is not always clear to older people, but the fact that they are able to name their quest in this way is certainly encouraging. The stigmas and embarrassments that plagued earlier generations of Australians, including my own, do not seem to plague theirs. Significant numbers of university students, especially the eighteen- to twenty-year-olds, announce that they are searching for spiritual meaning. I am not sure how other teachers respond to this in a secular educational setting, but I usually try to offer students some positive recognition that they are on a worthwhile path.

I sense a real revolution in the making here, because the secular education system in which I work notoriously does not take the sacred dimension of our lives into account. When young adults tell me of their spiritual interests, I often have to wonder whether the university environment will support those passions, or whether it would be better for them to be developed elsewhere. Officially, the university does not set out to destroy faith, but it does not attempt to encourage it either. Its stated view, developed from an old-style liberal humanism, is that spirituality is a private matter, something that should not be 'imposed' upon the young by religious teachers. But our youth are increasingly finding this attitude frustrating, empty, vacuous. It does not provide them with life-enhancing values, but merely encourages an attitude of intellectual inquiry in which the moral and spiritual foundations of existence are never affirmed. Young adults want spirituality put back on the public agenda, and this will force secular leaders to rethink education and, even more challengingly, to rethink their personal relationship to spirituality.

For young adults today, spirituality is no longer a matter of private taste or personal concern. Many of my students talk to me about spirituality in worldly and public terms — as the basis for a new sense of human community, as a cure for racism, as an essential ingredient of the new ecological awareness, as an antidote to domestic violence and civil unrest. Spirituality for youth today has acquired a public conscience, with very little of the antisocial, pleasure-seeking flavour that it had for the university students of my own generation, in the 1960s and 1970s. Spirituality is still a deeply internal experience, but it is an internal experience that profoundly affects how we view nature and the world, how we see ourselves and each other. It is therefore felt to be internal and external, personal and public, at one and the same time. This revolutionary development changes the face of spirituality for those who have seen it as essentially private, and is also profoundly unsettling for those who have constructed the outer world as an exclusively secular domain.

It is because of the new link with broad public issues such as land use, race relations, social justice and environmentalism that youth spirituality deserves to be taken far more seriously than it has been in the past. The old cynical view that spirituality is merely a fantasy escape from the realities of the world, a pleasure-seeking journey into esoterica, no longer appears relevant, and adults who condemn youth spirituality on 'political' grounds are failing to see that spirituality has become central to political life for many young people today. Spirituality does not alienate them from the world; rather, it gathers the world to themselves, making the political problems of the day personal and internal by posing them in essentially spiritual terms. Spirituality may continue to be based on the personal, but it is no longer private. A lot of our familiar dualities and boundaries no longer apply.

The view is often put to me by students that if one relates to the world as an extension of oneself, as a field animated with life and meaning along the lines of the Gaia hypothesis, then one lives with profound sensitivity, care and concern. A kind of cosmic religious awareness becomes virtually synonymous with the ecological revolution. This is not romantic escapism but sensible ecopolitics. In the same way that feminism showed university students that *the personal is political*, so the youth of today, it would seem, are engaged in a further but largely unmapped social revolution whose slogan might well be *the spiritual is political*. Spirituality has reached the ecological and environmental agenda and is making progressive inroads into public education, public health and national social policy. Significantly, those few youth in today's society who remain connected with the established churches tend to become vitally interested in, and animated by, social justice issues. Sandie Cornish, a youth leader in religious ethics, summarises this attitude: "If Catholicism were no more than a personal set of values to be applied only in the private sphere, it would not be worth bothering with".[2] Churched and unchurched youth share the same passion: that if spirituality means anything at all in today's world, it has to mean social justice and political equity. The old idea of a quiet, personal devotion to God and allowing Caesar to get on with ruling the world has given way to a new holistic ethic in which spirituality is personal and social simultaneously.

THE MASS DEFECTION FROM ESTABLISHED RELIGION

Young Australians now seem to be making hard and fast distinctions between spirituality and religion. Obviously, while this is not true for all young people, some of whom continue to find a neat fit between spirituality and established religious practice, the overwhelming majority do seem to make this distinction. When young Australians talk about their hunger for spirituality, they make it clear that they are not talking about religion, and if I suggest to them that they might like to pursue their spiritual interests in a church context, they can become defensive, and even hostile. Spirituality for these youth means that which touches them, engages them, and urges them to their part in an unfolding sense of mystery. Religion, on the other hand, often means that which is routine, regulated, conventional, with no claim on their soul. Even two generations ago, religion and spirituality were seen as interlinked, with spirituality a product of religious belief, but today, the claim is being made that spirituality can be separated from religion and experienced apart from any religious tradition.

Recent surveys in Sydney and Melbourne indicate overwhelming defection rates among young people who have graduated from the Catholic secondary school system. At the Australian Catholic University in Sydney, a report has indicated that up to ninety-seven per cent of young Catholics abandon the practice of their faith within twelve months of completing high school. In Melbourne, the late B. A. Santamaria found this figure so astonishing that he set about to conduct a similar survey in his own metropolitan area. Santamaria's report confirmed that approximately ninety-four per cent of graduates from Catholic secondary schools had defected from established faith practices within twelve months of completing their education.[3]

This sent Bob Santamaria and others into paroxysms of despair. Why this mass defection and what was the point of a Catholic education system that produced these results? It seemed that rather than encouraging and strengthening faith, the system was inspiring rebellion and dissent. But, of course, young adulthood is a time of experimentation and individuality. As soon as the shackles are off, young people spread their wings and launch into journeys and discoveries of their own. And who is to say that, in abandoning their faith's practices, they have actually abandoned their faith? Chances are that at least some young adults who no longer practise their religion eventually return, doing so once they have children of their own and pledge at the baptismal ceremony to bring them up in the light of the faith.

By the time I see young adults at university, most have reached the point of defection from the churches. I conducted my own survey at La Trobe University in March 1998, in which I asked fifty of my undergraduate students who had enrolled in a course on Jungian psychology to respond to questions about faith and spirituality. An impressive forty-seven of these students indicated that spirituality was of vital importance to their lives, whereas only *one* student out of the fifty said that religion was important to her life. This one student turned out to be a Thai student with a Buddhist background who had recently converted to Catholicism. Many of the forty-seven students said they had come from religious secondary schools, but no longer saw themselves as practising Christians. These figures and realities suggest that a cultural revolution is in the making, but are we prepared for it? Something profound is going on, but we are still not sure what it is.

Many adults within the established churches who are aware of this tidal wave of interest in youth spirituality are, perhaps understandably, suspicious of it. I have been told by some priests, religious educators and religious broadcasters that youth spirituality represents an underground conspiracy against the church, designed to undermine church tradition and to attack the authority of the Vatican. The claim is frequently made that spirituality outside the church is part of the New Age spiritual movement, but I think the New Age, as an identifiable subcultural entity, represents only a narrow portion of this unchurched spirituality, which is widespread and almost universal in youth culture. I don't think we can blame this spiritual revolution on the New Age, although the New Age does try to exploit the spiritual hunger of many young people, if they can be lured into the expensive technologies and cults that are for sale in this consumerist popular movement.

I have also heard priests announce that the phrase 'I am interested in spirituality' when uttered by these unchurched youth is actually a code for, 'I take drugs and am getting high on drug abuse'. This is a very serious allegation, but as yet I have not seen much to support it. To my students, this view is laughable, indicating just how out of touch the churches are, since spirituality outside the familiar forms of religion is still denied or berated — especially by conservative voices in the church, who are quick to dismiss unchurched spirituality as devil worship, ignorance, narcissism or drug culture. For religious conservatives, true spirituality can exist only within the church, and everything outside it is either mad, bad or morbid. But the churches have to face the fact that they no longer hold a monopoly on spirituality, and that the key term 'spirituality' has taken on new meaning in the life of the broader community.

A NEW OUTBREAK OF SPIRITUAL FEELING

After writing the above words, I came across the following passage from Diarmuid O'Murchu, in his *Reclaiming Spirituality*:

> *For many people it is virtually incomprehensible that spiritual yearnings, feelings or values can arise apart from the context of formal belief; in other words, religion is perceived to be the only fountain from which spirituality can spring forth. Fortunately, human experience suggests otherwise and has done so over many millennia ... It is not a realm of experience that has been researched or studied systematically as has happened in the case of formal religion. Consequently, we rely on anecdotal evidence, which is now becoming so widespread and compelling that we can't afford to ignore it any more.*[4]

I can only concur with this, though I am not sure that I share the writer's celebratory tone. But I certainly agree with O'Murchu that youth are being led away from established religion not by New Age gurus or evil magicians, as some conservatives imagine, but by something far more profound and interesting:

> *This new spiritual resurgence is not something planned by a specific group of people or by some new organisation that is seeking to undermine the significance of churches, religions or the culture of*

*traditional faith and belief. This is a proactive rather
than a reactive movement. Many of the people
involved in this spiritual reawakening have little or no
familiarity with formal religion. These people are not
anti-religion and should not be confused with those
who denounce religion because of some past hurtful
or destructive experience.*[5]

Again, I agree with the gist of what he is saying but cannot
endorse all of it. It is very true that many of the young
Australians I have in mind do not come from religious
backgrounds, so are not merely rebelling against their
upbringing. The sons and daughters of feminists, Marxists,
socialists, atheists, scientists and rationalists who espouse
no religious faith whatsoever are expressing the needs of
the spirit and are anxious to pursue a spiritual life. I do not
think the situation is as straightforward as O'Murchu would
like to believe. We are dealing with complex social issues,
which may include a creative explosion of the Holy Spirit,
but which also involves sociopolitical processes and the
protest of the young against the old.

But I see in this outbreak of spirituality a desperate
attempt by youth culture to support itself against the
encroaching tide of destructive materialism. The widespread and almost incantatory use of the word 'spirituality'
could well be an urgent measure against the nihilism that
has swept through the so-called 'Generation X' and the
subsequent generations brought up on junk food, violent
video games and internet pornography. Even by uttering
the word 'spirituality', young people seem to wish to
evoke some kind of protective talisman that will protect
them from the virus-like spread of consumerism. Whereas,
in the past, peasant-folk in Europe would make the sign
of the cross to ward off evil, youth today utter the word
'spirituality' to similar effect, hoping that some good will
guide them and some hidden reality protect them from
debasement and despair. This may be why they become

defensive and vague when adults such as myself question them about the term 'spirituality'. They simply cannot afford to have that talismanic word analysed in a critical way, because it is a sort of buffer against the forces of commercial and social darkness.

Religious leaders and educators may dislike the current use or misuse of the term 'spirituality', but I see it as a return to the radical, original uses of the word 'spirit' in the days of the early Christian church. For St Paul and the first Christians, spirit was a term of both protest and affirmation. It was a protest against both the Jewish religious establishment of the day, which was felt to be degenerate and empty, and the worldly authority of ancient Rome, which imposed upon other countries its own hegemonic imperial rule. It was also an affirmation of a truth beyond corrupt religious and political institutions, a truth that belongs to a higher order of human reality and to a future and greater manifestation of spirit. We must not forget that early Christianity must have looked very much like a New Age cult to the religious establishment of the day.

Today's imperial authority is the political authority of the multinationals and the economic forces of international oppression euphemistically referred to as 'globalisation'. Youth rightly fear these 'economic rationalist' forces that sweep across regions and countries, converting all places into the same anonymous no-place, where the pagan shrines are those of the fast-food chains and mobile-telephone towers.

THE CRISIS IN UNDERSTANDING AND THE DEMAND FOR INWARD KNOWING

Youth are making the same accusations that St Paul made in his own day: that the living spirit is not felt to reside in established religion, so must be found somewhere else. In protesting that the church is dead, these youth are not blaspheming against God, because they have not been allowed to see or witness the presence of the divine in religion in the first place. The spirit may still be present in the church, but it is tragically entombed in dogma and lost to an archaic theological language that has little impact on the contemporary imagination. If the spirit is not felt to exist in theology or church, it is as good as dead to those who fail to see it. We often hear from youth that the Mass or Eucharist is impossible to understand, that the purpose of the crucifixion has not been explained to them, that they do not understand this emphasis on pain and suffering. Young people are confused about the meaning of original sin, salvation, redemption, grace, resurrection, transubstantiation, confirmation, reconciliation, confession. Adult educators may have explained the terms to them once, but because our present age does not speak this language, these ideas do not take root easily in our minds.

Our Western crisis in religious faith is partly a crisis of language and representation. It is not that we have lost our capacity for spiritual feeling (that, clearly, is not the case), but we have lost our ability to locate this feeling in the old theological forms. The old religious world view no longer resonates with the understandings of the young or of the secular world in which they live. Theology has been famously defined as 'faith seeking understanding', but modern people seem to see our religion as a 'blind faith' where conscious understanding is ignored or not encouraged. Secular society is inclined to dismiss theology as mumbo jumbo because theology fails to speak to it. There is not enough emphasis placed on what all the symbols and images might mean to us today or how we might begin to get a personal connection to theology's stories and rituals. Western religion will have to recognise that we need to have much of our religion translated into modern terms and linked to everyday life situations. That is to say, faith will have to be based on a personal experience of spirituality.

In the past, youth did not protest too much when they failed to understand religious language, because the church held fearsome moral authority over their lives and youth were threatened with punishment and eternal damnation if they did not submit to church authority. But today, youth are more experimental, with more trust in the integrity of their own experience, so that the old threats of hell fire no longer create guilty conformity to church expectations. Also, church authorities previously ignored the criticisms of youth — youth were considered too young to understand the difficult world of theology, and their criticisms were lightly dismissed, or viewed with scorn. But today, we can no longer afford to respond in this magisterial and dismissive way, since more and more people, and not just the young, are asking what the point of all this religious language is, what does it mean, and why should I be concerned with it? The church has lost much of its authority, but it still holds an essential religious mystery that must be conveyed, though obviously not in the old authoritarian manner.

We have to recognise that we can no longer compel people to believe any more, since the impact of science and education over the past few hundred years has been to replace belief with experience and experimentation, which are the new standard-bearers for truth and knowledge. If religion wants to have any relevance for the young, it will have to go the way of experience and inward knowing, since belief has been eroded as a fundament of our culture. We must first show the young the logic upon which religion is based, and encourage them to experience the presence of the divine in their own lives. Only then might they wish to believe, but we must never assume that belief or devotion will be embraced without the support of an attendant spirituality that makes belief possible.

THE CHURCH IN TRANSITION: FROM DEVOTION TO SPIRITUALITY

Our Western religious tradition has never been particularly strong in the art of cultivating spirituality in its followers. True, in the monastic traditions, the cultivation of spirituality has been and continues to be a major religious priority, but the parishes that minister to the laity have not had the resources or the knowledge to work in this way. The conventional church approach has been to compel belief and demand conformity, not to cultivate spirituality. Over recent years, I have spoken with many religious people, including Protestant ministers and Catholic priests and nuns, who quietly confess to me that there is too much doctrinal form and not enough spiritual content in institutional religion. In my own city, Melbourne, the current leadership in the Catholic Church is still concerned with imposing an old-fashioned style of worship that is based on devotion to the paschal mysteries and loyalty to the institution of the church. This is exactly the opposite of what youth culture and secular culture are looking for at the present time, and it would seem almost perversely self-destructive for churches to persist in a style that generates dissent and opposition.

But in their urgent call for direction in spirituality, youth culture in Australia has caught the church by surprise, and it has caught it at its weakest point. It is not just a matter of 'modernising' church practices in order to regain contact with society: deleting Latin, bringing in guitars and rock music, reducing rituals, even introducing language that is inclusive of women will not ensure that contemporary culture is drawn in and that the church can find renewal and resume its leadership role. On the contrary, it is angels, rituals and mysteries that many people want to discover, and that many sorely miss when the modernised church takes them away. A friend of mine attended a party where a Catholic and a follower of the New Age were comparing notes about religion. The Catholic explained how his church was attempting to modernise, with more emphasis on the rational and moral basis of faith and less emphasis on rites and mysteries. The New Age follower said that that sounded strange to him, because rites and angels were precisely what the New Age was about, and one reason why it has become so popular and appealing. Religions of all persuasions are, clearly, floundering in the dark today, unable to determine which way to develop and in what direction to move in order to regain their connection with the spirit of the time.

My own view is that the demystification of church services, the reduction of ritual, and the emphasis on plain language and simple moral lessons is a huge mistake. This tends to throw the baby out with the bathwater, and if people feel that they are being delivered morality without an abiding sense of mystery, they will probably feel that they can acquire a moral education more readily and easily from secular systems than from religious ones. For instance, the doctor, the educator, the social worker, the counsellor, can all teach a morality of life, and these secular authorities are far more plentiful today than priests and nuns. The only true way that religion can claw back authority and meaning is not to shed its mystery but to show a new way into its mystery. The problem is about access and entry, about the existential and human experience of symbols, images, rituals and religious narratives.

I would suggest that rather than being 'modernised' in the sense that is synonymous with demystification, the people want the churches to be 'monasticised' — turned into local monasteries that teach reflection, prayer and meditation, offering a transformative, inward experience of the sacred. This is, paradoxically, how churches can regain contact with the world: not by diluting the message even further to accord with a disenchanted sensibility, but by providing a sturdy and solid spiritual brew, one that is based on monastic tradition and derived from the traditions of mysticism within the church.

Currently, young people are feeling that they must turn to India and the East if they are to find a contemplative path that encourages meditation and spiritual exercises. In particular, Buddhism is attracting many of our young people, and is the fastest-growing religion in Australia today. The East has primarily been an introverted culture, and its knowledge of the psychology of religious experience is sophisticated and highly developed. But while the West, and its public or non-monastic church, has been primarily extroverted in its focus, we do have our own intraverted and psychologically advanced mystical tradition, even though much of it has been lost or ignored. To regain contact with youth culture, Western religion will first have to regain contact with its own mystical roots, paying particular attention to the Johannine Gospel and its arresting image of the Cosmic Christ. Twentieth-century Christology, especially in Protestant discourses, has been preoccupied with the discovery of the historical Jesus through demythologisation, but this tendency, governed largely by a rationalist ethos, will have to be complemented by a renewed emphasis on mystery and sacramentalism.

We have a remarkable mystical tradition to rediscover, which would include such important figures as St John of the Cross, Teresa of Avila, Hildegard of Bingen, Jacob Bohme, Meister Eckhart and William Blake. Although these figures may at first appear 'old', on closer examination they are revealed to be hauntingly contemporary, since they are dealing with the same issues that are foremost today: how to get beyond the dogma and arrive at a transformative experience of the sacred. In more recent times, the Christian mystics who can provide guidance are Thomas Merton, Bede Griffiths and William Johnston. Johnston's recent great work *Mystical Theology: The Science of Love*[6] is an important resource for young and old alike in our recovery of our contemplative tradition. The task today is not to confine mysticism to the monasteries but to bring the monastic life to the people, where it is so desperately needed and sorely required.

TOWARDS A NEW THEOLOGY OF THE HOLY SPIRIT AND DIVINE IMMANENCE

Youth culture is interested not only in the mystical sources of religion but also in the presence of the Spirit in non-Western and unfamiliar traditions, such as indigenous spiritual traditions and Eastern religions. Again, this is a shock to conventional Christian taste, which has always emphasised the primacy of our own tradition and has generally been suspicious of the comparative study of religions. Beneath this suspicion, it has to be admitted, has been the lingering sense that our own religious tradition is superior to other traditions. This view has been radically questioned by Vatican II Council, which has emphasised the universalism of the Spirit, thereby opening up the possibility of interfaith dialogue and creative conversations between and across religious traditions.

But also, in the world outside the church, youth have been exposed to the powerful influence of post-modernism, with its primary emphasis upon diversity and plurality. We should have an instinctive fear of single answers, absolute dogmas and exclusive religious pro-grammes, particularly in a time that has experienced the horrors of various totalitarian and absolutist systems at both extremes of the political spectrum. We cannot go back to the old days of single positions and non-inclusive theologies; Father Tony Kelly has written persuasively of the need for increased openness and conversation in his book *An Expanding Theology: Faith in a World of*

Connections,[7] which provides a wonderful antidote to the bigotry and narrowness of the past.

To make itself capable of dialoguing with the present social situation, the church has to sacrifice its own claims to exclusive truth and begin to insist on the plurality and diversity of the living Spirit. At the same time, it has to abandon the emphasis on belief and start working at a more primal and deeper level, on the in-dwelling experience of the sacred. These two elements — the *expansive nature of the sacred*, and the need for a *compelling experience of the sacred* — seem to me to lead us directly to a new theology of the Holy Spirit. My own sense is that a theology of the Holy Spirit is what contemporary culture longs for, and that this Spirit is what guides it at present, tragically unsupported by the institution of the church, which as yet cannot recognise what is taking place. The youth crying out for spiritual direction are not rebels or conspirators; rather, they are the prophets of a new religious dispensation, one that is only now taking shape in the collective psyche. The popular and ever-growing Pentecostal and Charismatic movements, which are especially attractive to young adults, must surely be seen as one expression of the increased hunger for the direction and presence of the Holy Spirit. However, I am not sure that these movements are always authentic; they seem to become fatally entangled with the egos and ambitions of the charismatic leaders involved, and as such, they are more symptomatic of the need for spiritual presence than they are expressions of this presence.

But if the Father represents our awareness of God beyond us, and the Son represents God beside us, then the Holy Spirit governs our experience of God within us. It is the presence of God within our lives that is unfolding in society today, and this calls for a new theology and a new religious understanding. A theology of the Holy Spirit must, obviously, be based in spirituality, and that is the deep hunger of our time. Appeals to the faith of our fathers, with its familiar focus on a God beyond us, no longer attract young people today, with their 'unholy' desire for inner experience. One priest has said to me that youth are looking for what he calls the 'f.i.f.', or funny internal feeling, and that may be so, but conservatives must not trivialise this simply because they fail to understand it. The radical cry of our youth today is precisely captured in a line from Bertolt Brecht's *Life of Galileo*: 'God is ... inside us or nowhere'.[8] As in our own bold, sceptical age, Brecht's scientist Sagredo asks, "Where's God?", and the answer given by the cosmologist Galileo is, "Inside us or nowhere". People today are prepared to believe in a God 'out there' only if they can first sense the presence of a God 'in here'. This is what gives our time its radical, inquiring and unconventional quality and its uncompromisingly psychological and mystical emphasis. We are prepared to risk all, to give up the traditional emphasis on a transcendent God in heaven, in order to get to know the sacred presence at the core of our own lives.

TAKING RISKS WITH FAITH AND TRADITION

Religious conservatives, quite naturally, do not like the sound of this at all. What if we give up our inherited faith, only to find ourselves consumed by an abyss? Indeed, our modern culture has already experienced this void, and it has been called Existentialism, a modern philosophical tradition that has shared much with Relativism, Constructivism and the so-called 'Death of God' movement in theology. Existentialism has been around for over a hundred years, and our culture has moved on from this nihilist and negative stance. Existentialism said: there is no meaning in the universe, other than that which is 'man-made' and imposed on the universe. Meaning is not discovered, just 'invented' to allow us to live comfortable lives and to enable society to function. Modern philosophy has had its hundred years in the wilderness, its long interval in the God-forsaken wasteland of meaninglessness, and now it waits on the miracle of the Holy Spirit to renew our faith and reignite our passion for the divine.

Clearly, a church that still speaks the old, premodern language of dogma and belief will not answer the urgent needs of the postmodern present. But a church that is willing to sacrifice some of the old ways and take risks with faith may recover its philosophical and intellectual leadership. Cardinal Martini, the popular Bishop of Milan, is prepared to allow the Catholic Church to provide precisely this leadership role. In his various books and lectures, Cardinal Martini speaks of the need to seek spiritual renewal, calling on believers to renounce what he calls 'our conventional faith', in order to discover a 'deep faith' that wells up from the mystery of our being, from the ground of our unknowing. Whoever would have imagined, even twenty years ago, that an important Cardinal and Bishop would be entreating Catholics to let go of conventional belief and allow the Holy Spirit to renew our lives and provide a new foundation for faith? Naturally enough, cynics and realists within the church are saying that the official church can never afford to risk conventional or routine faith, lest the millions of believers disappear, leaving only a few mystics and monks in the church.

In the series of talks I attended at St Mary's Church in Melbourne, Cardinal Martini actually apologised to the people on behalf of the new or renewed church. He indicated that the church had got it wrong, that the politics of fear and the theology of compulsion were not a platform for the church in the future. Rather, he said, the theology of grace had to be adopted as the central religious platform. He also indicated that, for the faithful, risk-taking in this way is not so terribly risky, for even in the moments of our greatest doubt and despair, we are able to feel the presence of the Holy Spirit. But we must take risks, for two reasons: to fulfil our urge for a personal journey, a personal commitment to faith, and to renew and strengthen the Western tradition in which we operate.

The Second Vatican Council papers of the 1960s spoke candidly and pointedly of "the split between the faith which many profess and their daily lives", but in view of Cardinal Martini's teachings, I think our 'split' could be refashioned as the split between a doctrinal faith that we profess and a personal spirituality that we experience. The document on 'The Church in the Modern World' suggests that we have to rearrange our daily lives to fit with our faith, but it does not suggest, more radically, that our inherited faith structures may have to be changed to fit in with our contemporary spiritual experience. This is what has been left out, and is what needs to be considered, perhaps in conversation with Protestantism, which knows a great deal about 'revisioning' the faith. For present purposes, I would like to offer two definitions. Firstly, the 'doctrinal faith that we profess' is an inherited, routine Christian faith, which can be a source of strength and stability, but which can be external to our experience, and hence easily abandoned without much moral argument or conscience. In fact, youth find such abandonment 'liberating'. Secondly, the 'spirituality that we experience' is a deeper religious faith, based on an intuition of the presence of the Holy Spirit, in which one's life is experienced as sacramental and as touched by the breath of the sacred. This spirituality is existential, life-changing, often painfully achieved, even against one's will, and it can never be abandoned, because it is our own 'true self' (according to Thomas Merton).

Theologian Frank O'Loughlin is correct in asserting that our religious status in the future "will be more a matter of 'being made, not born'". Children born into religious families are born into religious or cultural forms, but these forms need to be renewed by personal spiritual experience if they are to be understood and respected.

People will need to come across Christianity and come to Christianity in ways different to the past. Our giving 'an account of the hope that is in us' will be much more important. This new social situation will affect the numbers of people making up the Church and it will change the Church's relationship to the wider society.[9]

Western religion in the past has relied on a high degree of conformity and routine religious practice, often set in place by fear rather than arrived at by conviction. The way ahead will have to emphasise grace and love, and this will necessarily involve a religious style that encourages, rather than represses, personal variations on the religious theme and unique expressions of the religious calling.

In reality, there can never be a 'tight fit' between formal religion and personal spirituality, because the former is collective and formal, while the latter is informal and personal. Even the most formal religious believer is constantly having to engage in adjustments and translations. Religious terms have to be 'translated' into personally meaningful categories, and the structures of religion have to be 'filled out' with anecdotes, narratives, and metaphors of lived experience. Women are our teachers and guides of this art, since they have been engaged in spiritual translations and adjustments for centuries of patriarchal religion.

THE LONELY PATH OF INDIVIDUAL SPIRITUAL EXPERIENCE

The failure of many contemporary individuals to find a neat fit between their spiritual experience and established religion is now so widespread as to be almost endemic. It may be instructive to review a biographical statement from one of my students, who has written succinctly and briefly of her spiritual development. This is what she says about the relationship between religion and spirituality in her own experience:

> *I had been confirmed an Anglican, and whilst I loved the ritual, the mysteries of Christianity were so mysterious they remained meaningless for me. The question of whether God was good, evil or both was never satisfactorily answered. The Bible was contradictory and the church's creed contained no resonance that made my heart sing, that made me feel any personal power, no love for the natural world at large or the people around me. I maintained a constant dialogue with this masculine Christian God, but received no response in return. Eventually, frustrated and annoyed that I could not belong, my church attendance drifted away into nothing, leaving me with a huge inner void.*

There are several salient and typical points made in this paragraph, which is why I think it has general significance. The student reveals an attitude that is not directly hostile to religion, in fact, she indicates that she "loved the ritual" in church services, but she is disappointed by the church's inability to speak directly to her condition. As with the majority of people today, she is by nature questioning and critical, and she asks for the meaning of the ritual she loves, but such meaning is not forthcoming. She tries to stick with it, but eventually finds herself losing her connection with the church service and the community. She thus becomes one of the rapidly increasing majority of unchurched Australians, who do not lack spiritual sensibility but who are unable to remain within a structure they fail to understand. There are also other familiar aspects here, including the reference to the masculine or patriarchal image of religion, which she, as a woman, finds alienating. There is a reference to the need for celebration and joy, which she does not find. There is a need for her own individual integrity and pathway to be affirmed, yet instead, she is simply one of the flock who must submit to a collective and already revealed faith.

The problem with conventional Christianity is that it fails to generate in people a sense of adventure or risk, a sense that the personal journey matters and that the individual experience has real theological meaning. Conventional forms of Christianity seem not to be interested in personal risk or adventure, because the great truths have already been revealed, and it is simply a matter of devoting oneself to what is already known. This is how our tradition has become emptied of spiritual substance, because the quest or challenge of igniting what Martini calls a "deep faith" has been missing and the mystical fire has not been kept alight. It is significant that this student has found her way towards Indian religions, in which the experience of meditation and contemplation gives the individual a sense that she is capable of a true relationship with a living sacredness.

This student's spiritual statement ends on an ominous note: "my church attendance drifted away into nothing, leaving me with a huge inner void". Defending against this huge inner void is what many young people mean by 'spirituality'; it is whatever combats and reduces the crippling sense of alienation and meaninglessness. When youth undertake personal spiritual journeys, they often sense the possible dangers ahead, but nevertheless they go forth like knights in search of the Holy Grail, with only the courage of the spirit. Parents often wish that they would settle down and not be so endlessly restless. Church leaders and religious educators would like them to be more conventional and less attracted to the road less travelled. But some strange sense of quest and adventure beckons them, and they are being drawn by a force most adults do not see and therefore do not understand.

At the outset of their spiritual journeys, many youth believe they can supervise their own spiritual development and chart their own spiritual course. It is just as well that they possess such unbounded optimism, because otherwise they might not set forth at all. At any moment, the youth can become overwhelmed by existential terror, since he or she has exposed him or herself to the high seas of the dark unknown, and archetypal forces in the psyche can readily diminish and override the relative insignificance of the personal self. Youth optimism must be tempered by the social fact of increasingly high rates of youth suicide, and at least some of those individuals who end up in suicidal despair began with personal enthusiasm for their spiritual journeys. To negotiate the spiritual path requires enormous inner resources and intuitive abilities, and not all people have the necessary moral genius to succeed in this task. This is why a cultural solution (ie. a renewed religious attitude) is urgently required for our spiritual problem, since not all of us can embark on an individual spiritual journey.

Youthful confidence is tested very early, and with these tests come a rapid ageing or maturing process, where everything gets toned down quickly, especially if the personal spiritual journey coincides with having to make one's own material and economic way in the world. But the young adventurer learns quickly that truth cannot be made, only found or, at best, rediscovered. This disappointing realisation always knocks some wind out of the sails. The whole notion of originality, invention, and creativity is thrown into doubt. There is nothing new under the sun, but perhaps there are new or original approaches to age-old wisdom. The quest becomes no longer a bold search for new truth, but an individual search for established or perennial truth. With this realisation, there is sometimes a change of attitude towards tradition, and a softening of the earlier attitude towards churches and religious organisations, which are looked upon with a new sense of compassion and shared humanity. The notion of an individual journey as a protest against tradition becomes replaced by the idea of an individual journey to renew or revitalise a tradition. Some of the hubris and arrogance disappears, and ordinary people can relate to this headstrong person again.

Personal pride is punctured still further when the young adventurer realises that this journey cannot be conducted alone. To some extent, the 'personal spiritual journey' is a contradiction in terms, since the great spiritual truths are collective, transpersonal — anything but personal: they are collective, ageless, transpersonal, shared. Spiritual truth is still largely an oral tradition, even today, for spirituality is best conveyed by word of mouth. One can reach great stillness and peace in meditation and solitude, but nothing delights the heart more than insightful conversation with a spiritual guide, or mentor. It is conversation and dialogue for which our heart longs, and this realisation draws us back into community again. Scaling the icy peaks of spiritual solitude becomes less attractive when we listen to the desire of the heart.

INTEGRATING THE LESSONS OF YOUTH SPIRITUALITY

It is apparent that youth spiritual experience has much to teach our culture in general and our religious tradition in particular. To our mainstream secular culture, youth spiritual experience says that secularism has failed, materialism does not work and rationalism (whether of the economic or philosophical variety) is inadequate. Youth spiritual experience is a protest against secular humanism and rapacious consumerism, which pathetically attempts to 'win back' its lost spiritual enchantment by generating new realms of experience through technology, drugs and entertainment. Youth spiritual experience challenges society to recover its spiritual life and its religious imagination. It also represents a challenge to academic postmodernism, with its dread of essences and its institutionalisation of relativism and nihilism.

Youth spiritual experience also represents a serious challenge to Western religious tradition. Firstly, it teaches that the spirit has got out of the bottle, and that organised religion no longer holds a monopoly on spirituality, a word now used freely and often without any reference to the churches. Secondly, it shows that spirituality is an existential and practical issue, involving not merely knowledge of theology or familiarity with Scripture, but knowledge of the self, of the psyche and of life itself. Spirituality is less concerned these days with an abstract faith in the afterlife than with practical concerns with this life. Young people are looking to spirituality to teach them how to live, how to be in the world, and how to know themselves in relationship to others. Spirituality is today a 'care of the soul', an understanding of life that comes closer to therapy than to theology, closer to psychology than to metaphysics. It is this psychological spirituality that youth are craving beyond all else at present. If organised religion cannot reveal this inside dimension, it will be violently rejected by a youth culture that cares more about stemming the tide of disintegration than about preserving the traditions of theology. I do not think that youth culture wants to bring down religion for the hell of it, but it is prepared to risk a great deal in order to have the spiritual crisis of the present adequately addressed.

To heal the split between spirituality and religion, between youth culture and established culture, between experience and faith, will require enormous courage from those on both sides of this schizophrenic divide.

The important thing is for conversations to develop across these divides, so that each can be informed about the other side, and each can know what the other side is about, what its motivations and interests are, and what it sees as the truth. Western religion is currently engaged in conversations across various faith traditions, including conversations between rival traditions within Christianity and, more broadly, between Christianity and indigenous religions, Islam, Judaism, Buddhism, Taoism and Hinduism. However, in addition to these important 'interfaith' dialogues, there is a dialogue we are not having: an open, non-suspicious dialogue with our own youth culture and, by extension, the wider secular or disenchanted culture in which youth culture is predominantly situated. It is crucial that we begin, and maintain, a dialogue with the 'unchurched' majority about meaning, spirituality and values. The community of believers must share the comfort of faith with the disaffected, the secular and the needy. Faith is suspiciously weak if it cannot be 'tested' against the claims of contemporary social experience. Karl Rahner enjoins contemporary theologians to address the 'unbeliever' in ourselves, and if theological inquiry were conducted in this spirit, it would find that it no longer merely talks to itself in a cloistered environment, but that it speaks also to the urgent needs of a sick, hungry, increasingly desperate world.

8

Religion and the New Paradigm

Religion will not regain its old power until it can face change in the same spirit as does science. Its principles may be eternal, but the expression of those principles requires continual development.

— *A. N. WHITEHEAD*[1]

In this chapter I will explore further aspects of the split between spirituality and religion, review some of the negative consequences of this split, and consider the possibility of a future rapprochement or reconciliation between popular spirituality and formal religion, which would lead to the construction of a new paradigm for Western religious experience. We need to draw up future scenarios and new social visions, in order to heal the dangerous rifts that are threatening the integrity of psyche, spirit and society. First, I would like to revisit the problem of community in a world that has come to privilege personal spirituality above communal religion.

BEYOND INDIVIDUALISM: THE NEED FOR COMMUNITY

As we have seen, there is a marked tendency today to assume that spirituality is 'good', and religion is 'bad'. The popular view is that religion is institutional, narrow and authoritarian, whereas spirituality is individual, expansive and liberating. A recent statistical survey in the United States indicates that this kind of rift is now characteristic of contemporary experience in Western societies:

> *As spirituality has become differentiated from religiousness ... it has taken with it some of the elements formerly included within religiousness. Therefore, recent definitions of religiousness have become more narrow and less inclusive.*[2]

Historically, religion has been both institutional and individual, and this tendency to equate religion with dogmatic and oppressive institutionalised structures is a very recent development, arising from the beginning of the secular period. To some extent, modern sensibility has created a false dichotomy between institutional and individual life, viewing these as somehow contradictory rather than as complementary and mutually beneficial. Some institutions may oppress individuality and human difference, but for the most part, institutions are complex and differentiated structures in which individuality survives and may even be encouraged.

I am conscious that institutions can carry very negative projections, and in an individualistic modern world, they may reap more than their fair share of criticism. In the Australian context, it could also be that our social ethos has lent this religion versus spirituality dichotomy extra weight, since our national character has from the beginning been anti-institutional and anti-authoritarian (as expressed in our folk anthem 'Waltzing Matilda'), and what is 'good' in life supposedly arises from the heroic achievements of the battling individual, while the collective institution is felt to generate only oppression and limitation.

But I think that individualistic spirituality gets an unfairly good press because it accords with the prejudices and tastes of the time. When we extol the virtues of the individual journey, we conveniently forget how isolating and alienating this journey can be. There is no guarantee, when we cut loose from the community, that we will end up in a creative or happy place, and people on spiritual journeys can often feel hopelessly bereft and in desperate need of human comfort and solace. But no, we soldier on, continuing to advocate spirituality above religion. There is every chance that our current preoccupation with casual spirituality will contribute to further disintegration of social bonds and breakdown of community. If unstructured spirituality is the way of the future, we have to ask where this leaves our instinct for community and our very human need for shared identity and group coexistence.

SPIRITUAL BONDAGE AND SUFFERING PROJECTED UPON 'RELIGION'

Moreover, we know that 'spirituality' is not all that it is made out to be. Authentic spirituality involves loss of self, displacement of the ego, and sacrifice. While spirituality may lead to a deep sense of connectedness to the sacred, and thus to deep security and spiritual confidence, it always comes at considerable cost to our self-centred lives and our innate narcissism. The popular notion that it always 'feels good' is a complete fabrication, or what psychoanalysis might call a defensive idealisation to avoid facing the reality. The New Age slogan 'follow your bliss' is more a product of consumerist capitalism than it is a genuine indicator of the spiritual life.

Spirituality liberates the spirit, but it very often has a negative impact on the ego, especially if the ego has not made adequate provision for the spirit in its concept of life. Spirituality connects us to a larger centre of authority, relegating the ego to a subservient and passive role. The ego must reflect upon and attend to a life that is Other than its life. This can be excruciatingly painful and disorienting. An Other life breaks in upon our life, and we have to surrender and renounce control. Spiritual rebirth must always be preceded by a 'death' of the ego, and this death is powerfully symbolised in the sign of the Cross and in Christ's Crucifixion, which so many people find 'morbid' or 'negative'.

I have spoken to many people, especially intellectuals, who find the iconography and imagery of religion abhorrent and repulsive. They say that the church is involved in a cult of suffering, that the images of death and sacrifice are morbid, and that the eucharist or communion, with its emphasis on the broken body and the blood of the redeemer, is sado-masochistic and perversely mediaeval. It is clear that these images and rituals do not suit 'modern' taste, with its denial of death and its rejection of darkness and suffering, but these images speak to the eternal condition of the soul and spirit, which is not terribly interested in what is fashionable or what is rejected by modernity. But in rejecting or abhorring these so-called 'negative' images of religion, we may be rejecting our own consciously lived suffering, and hence our own entry into the mystery that leads to spiritual renewal and transformation. We could be rejecting religion not because it is irrelevant to our lives but because it is too close to a truth we cannot bear to understand.

Another typical complaint against religion is the view that religion is authoritarian, that it sets rigid boundaries to our experience and is heavy on morality. If we leave aside for a moment the problems besetting the actual church and its historical condition, we might again ask what aspect of our own psychological experience we are projecting upon the institution of the church. Authentic spirituality leads to an encounter with the living Spirit, and this Spirit is indeed a separate 'authority' within the self, which bids us to attend to realities to which we otherwise would not attend. This sacred presence can be experienced as 'authoritarian', especially by those people who assume that life is primarily about doing what you like. The hunch I have is that the negative side of this spiritual experience is split off from 'spirituality' and projected forcibly upon 'religion'. Again, I am not wishing to defend religion against all criticism, some of which is justified, but I am genuinely amazed by the amount of negativity heaped upon the church, much of which strikes me as deriving from unresolved personal problems and popular projections.

Spirituality imposes a new logos, a new law and order, upon subjective experience. It may well be that religion in the past has exaggerated this egodystonic sense of foreboding or dread, this sense of being 'taken prisoner' by another power. But being overtaken by a greater authority, having to submit to a force mightier than ourselves, is central to spiritual experience and cannot be denied, despite its inconsistency with the modern notion of free will and personal autonomy. When people look to the church or religious tradition and see only a negative force that wants to control them and rule their lives, are they perhaps experiencing this split in projection?

I am interested in, and suspicious of, the way in which the sacred has been deprived of its negative aspects or dimensions, and reframed as a source of pleasure or eternal delight. The image of the sacred as stern judge, senex or ruler has been forcibly repressed today, because popular taste has no room for it. The source of restriction and boundary is felt to be human rather than divine, arbitrary rather than essential.

This represents a very dangerous state of affairs, because it suggests that morality, ethics and inhibition is entirely artificial and man-made, whereas 'spirituality' itself is boundless and joyful. In advocating spirituality and rejecting religion, there appears to be much more going on than just a refusal to engage with a social institution. We are witnessing a splitting of the spiritual experience: a celebration of its joyful aspect and a denial of its attendant moral and ethical demands. The spiritual bond is paradoxical: it releases us from human alienation and binds us to the cosmos, but it also demands a binding agreement to live in strict accordance with the spiritual laws of creation. Despite popular opinion to the contrary, spirituality cannot be cut loose from its historical basis in ethics and morality, and the joy of linking with a God who inspires me is simply the flip side of the pain generated by a God who summons me into His service. Spirituality is in danger of becoming a fantasy-construct (as Freud imagined it to be), if it is not mindful of the moral restrictions and inhibitions that are integral to any experience of the sacred.

THE DISAPPEARANCE OF SIN AND EVIL

The loss of the central importance of the moral perspective derives not only from the pleasure-seeking and ecstatic aspect of contemporary spirituality, but also from the modern world view that the self and creation are all essentially 'good'. Contemporary awareness has lost the meaning of sin, especially original sin, because of our new and naive commitment to the goodness of creation. This naive positivity has an important contribution to make, and is a logical counterbalance to our historical overemphasis on evil and sin, but it has in turn created a new one-sidedness that leads to distortion and untruth. Today, the emphasis is not on original sin but 'original blessing', which sits nicely with the new ecological turn of popular spirituality. Youth culture and secular culture celebrate the goodness of the world, the wholesomeness and purity of sexuality, physicality, spontaneity, instinct and the sensuous life. But if everything has become good, where has evil got to?

This seems to me to be one of the keys to modernity, and one of the basic premises that explains so much about our contemporary world: the loss of passion for moral philosophy, the lack of interest in a personal God, the disregard for a divine act of redemption and, at the same time, the outbreak of violence and rage in our time, and the relative ease with which evil is released into the world and reigns supreme in it. Since the modern world view has decided that there is no evil, it has also decided that there is no need for protection against evil and no need for a redeemer to save us from our sin. These theological ideas are remote from the secular mind, which sees the religious-moral dispensation as out of touch with the present and lost in the superstitions of the ancient past. Again, sin and evil are seen as inventions of an oppressive culture or religious institution, not as central to the experience of spirituality. Many of us consider that the churches are labouring under mediaeval delusions, and that the goodness of everything is patently apparent and must be celebrated and enjoyed.

The contemporary pendulum swing against a religious culture steeped in the awareness of evil and sin, and that subscribed to a fall-and-redemption cosmology, is now headed into a glibly superficial awareness in which there is no perception of the reality of evil at all. I especially find this problem in youth culture, where there is often little respect for inhibition or restriction. There is a sort of primitive sense that if something 'feels good', it must be okay. I do not think we are becoming immoral so much as amoral; we are forgetting or losing the moral sense. To draw attention to moral matters is considered boring, because there is no guiding moral force in the universe and no threat of having to atone for immoral actions now that our culture has rejected both the idea of a punishing God and the idea of hell or eternal damnation.

Evil and sin do not go away just because we have stopped noticing them. On the contrary, they hold more sway than ever before, because they work below the threshold of awareness. In the language of the fundamentalists, 'Satan' (as the personification of evil) reigns supreme in our culture because he is not even noticed or observed. I think that a lot of what the fundamentalists say is almost half-right, except that they think in such ridiculously concrete terms that the modern intellect recoils from their utterances as the babblings of an idiot. But evil and sin are basic human realities, and if we repress them, they only arise to assault and defeat the common good with even more power and devastation than before. It is the old Freudian adage: whatever is forcibly repressed eventually returns in altered form and with more primitive and destructive force than when it was held in consciousness.

It may be no accident that, as many of us in 'civilised' societies subscribe to the theory of goodness in its secular or quasi-theological guise (in 'creation theology'), random acts of violence, anonymous crime, terrorism and street horrors have steadily increased. Our naivete is frequently exposed as naive and stupid. If the lessons about human and social evil have to be learned all over again, if we have such short memories that we fail to call to mind the Holocaust, world wars, colonial tyranny and racial genocide, then our contemporary secular and/or spiritual awareness becomes morally and politically worthless. We must always labour to identify human evil and work to transform it. That is what traditional religious ritual is all about, and I fear that we disregard this to our personal and collective peril. We should ground our new enthusiasm for spirituality in the practical soil of ethics and moral awareness, and this grounding inevitably leads us to a rapprochement or reconnection with our abandoned religious tradition.

FACING A CONSERVATIVE RELIGIOUS TRADITION

> *If anyone has ears to hear, let him listen to what the Spirit is saying to the churches.*
>
> — *REVELATION 2:7*

I would be among the first to agree that our religious tradition needs to be radically transformed. As David Millikan has said:

> *Christianity in the West tends to have a conservative tendency to move with painful slowness in response to the changing needs of people. Like all religious systems it tends to be more intellectually imperialistic than is warranted.*[3]

While the substance of religion is eternal, its forms and structures are historically constructed, and the language and forms that continue to govern our religious tradition are derived from ancient and premodern awarenesses. Our religious language is archaic, the stories and narratives are dualistic, the imagery is patriarchal and sexist, the iconography of the spirit is literalistic, and the discourse about the person of God is so ancient that it is little wonder all but a few have abandoned the faith practices and structures on offer. Western religion is, in certain respects, a living fossil that has not caught up with the recent several hundred years of history, and there is much in it that any intelligent person would find objectionable. The theology is supremacist and otherworldly, based on the supposed 'triumph' of spirit over matter, resulting in negative and hysterical views of the body and sexuality. There is an innate loathing of the flesh, a fear of the feminine, a devaluation of nature, and a transcendentalist emphasis that is at odds with modern consciousness, the incarnational thrust of history, health awareness, psychotherapy, and the social experience of gender.

Only a few can overlook the outdated cultural forms and decayed structures and find solace and comfort in the mystery at the heart of Western religion. Sometimes I achieve this equanimity, but I am always painfully conscious of the gap between what religion is and what it could be if it started to unpack its cultural baggage and enter further into the modern era. My dismay is often tinged with anger, because I see an entire global institution devoted to the life of the spirit that has not managed to communicate with our time or to give a decent account of itself.

SHARING THE BURDEN OF CHANGE

It is clear to me that we cannot expect isolated individuals to carry the burden of spiritual or cultural change, and yet that is what is happening in the modern world. Through timidity or blindness, the churches are not leading the spiritual revolution in our midst. Meanwhile, many unguided and untutored individuals, especially among the young, are being crushed by the burden of history and the demands of the spirit of the time. Not all us have been blessed with moral or spiritual genius, making individual solutions to our problems not only difficult to achieve but also relatively rare. The burden of cultural transformation has to be shared by our collective institutions, not merely passed over for numerous and sundry individuals to sort out. We require a 'cultural solution' to the spiritual difficulties of the time, and this means that our religious institutions have to catch up and assume some leadership in facilitating the birth of the new cultural and religious paradigm.

IS RELIGION PREPARED TO CHANGE?

In thinking about a possible rapprochement between popular spirituality and religious tradition, we are faced with many difficult questions. Will Western religious tradition adapt itself to the new spiritual environment, or will our tradition adopt a siege mentality, striving to preserve inherited religious forms even if this proves self-destructive? Will religious tradition allow itself to be reshaped by the *zeitgeist* or spirit of the time or will it argue that significant change is destructive to faith and an assault on its core values and visions?

Obviously, I am on the side of change, because I see this change as instigated by the creative power of the Holy Spirit, which works through time and history to beckon us to new and more fulfilling forms of religious experience. I am conscious, however, of also being seen as heretical and dangerous by some authorities within church traditions, who see change not as authorised by the Holy Spirit but merely as encouraged by radicals and stirrers seeking change for its own sake and destabilising traditions out of some hidden destructive urge. So the further questions arise: is spiritual change actually supported by the sacred, or is this change merely instigated by human fashion, social frailty and revenge? What is the relationship between change and the sacred?

None of these questions has simple answers, and they can be responded to only paradoxically. I think that the sacred exists both within a tradition and in the revision of that tradition. Within Christianity, I feel that Catholicism is vitally important, because it contains the wisdom of tradition, with roots going back to the very beginnings of our era, and its powerful sacramentalism and spiritual substance links us with the heart of the spiritual experience. Nevertheless, none of this substance or mystery exempts it from due criticism, and I also value the Protestant tradition for providing us with an ongoing critique and revaluation of our spiritual tradition. I can never subscribe to the rivalry between Catholicism and Protestantism, which strikes me as infantile and silly, because both sides have important truths and contributions. We need both a tradition and a critique of that tradition as we move into a new millennium and a new religious dispensation. I am also made aware on an almost daily basis that today's Catholicism is deeply divided between a strong core tradition that resists change and a very popular wider tradition that encourages change and is deeply frustrated by the refusal of the stalwarts to be guided by the spirit of the time.

An ancient Chinese curse reads: 'May you live in interesting times', and ours is certainly an interesting time, in which we can feel alternately blessed and cursed by the changing conditions of truth in our culture. Although dogmatic conservatives appear to appropriate the sacred for themselves, it represents a colossal error to suppose that the sacred is synonymous with rigid, unchanging cultural conditions. There is no room today for any complacency regarding the future of our religious institutions. Bishop Spong has declared that Christianity must change or die, and I am inclined to agree with him.[4] If our religious structures do not accommodate change, then change will just roll over our structures and destroy them. Some maintain that this catastrophe has already happened, and that the churches are merely fossilised remnants of a former cultural order. But I firmly believe there is life left in our religious traditions, and where there is life there is hope. I remain hopeful that 'spirituality' and 'religion' can become related again.

THREE VIEWS ABOUT RELIGIOUS CHANGE

With regard to the relationship between new spirituality and old religion, I discern basically three views or attitudes. One is the radical view that new spirituality will destroy the old structures of religion and the limitations of the past. This view is strongly expressed in contemporary youth culture, with its enormous frustration with the old patterns, its eagerness to overturn what stands in the way of progress, and its hostility towards what it fails to understand. I often hear youth calling for a new kind of cosmology, one free from the encumbrances of patriarchal ideology, and free from the debilitating dualisms of masculine versus feminine, spirit versus body. We need a new religion, they often say, because our present religion merely keeps replicating the dualisms and splits that have a debilitating effect upon life and society.

The second view, upheld by religious conservatives, is that we already have a perfectly good religious tradition, so why mess around with it and possibly disturb its original integrity? This view is deeply suspicious of reform and resistant to change. It interprets any call for change as narcissistic and irresponsible. The call to change arises from mere ignorance of the value, complexity and historicity of religion. This view essentially says that the faith has not failed the people but, rather, the people have failed the faith. It does not recognise that eternal truth must be constantly reformed and re-expressed to meet the changing conditions of culture, and it says that anyone can access this eternal truth if they have the patience or humility to attend to it. This view holds a basically resentful opinion of modernity, and is dismissive of our contemporary unwillingness to make the 'leap of faith' that would make conformity to tradition possible. The conservative attitude relies heavily on the suggestive or coercive power of authority, employing fear as its key weapon against the threat of change.

Then there is a third view, which is where I tend to be situated. This view says that change and tradition must coexist. It points out that no living tradition is ever static, but is always being modified and corrected by changing historical conditions. This view regards rigid conservatism as self-destructive, because clinging to outworn forms will render the tradition obsolete, out of touch with present and future needs. Any tradition that constantly looks backwards can hardly be expected to have a future. On the other hand, this view regards full-blown radicalism with suspicion as well, since there can be no authentic future spirituality that is not grounded in the soil of the past and nourished by the tap-roots of tradition. If we want to keep faith with the future, we must also remain grounded in the past, and this view asserts that the demands of the past and the claims of the present (and future) need to be balanced and properly integrated.

This third view sees religion as a paradoxical reality: it enshrines what is eternal, but its forms and structures, in so far as they have been shaped and created by society and culture, are not eternal. The spiritual essence and mystery of religion is eternal and unchanging, but its institutional body, its interpretation of scripture, its credal attitudes and doctrinal teachings, are culturally dependent and subject to change. This is why the notion of papal or ecclesiastical infallibility is an embarrassment to modern taste and an outrage to the intelligence of our time.

THE DECONSTRUCTION AND REVITALISATION OF TRADITION

But if we agree that there is an urgent need for new structures, emphases and directions in religious awareness, then we have to plan for such reconstruction. I hold out little hope for the radicals who want to abolish the old religion and develop a new one. There is much more sense and practical opportunity in the idea of paradigmatic change upon a traditional base. New religions do not develop out of thin air; they are always grounded in the experience of the past. Christianity was so close to its parental background in Judaism that many still consider it to be a kind of successful, universal Jewish sect. Jesus said that he came not to overturn Jewish law but to fulfil the law and the teachings of the prophets. The same is true of the growth of Buddhism from the fertile soil of Hinduism: the new form evolves out of the old tradition, and is deeply respectful of that tradition, even as it attempts to define its own separate identity and direction. New-fangled religions rarely succeed, simply because religions are organic things, requiring roots, soil, ancient history and psychological background. Recent attempts to found new Western religions, such as Theosophy, Anthroposophy or Christian Science, often have dynamic brief histories, but they rise and fall rapidly, because they lack the substance that comes from groundedness and depth. That is why I am committed to the idea of finding a new vision that is based on the old.

What is needed is a reworking of the tradition we already have, with a reversal of some of our values and attitudes and a deconstruction of our ideological baggage. The Anglican Archbishop of Brisbane, Peter Hollingworth, wrote recently:

> We have to deconstruct much of the philosophical framework of our more recent past. This has led us to segment our society by saying 'this is sacred and that is secular, this is natural and that is supernatural, this is spiritual and that is material.' I think this is a series of ludicrous dichotomies which the ancient world would never think to do and the non-western world of today would look at askance.[5]

It is true, as Hollingworth says, that Eastern traditions such as Buddhism, Taoism, Yoga or Zen know little or nothing of our typically Western dualism between the spirit and the body, which is part of the reason so many of our youth find these foreign paths attractive and richly rewarding. But the truly rewarding and creative path, I believe, is not to abandon our tradition because it is dualistic, but to unpack and deconstruct the dualisms in our own tradition, thereby redeeming, rather than condemning, the religious tradition we have inherited and for which we are historically responsible.

To reform a tradition from the inside often means going back to the sources of that tradition and working them in a new way. Central to this task is the scholar's art of showing how the conventional forms and attitudes, which have become synonymous with the tradition, are somehow 'inconsistent' with the original sources, and new forms can be developed that are closer to the original sources. This is a very effective method if it can be developed and sustained, because the 'new' thereby frees itself from the stigma of being arbitrary and is able to reveal itself as the legitimate expression of the original message. Martin Luther was an effective reformer because he went back to the roots in an attempt to reinterpret them, arguing that basic aspects of the original wisdom had been obscured, and that a programme of reform would lay bare the original wealth of wisdom that had become 'clouded' by literalism, misreading and layers of ecclesiastical culture.

The reformist exploits all available ironies and inconsistencies deriving from the paradox that while religion enshrines what is eternal, its own forms and practices are not eternal. The reformist exposes us to the possibility of a gap between original revelation and cultural practice, and shows that original revelation is always 'greater' than any cultural attempt to contain and enclose it. True, this strategy creates a general atmosphere of insecurity, calling into doubt the possibility of culture ever getting it right or being able to express or contain the truth, but it serves as a powerful educative force to everyone, reminding us that it is never humanly possible to contain or grasp Absolute Truth. This strategy also generates enormous spiritual excitement, because it breaks the monopoly of the past, showing how the closed circuit of ecclesiastical tradition can be opened and establishing a new gradient upon which the future can be constructed. Effectively, the reformist is saying that there is a better way to serve our original revelation.

What reformist scholars have to show, and what many creative thinkers are already revealing, is that the dualism between body and spirit is a cultural imposition on our religious tradition, not intrinsic to it. We also must show that the dominance of the sacred life by men is cultural, not intrinsic, as are cultural additions such as celibacy and negative attitudes towards the body and sexuality. What previously was regarded as written in stone must be transformed and changed. We have all sorts of theological and cultural work to do, and reversals and deconstructions to be performed, before we can separate our superimposed patriarchal ideology from the core substance of our living religion.

THE NEWLY EMERGING PARADIGM

It may be useful to outline what I see as the huge paradigm shift taking place in our culture, which is already being felt across numerous sections of society. This paradigm shift is archetypal, which means that it is universal, not confined to any one field of experience or specialised area of knowledge.

THE PARADIGM SHIFT IN WESTERN CULTURES

OLD CULTURAL FORM	NEW CULTURAL FORM
dualistic, spirit above matter	holistic, spirit and matter together
transcendentalist	incarnational, immanental
God in the world seen as 'pantheism'	panentheism, the world is in God
patriarchal, masculinist	inclusive, non-patriarchal
anthropocentric, human-centred	environmental and contextual
religion separated from the state	religion engaged with political process
hierarchical	democratic
authoritarian	compassionate
human being dominated by sin	human being both sinful and graced
exclusive, tribal	inclusive, global
ethics based on *perfection*	new ethic based on *wholeness*
religion as a moralistic 'high-jump bar'	religion as empathy and acceptance
religion based on doctrine/tradition	tradition complemented by experience
fundamentalist interpretations	hermeneutic complexity and fluidity

The column on the left is what youth and secular culture call 'religion'. The column on the right is what they generally call 'spirituality'. The old cultural paradigm is regarded as oppressive, while the new paradigm is linked to optimism, vision, and the future. For youth and secular culture, religion is 'guilty until proven innocent', and we prove it innocent by showing how it reaches beyond itself to the goals and values in the new paradigm. If religious educators want religion to come alive for youth today, they will have to teach the cutting edges of change, showing how religion is willing to risk its established dogmas in a bid to encompass a living and transformative spirituality.

But to the extent to which religion already possesses a spiritual foundation, it is at any moment in transition across both these paradigms, and therefore contains both elements (old formalist and new inclusivist) at the same time. But youth and secular culture tend not to see this internal fluctuation, partly because they are not receptive to the creative dimensions within religious tradition and partly because the spiritual, progressive, expansive aspects of tradition are not easily seen by or clearly modelled to the community. That is to say, if creative change is going on in religion, the majority of people know nothing about it, and the old stereotypes and limitations will stick until there is public renewal and change. Scholars and educators therefore have a moral responsibility to show students and the public how religion is changing, and how it is reaching beyond self-concern and self-interest, beyond dogmatic formalism, to engage with the time and the community.

Arguably, the West has been reaching towards a new cultural paradigm at least since the beginning of the Christian era, but somehow, we always fall short. We lose confidence in the grace and fluidity of the spirit and instead start to focus attention on the letter of the law and on our own institutional and intellectual structures. The new cultural form is actually very close to Christ's original message of redemption, hope, love and inclusiveness, whereas the left-hand column reflects the rigidity that is the bane of any institutional structure, whether secular or sacred. The purpose of prophets, saints, mystics and visionaries is to constantly draw attention to the original goals and inspirational visions that have always been central to the aspirations of Western culture and religion but that become clouded or lost beneath the dead weight of dogma and fear.

I think it is, essentially, fear that dominates the left-hand column, whereas love is the central pillar of the new paradigm. It will probably always remain 'new', nascent, just over the horizon of cultural possibility, to the extent that fear keeps pace with love and sometimes even replaces it (in fundamentalism, backlash regimes and fascism). So the 'revolutions' and 'renewals' in Western culture are always the same: a movement towards increased love, fairness, and democracy of the spirit or state. The same ideals keep presenting themselves, to be met by the same or similar obstacles. However, the historical and social conditions of these revolutions are constantly changing, and the emphases or points of change are always different.

THE MISSING TRINITY IN WESTERN CULTURE: WOMEN, BODY, NATURE

In our time, the central emphasis in spiritual change involves the overcoming of the dualism between spirit and matter, and the resolution of the many problems to which this dualism gives rise, including the denigration of the body, the control and manipulation of women, the demonisation of sexuality, and the abuse and desecration of nature. All of these problems are bound up in a dualism that prevents us from understanding the radical implications of the Incarnation, and of the necessity for continuing Incarnation. The entry of the Spirit into time, history, flesh and embodiment means that the objects and persons of this world are sanctified by this same arrival or presence of Spirit. The 'descent of Spirit' is the major insignia of our time, and wherever this movement is felt, the old dualisms in which Spirit has been kept apart from the realm of manifestation are exploded, collapsed or reversed. Hence the old sacred order, which has failed to further the incarnational unity of spirit and matter, looks spurious and doubtful to those who have become inspired by the new (or perennially new) paradigm.

Because our Western religious tradition is so bound up in, and so much a product of, a patriarchal and dualistic culture that seems to have passed, youth look upon our institutional religion and see only the works of man, not the presence of God. They constantly point out how strongly patriarchal and masculinist our religion is. They see a religion based on God the Father, and ask why not also God the Mother? They dislike this editing out of the feminine, and the downgrading of women, the body and nature. Youth culture argues, in a sense, that women, the body and nature constitute the missing Trinity in our Western religious, philosophical and sociopolitical world view. I think they are right that this is the voice of the *zeitgeist* or spirit of the time.

I indicated earlier how creative scholarship and research must continually reinterpret the core tradition in the light of new and pressing truths of the day. Cynics might say that we reinvent the past to suit the needs of the present, but we could respond that we redeem the past by showing it to be boldly, even radically contemporary. By reinterpreting and reimagining the core tradition, we rescue it from its conservatism, releasing new and exciting potentials that enable us to move forward with confidence into the future. We redeem the past not by killing it off (as in wild radicalism), nor by replicating it in the 'same old' way (the imitations of rank-and-file clergy), but by dreaming it onwards to new possibilities. One example of this liberating activity is the work of theologian Sallie McFague, who argues in *The Body of God: An Ecological Theology* that the original Christian vision is far more radical than the institutional edifice that has grown up around it.

McFague addresses herself to the contemporary need to oppose the dualism of spirit versus body, and to recognise the embodiment of the Spirit and its incarnational intent and movement:

Christianity is the religion of the incarnation par excellence. Its earliest and most persistent doctrines focus on embodiment: from the incarnation (the Word made flesh) and christology (Christ was fully human) to the eucharist (this is my body, this is my blood), the resurrection of the body, and the church (the body of Christ who is its head). Christianity has been a religion of the body.[6]

McFague argues that of all the world religions, Christianity is the one that most dramatically emphasises the incarnational dimension, and she points out how 'shocking' it is to worship an incarnational God who takes on flesh and participates in culture and history. She sees the life of Jesus, despite the plethora of otherworldly interpretations that have often represented it, as having been a deeply sensual experience. Moreover, she argues that Christianity announced its non-dualistic vision in direct contradiction of the prevailing ethos of its time and place:

Christianity during the first-century Mediterranean culture, which was noted for its disparagement of the body and its otherworldly focus, defiantly proclaimed its message of enfleshment.[7]

In view of the important claim that Christianity is a "religion of the body", the irony of the problems Christianity has had in its relationship with the body is apparent. McFague notes this paradox:

And yet, the earliest Christian texts and doctrines contain the seeds that, throughout history, have germinated into full-blown distrust of the body as well as deprecation of nature and abhorrence and loathing of female bodies. If Christianity is the incarnational religion, its treatment of embodiment, nature, and women is very strange indeed.[8]

McFague works to expose the ironies and riddles that can be unearthed from Christian tradition, in the hope not of debunking this tradition but of releasing new potentials for its growth. She argues that we have to strongly oppose the 'otherworldly' character of the Christian spirit, instead dragging it into creation and embodiment. Why must spirit be afraid of nature? Is its masculine power threatened by the might and majesty of maternal nature? McFague argues that the spirit is not afraid, but our cultural (patriarchal) conception of spirit is afraid of the realm of *physis* and matter — a gap created by dualism and oppositional thinking. It is as if historical Christianity has failed its own incarnational mystery, or has not yet realised or understood the radical implications of the sacred having entered time and human form. Fear is still preventing the Catholic Church from ordaining women priests, or from recognising that priests, like all of us, must consciously engage their sexual lives.

McFague insists that the incarnation ought to be taken seriously, and that it should be taken spiritually and symbolically, to include the entire realm of manifestation and of the body and matter. McFague announces: "We will suggest that the primary belief of the Christian community, its doctrine of the incarnation, be radicalized beyond Jesus of Nazareth to include all matter".[9]

The dualistic conception of spirit and matter is a kind of persistent cultural illusion, and one that creates enormous social and personal damage. The patriarchal image of God and of spirit can no longer be supported, and just as spirit needs to embrace matter, so does our masculine image of God need to embrace and include the image of God the Mother. We must experience God again as mother, nurturer and sustainer, and not only as judge, law-giver and authority. When God is discovered simultaneously as immanence and transcendence, nearness and distance, Mother and Father, then we will have found the right religious vision for our time and for the generations to come.

The rejection of Western religion's disregard for the sacredness and sanctity of nature, the body and women appears fundamental to contemporary culture's rejection of Christianity. In this passionate rejection, youth and secular culture may be deeply inspired, not simply rebellious or heretical, for the ground of nature is itself the most visible and solid ground for spiritual activity.

Contours of Australian Spirituality

AN INTERNATIONAL VISITOR IN SEARCH OF AUSTRALIA

I am sometimes told that the tag 'Australian spirituality' represents a contradiction in terms, since the word 'Australia' signifies everything that is modern and secular. But is Australia as boldly secular as it sometimes claims to be? Let us imagine the hypothetical situation of an educated international visitor who is coming to Australia for the first time, and who would like to discover something about its essential character and meaning. The visitor has done some preparation, by reading Manning Clark's *A Short History of Australia*, Patrick White's *The Tree of Man* and a selection of poems by Judith Wright. The visitor — let us assume he is an American male — has also seen some Aboriginal art, at an exhibition in New York, and is now reading Les Murray's *Selected Poems* in his Sydney hotel room.

After Les Murray, he intends to explore the writings of Tim Winton and Rodney Hall. Meanwhile, he is perusing the pages of a book of cartoons by Michael Leunig, and the cartoons look more like modern expressions of theological questions than satirical comments on the politics of the day. Moreover, he discovers that this popular artist has also published a book of prayers, the tone of which is naive rather than cynical. The visitor has also just purchased a musical compact disc entitled *Spirit Returns*, by the folk-rock group Goanna.[1] The epigraph quoted on this disc is from Lionel Fogarty: "The spirits are all still there in the rain the wind the bush walkin' talkin' singin' dancin' in the land".

Not surprisingly, the visitor has reached the conclusion that Australia must be a very spiritual country, and he is keen to discover more about the nature and direction of this spirituality. What is the relationship between this cultural spirituality and organised religion? Is this spirituality Christian, Buddhist, pantheistic, pagan or theosophical? Has this spiritual feeling come from the Aboriginal cultures, and is it in some way a continuation of Aboriginal cosmology in the present-day society? Has it been imported from European cultures? Is it related to the popular spiritual movement that began in California? Is it a product of Australia's close proximity to Asia and its powerful religious forces? Has a nation made up of transported criminals become a nation of mystics? What, in short, is the contour and history of Australian spirituality?

Most of the recent writing on Australian history and society completely ignores this dimension of Australian experience, and so our visitor is none the wiser. Books on Australian literature and art never appear to mention spirituality, and even writings on Patrick White or Les Murray somehow manage to ignore or bury in obscure academic jargon these important questions. On the other hand, popular New Age books on spirituality deal only with authors' personal experience, never seeming to engage cultural or historical questions. Spirituality is approached by these authors in a kind of social vacuum. Outside art, literature and music, or the primary ground of cultural imagination, there seems to be no public discussion or social integration of the spiritual questions.

Initial forays into social interactions have not proved encouraging. In a public bar across the street, his statement that Australia seemed like a very spiritual country was met with incomprehension and denial. "A spiritual country?" "There's not much spirituality around here, mate." The Australian said he had never read Les Murray's poetry, though he enjoyed his coverage of soccer on SBS television. This left both of them mystified, so they changed the subject. Later, the visitor struck up a conversation with a university student in a fashionable bookshop. "Actually," the student told him, "we are in the postmodern world now, and we believe that everything, including spiritual truth, is merely an oppressive myth imposed by patriarchal authorities upon the people. But we respect the spirituality of Aboriginal people here, because it is intimately connected to their experience of the land. As a society, though, Australia is disenchanted and irreligious, and we like it that way — it keeps us free from fanaticism and religious passion. It is the absence of religious feeling that allows us to be tolerant and pluralist. Multiculturalism works only because we have no religion."

Our visitor has to revise his earlier conclusion that Australia is a very spiritual country. He realises that the Australian situation is much more complex than he had imagined. There seem to be two different Australias: an Australia of the spirit, expressed in art, music, literature and Aboriginal cultures, and an Australia of public or consensus reality, using different language and based on entirely different expectations about the world. Which one is the real or true Australia?

THE DOUBLE LIVES OF AUSTRALIANS

Someone might suggest to the visitor that we live two vastly different lives in Australia: one at the surface and one in the depths. The split has nothing to do with education or upbringing, though the educated Australian may be able to give more complicated explanations of why we are not a spiritual culture and why we have rejected religion. The national psyche is split between two levels of reality, and the spiritual level is encountered only in individual or private experience; it is never engaged at the social or public level. Privately or personally, Australia is enchanted, haunted, and steeped in religious feeling, and this is the life that our best artists articulate and explore. But publicly and officially, we are postmodern, proud of our social cleanliness.

In Australia, life at the surface is resistant to the depths. Our depths are hidden and silent, and we are embarrassed, even angered, by the artworks and artists that expose these depths. The strength of our reaction to revelations of our spirituality depends upon how split we are. If we are mildly split, we allow artists a degree of 'poetic licence' to articulate our soft underside. If we are deeply split, however, we can become hostile towards artists who give voice to the spirituality we deny. Witness, for instance, the early reception of Patrick White, with critics outraged by his religious statements about Australian experience, which contradicted all the public and official designations of Australianness. And as Manning Clark's work became more prophetic and interested in unveiling Australia's repressed religious side, secular critics were savage. Eventually, Clark confessed in an ABC radio interview with Terry Laidler that he could no longer stand to be in the presence of unbelievers.

Most Australians are what I would call moderately split, or gently divided, so that our other side eventually does make an appearance. If, for instance, our visitor friend is still interested in analysing us, he might encounter small glimpses of the hidden spirituality. He might be told of some strange or emotionally moving experience we have had in the bush, or an upwelling of deep compassion for our fellow man as we assisted in the battle against a devastating bushfire, or how serenity and clarity overcame us while we sat beside a dying loved one, or how some revelatory dream prompted an eerie feeling of *deja vu* when it appeared to come true in reality.

When we Australians relax and are allowed to feel, our feelings are often religious, but our pronouncements are mostly secular. The split is between thought and feeling, as if in Australia you can have as many religious feelings as you like as long as you do not talk about them in religious terms or name them as 'religious'. There is enormous fear in the Australian psyche: fear of religion, fear of the unknown, fear of an authority greater than our own. Some of this fear is well founded; religions in the past have been tyrannical and dictatorial, and they have imposed a culture of conformity and compliance, under threat of hellfire and damnation. Australians have overwhelmingly rebelled against this style of religion, and I like to acknowledge our courage in this regard. We have the strength of character to reject what we do not like and accept the consequences, and we need to celebrate that fact.

THE OLD PUBLIC STORY AND OUR DUAL LEGACY OF DISENCHANTMENT

For too long, we have been the prisoners of an old story about ourselves, a story that has systematically cut us off from the spiritual half of our selves. The governing values that have determined official Australian consciousness have been secular and reductionist. We have failed to take the sacred into account, because it has not been part of our map of the real. Australia is what classical anthropologists would describe as a 'shaming' culture,[2] and if confessing to some strange feeling would put us at odds with the status quo or set us apart from others, we are very reluctant to do so. It has not been seen as permissible to publicly acknowledge the sacred, and to the extent that we are a nation of conformists (despite our national self-image as rugged individualists), we eschew the spiritual in order to comply with the old story.

Some of us have been duped into believing that the sacred is dead and that only human design and social engineering govern reality. Others have been duped by lifeless versions of institutional religion into believing that God is so far removed from human affairs that the divine has no determining role to play in our immediate personal and social experience. We are the inheritors of a legacy of disenchantment and loss of spirit. We are the products of an intellectual tradition that has been constitutionally opposed to the sacred and the mysterious, and of a tired religious tradition that has lacked the courage to discover the workings of the divine in the here and now.

Far too much of our religious tradition has been fixated upon the workings and miracles of the divine in the ancient past, so that we have participated in a sort of cult of Jesus to the detriment of the continued workings of the Holy Spirit in the present. We are supposed to 'believe' in the miraculous transformations of biblical times, viewing our own time as mundane by comparison. Moreover, our imported religious traditions have suffered from a constitutional blindness towards the sacredness of the ancient Australian landscape and the religious traditions of its indigenous peoples. It is little wonder our traditional religions have been declining, for they have lost the spiritual vision that is needed to track the sacred in the present and to bring the spirit into living focus.

Whether we turn to church, university, political system, law, hospital or workplace, we find widespread dissatisfaction with the quality of public life and disenchantment with our official consciousness. We are witnessing the death of one public story and the birth of another story, and no part of society can be immune from such a transformation. We have outgrown the narrative that used to contain our lives and provide meaning, because it is too narrow and we have matured. We no longer want life to revolve wholly around the rational mind or ego and its wishes and desires.

A new star has risen in our heavens, and we are hoping that we can find a new orientation in relation to it. A kind of Copernican revolution of the spirit is upon us, as we see that our little Earth, the personal ego, is not the centre of the universe after all, and that the human ego's role is, actually, to serve a larger purpose and fit into a greater design. We could probably define spirituality as all the cultural forces and mechanisms opposing the alienation of the ego and the self-imposed isolation of the rational intellect. We desperately require a larger story, one which allows us to shed the illusions of the separate ego and join together in celebration of our spiritual unity.

THE POSSIBILITY OF RE-ENCHANTMENT

In examining the possibility of a common spirituality or shared purpose, we venture onto difficult and sensitive ground, as far as our old public story is concerned. The distinguished writer and literary figure Robert Dessaix has recently explored our spiritual dilemma in a paper called 'Some Enchanted Evening', delivered to a literary audience in Melbourne. Is re-enchantment possible in Australia? he asks. In exploring this critical question, he encounters a double standard in our official Australian attitudes, which is hardly surprising, given the split character of the national psyche. In contemporary multicultural Australia, people whom we would call 'ethnic' or 'indigenous' are allowed their public enchantment, but so-called ordinary Australians must remain in the shipwreck of reason, by public consent and at the risk of reprimand.

Robert Dessaix reflects that if he were to announce his involvement in, say, spirituality or "magic incantations", "it would embarrass you". "Unless, of course," he adds, "I happened to be indigenous or multicultural", in which case:

> ...I think you'd probably compose your face and hear me out, politely suspending your sophisticated disbelief. You would, in other words, permit me my enchantment. You would probably even applaud me for revivifying my traditions. (However, if you applauded too loudly, I might accuse you of patronising me, and if you showed too much sympathetic interest, I might accuse you of appropriating my discourse.)[3]

He continues: "I wonder if the time might not have come for us to allow ourselves much more enchantment in our lives than we do".

SHARED MEANING IN AN AGE OF MULTICULTURALISM

The new challenge is to achieve a shared public meaning and a unity of purpose that is clearly absent from our present social system. The educated elites in our society regard such national unity with enormous suspicion, regarding any call for cultural or spiritual unity as a call to uniformity. To be fair to this educated view, our cultural unities of the past have been limited. Our earlier sense of nationhood was based on experiences arising from bush culture, and we created a national 'ideal' that was judged by later generations to be xenophobic and sexist. We also upheld an idealised image of masculinist Australian experience that was unnecessarily narrow. Not all men fitted into the national stereotype of the ANZAC digger, who was bold, resilient, laconic and stoical. Most men did not fit this national image, which also made little room for women, recent migrants, people from non-Anglo countries, homosexuals and Aboriginals.

Similarly, we celebrated a folksy image of the Australian landscape, typified in Banjo Paterson's poetry and bush ballads, which excluded both the sacred mystery of the land and the ancient Aboriginal story that had already imagined and possessed it. Over recent years, we have exploded our former images of nationhood and selfhood, viewing these as tyrannical to the extent that they have excluded so much social and human reality. We have been celebrating plurality, diversity, everything that opposes and transcends our former social unities. The rational intellect sings the praises of plurality, noting especially how such plurality frees us from the tyranny of any 'single view', any single church authority or any one version of absolute truth. But the national soul is not nourished by a plurality in which no universals are affirmed, and so is inclined to see plurality as chaos or fragmentation. Now we have to discover what we have in common rather than what separates and differentiates us. The challenge for Australia is to abandon the negative uniformities of the past in favour of new, positive unities that can give us common purpose and shared enchantment.

The achievement of a multicultural society can hardly be underestimated, since it has taught us how to get along with one another and how to support and tolerate difference. Many countries continue to exhibit the xeno-phobia and racism that thrived in Australia some fifty years ago, so Australia's must be regarded as a real cultural achievement. But at what price have we achieved this secular tolerance? Robert Dessaix argues that we are: "living through the meltdown of pluralism and multiculturalism as we knew them — the ideology, as I would think of it, of the ultimate arbitrariness and meaninglessness of everything". If we agree with the description of multiculturalism as an ideology of the "ultimate arbitrariness and meaninglessness of everything", we could say that it represents a cynical manoeuvre on the part of both government and high culture.

As an ideology championing the maintenance and celebration of difference, multiculturalism represents an excuse not to bother about the complex and difficult task of identifying the moral and spiritual bonds between us. Since our secular elites are made to feel uncomfortable by religious and spiritual questions, multiculturalism allows them to sidestep the pursuit of meaning altogether, while at the same time, the unconscious religious belief of our time — economic fundamentalism — reigns politically and socially supreme, unchallenged.

Multiculturalism does not foster a common or shared enchantment, because its ethic is based on mutual tolerance of those who *remain* Other and outside our own experience. The system is tolerance, not creative integration or engagement. Our current ethic seems to say that if you do not bother me, I will not bother you, and that is how we 'get along' in this country. If Australia were plunged into a sudden economic or political crisis, would we find ourselves unable to focus on a shared set of values to handle it? In other words, a group of randomly gathered ethnic communities does not constitute a living culture unless some psychospiritual bonding has occurred beyond material and financial connections. Beyond economic considerations what is there to bind us all together? What myths and symbols do we share that foster respect for each other and for a common set of ideals?

The new public story will go beyond the fact of our plurality to discover a common stock of shared meanings. In his book *The Culture of Hope*, Frederick Turner writes about the postmodern world in these terms:

> *The theme now becomes unification; not the disap-*
> *pearance of cultural differences, but the emergence*
> *of larger concepts, of logic, science, money, law, and*
> *art that could contain the diversity and make sense*
> *of it.*[4]

The new unity will have to be inclusive rather than exclusive, fluid and permeable rather than fixed and unchanging, celebrating our continued diversity yet recognising the essential unity that links us all. In other words, the new unity cannot be a conservative backlash against our avowed diversity, but must be a further development within and beyond our contemporary recognitions.

RELIGIOUS CONVERSATIONS AND COMMONALITIES

Secular multiculturalism is interested in spirituality only in the sense that the spirituality of minority ethnic groupings is patronisingly respected. Secular multiculturalism offers another version of rationalistic thinking: "we", the architects of multiculturalism, know there is no basis for spirituality, but if "they", the various ethnic groupings, want to keep their spirituality as a sentimental reminder of their own traditional ancestry and identity, then let them have it.

A new public enchantment will never come about if this attitude dominates, because a re-enchantment can be achieved only if the organising consciousness respects the reality of the sacred and acknowledges the diversity of its expressions. Spirituality is not just some relic from the ancient past, but a dimension of our experience that is contemporary, relevant, and vitally important for mental health and social cohesion. An authentic, spiritually valid multiculturalism would recognise the need for diversity in religious expressions, but would also seek to engage these separate traditions in ongoing creative dialogue.

Religions and cultures have to risk the influence of each other; that is, historically, the best way for civilisations to endure and thrive. Meaning cannot be carved up into little segments and confined to cultural ghettoes. Interbreeding and mongrelisation create a stronger culture than do purity and division. It is the mongrel dog that generally proves to be healthier than the thoroughbred. Christianity has had a vigorous history as a world religion precisely because it has learned to be eclectic and adaptable, to borrow and absorb influences from countless mythological traditions and regional sources. The same must be the case for re-enchantment in Australia: public enchantment requires a willingness to borrow, exchange and integrate. Culture is about risk and cross-fertilisation producing ever-new hybrids and unities.

There is an urgent need in our society to exert effort towards developing a common bond with the sacred. There is a need to rethink our relationship to the land, to place, to history and to eternity. The bond that links us can only be a new kind of spirituality, one we all can share regardless of race, creed, colour or background. Only eternity is large enough to encompass us all and only the sacred is grand enough to remind us of our true destiny. A new kind of reconciliation is needed, both among our splinter cultural traditions and with our Aboriginal people, so that we can dissolve our disparities and unite in a common human purpose.

SPIRITUAL CHANGE, THE LAND AND ABORIGINALITY

Robert Dessaix concludes his speech with this suggestive remark:

> Is re-enchantment possible? This is going to sound like a terrible cliché, but I happen to think it is partly possible in Australia in a way in which it's not in most other Western countries, through re-immersion

in untransformed landscape and in listening to what
our indigenous Australians find magic in.[5]

Still, we need to unpack the cliché about landscape and renewal and open ourselves to this poetic truth. The sophisticated habit of referring to this idea as a cliché may well represent an intellectual defence against change, and a resistance to the transformative possibilities of the sacred as these are present in landscape.

Dessaix is right to suggest that a new enchantment can be achieved more readily in Australia than in many other Western countries. It is the influence of the land — savage, untamed and always honest — that punctures our ego-based story of the world, exposing us to the elements and to the wider cosmos, with which we feel we must now develop a new relationship. A country that is two-thirds desert cannot help but limit the scope of the greedy ego, rupture our innate narcissism, and expose us to mysteries that reside both within and beyond the envelope of rationality. A desert country inevitably gives rise to a desert mysticism: a desire to live beyond the self, to befriend and know the Other, to learn how to live authentically in relationship with the land and its indigenous people.

It is a harsh magic that we will discover here, poetically affirmed in Hope's image of a "savage and scarlet" spirit of place. The familiar, conventional, heroic ego is displaced by this untransformable landscape. We cannot reinforce the ego's story of limitless progress and enlightenment, but instead must listen to the testimony of rock, the wisdom of the desert, the eternal mind of a timeless country. Often without our realising it, we are forced to commune with forces beyond the self, and if we respond to it creatively, this communion can lead to a spiritual quickening. If we resist this communion, however, we can be fragmented by it, destroyed by the power of the non-egoic forces, lured beyond the safety of the ego's ground into a savage and scarlet madness. Our literature and culture suggest that both options are available to us: positive transformation by a spirit of place (as in the poetry of Neilson, Wright, Murray, Hope) or negative destruction by forces that we fail to understand (as in much of our classic fiction, including *Voss*, *Picnic at Hanging Rock*, *Evil Angels*, *The Fortunes of Richard Mahony*).

But spiritual renewal can be readily achieved here because our society is perched upon an untransformed landscape that interrupts our erstwhile sophistication, drawing us ineluctably into itself. As Dessaix says, we will have to listen to what indigenous Australians tell us about what they find magic in, but we do not have to steal their magic. The great difference between listening and stealing, appreciating and appropriating, is apparently lost on our intellectual elites, who continue to argue that Aboriginal spirituality is a taboo area, since non-Aboriginals can (it is supposed) bring only desecration or despair if they trespass upon it. These fears, as I have argued, are based on a cultural materialist view of the world.

Cultural materialism deals in objects, things and cultural 'property', and it argues that Aboriginal property is off-limits, because of the danger of it being appropriated for neocolonial uses. The secular architects of cultural sensitivity see only appropriation, not appreciation. They see only a parasitic and harmful relationship between white society and Aboriginality, mainly because they fail to comprehend the reality of spirit in all human beings and societies. However, this well-intentioned theory of cultural apartheid is completely mistaken. Spirit cannot be 'owned' by any one society, indigenous or otherwise, and any attempt to bracket off spirit as cultural property is doomed. When there is a deep wound in the national psyche, only spirit is large enough and powerful enough to bring about the necessary reconciliation.

Australia can move forward only if there is reconciliation in the depths, and this must be expressed in religious and artistic rituals. We need to listen to the land, appreciate Aboriginal relations with the land, and move towards a new, postmodern and postcolonial enchantment. Our relation to Aboriginality must not be parasitic, but should be creative and progressive, as our country moves into a new religious awareness that is a co-creation of Aboriginal and migrant Australians. But the very thing that could bring healing and renewal in Australia — a binding, inclusive religious awareness — is currently forbidden under the rubric of cultural sensitivity and non-exploitation.

I believe that the widespread idea that Aboriginal people do not wish to share aspects of their Dreaming with us is profoundly mistaken, a product of the prejudices both of the educated white classes and of young Aboriginal voices radicalised by a materialist system that urges them to adopt a victim mentality. Fear, suspicion and prejudice, all fostered under political correctness, treat sacred awareness as exclusive property, but the Aboriginal elders whom I have met throughout the country, especially David Mowaljarlai of the Kimberly region and Nganyinytja and Ilyatjari of central Australia, are insistent on sharing their traditions and stories with us. Such elders see it as their mission to educate and inform other Australians about their cultural and spiritual practices.

The Aboriginal elders with whom I have discussed these issues believe such sharing will strengthen, not weaken, their beloved traditions. If white people develop a spiritual feeling for the land, this will, according to Mowaljarlai, make them respect the land much more than they currently do, and such ecological sensitivity will benefit all living things. Nganyinytja wants us to develop a shared spiritual respect for the land, because, "If we cease to listen to the land, how can we hear each other?" Clearly, indigenous peoples are more than ready to show Australia how to become more ecologically and spiritually responsible.

A NEW RELIGIOUS ATTITUDE ARISING FROM BELOW

Officially and publicly, not a great deal is being done to facilitate the growth of an Australian spirituality. This is perhaps to be expected, since the secular government is concerned only with the development and maintenance of secular values, and while it certainly likes to promote the idea of an Australian ethos or character, this has fallen short of spirituality as such. Our religious institutions, too, have been slow to act on the Australian spirituality project, since these institutions are mostly colonial or neocolonial structures that have been more concerned with evangelical mission and imposing a religious dispensation from above than with listening to and being guided by the living spirit of this time and place.

To foster a regional spirituality requires enormous receptivity and openness, and yet, officially the churches have been, until recent times, in colonising mode. Unofficially, there have always been clergy who have been receptive to regional conditions, but they have often not been given institutional support or encouragement. However, this situation appears to be changing, because the institutional churches have been so profoundly weakened by loss of public support that they now appear more ready than ever to listen for a local spirit and to discover a local direction. Religious leaders who are breathing new life into the Australian church are mostly from the Catholic tradition, including Veronica Brady, Deirdre Brown, Eugene Stockton, David Ranson and Frank Brennan. Indeed, it is astonishing to find so few Protestants actively engaged in the pursuit of a regional spirit, a fact noted by Stephen Pickard and other commentators.

Currently we live in a rather tense in-between period, where it is patently clear that the old ways of being religious are not working but where we are still not sure of the future spiritual directions. It is a time of exploration and experimentation, with a loss of faith in the old methods and a new hope about possible future developments. The new religious dispensation will spontaneously rise up from below, not be brought down to us from above. We are concerned here with the psychodynamics of a collective psyche, and the gradual emergence of the inner life of a nation. That inner life, as Jung knew, will always tend to compensate the one-sidedness of the dominant consciousness, so that whereas Australian public life is secular and rationalistic, our inner life is quite naturally spiritual and even mystical, a fact often noted by Les Murray and John Shaw Neilson. The inner life will always embody those aspects that have been repressed by the governing style, and if the official religious attitude has been puritanical, body-denying, dualistic and patriarchal, then the compensatory inward spirituality will tend to be sensual, this-worldly, holistic and non-patriarchal.

What has been brewing inside the Australian soul is a new spirituality that will surprise both the secular establishment and the official religious tradition. The question is: will it be the government or the church who first opens up the new spiritual possibilities, unleashing the enormous healing potential that lies in wait within the sleeping land? Already we see that workplace culture and the mental-health industry are waking up to the healing and transformative possibilities of spirituality, but these are still largely sporadic and represent only marginal shifts in awareness. I have argued in this book and in *Edge of the Sacred* that it is the artists, writers and musicians who first gain access to the regional spirit, and who express that spirit powerfully in their creative works. It remains for many of us a strange enigma that so much of our high and popular art has adopted a decidedly religious tone and direction, although this is often unrecognised by the institutions of faith (mainly because it is often lyrical, sensual and bodily) and spurned or ignored by the secular art authorities and industries (who still do not have a language or framework to cope with the re-emergence of the sacred).

The miracle is that the secular keeps giving birth to the sacred, often against its will and in spite of its own judgement. This is why even 'religious' artists can be hesitant about their own religiousness and sometimes even deny its presence in their work, because it does not arise by dint of their conscious will but by virtue of their spontaneous creativity. Creativity occurs only if artists delve deep into the collective psyche, and in a secular society they automatically resurface with visionary symbols and mythical narratives. Any society that strongly represses the religious instinct will be plagued by a large group of visionary artists or prophets whose work attempts to restore the balance of life by giving expression to repressed elements. One could almost say that the best conditions for an outbreak of the religious impulse is to bury that impulse and then, by public attitude or government decree, forbid its expression.

The current situation in Russia and Eastern Europe indicates this same rhythm of repression of religious life by a fanatically secular regime, with the inevitable return of the repressed as soon as that regime has weakened or fallen apart. We in Australia have not been subject to a totalitarian Marxist oppression, but we have been subject to a kind of self-imposed secular, rationalist tyranny, the product of a youthful, arrogant, antitraditional consciousness that thought it could rule without the sacred. Its 'governance' consisted of concern for economic development, expansion of business and industry, and egoic development at all costs. This governing psychosocial structure is now in the process of breaking apart. Widespread public cynicism in our major institutions is only one side of this vast dismantling of our former ruling consciousness. There are countless numbers of Australians who have already tossed aside their secular attitudes of the national persona and their naive belief in mechanistic science and rational economics. This process is now so advanced that I doubt whether we can reasonably refer to ourselves as a 'secular' nation at all. This term hides and conceals far more life than it reveals. As Veronica Brady has put it: "Our society is not secular, as it likes to think".[6]

We are now disillusioned by a secularism that has promised so much and delivered so little. This discontent, and the public cynicism that accompanies it, is what I would call, after Martin Buber, holy discontent or sacred insecurity, in that this discontent is fuelled by a desire to create a richer life, with fuller moral and spiritual rewards. Therefore, I have argued in this work that the light is shining into our depths not because we have deliberately sought out a sense of the holy but because we have been forced, as our conscious framework has been collapsing, to recognise an unexpected holiness. We are becoming more religious as it were by default, by our surprising discovery of a buried inner life, the same religious inner life that made our artists of the 1940s and 1950s (White, Wright, Tucker, Boyd, Nolan) truly great. If we handle this uprising of spiritual life correctly, this buried treasure will make our young society great, ushering in a period in which Australia will blossom into a spiritual civilisation.

After the prophetic artists will come prophetic scholars and theologians, who will attempt to provide a more conceptual understanding of our developing spirituality. And as this cultural process unfolds, ordinary people will meanwhile be discovering for themselves what the national consciousness has excluded or left out. But the sooner our high culture can provide a spiritual framework for ordinary Australians, the fewer individual citizens will have to fall through the surface fabric of our society and into the disorienting and often overwhelming depths below. Mental illness rises in direct proportion to official cultural ignorance of the depths of the soul and the need for spiritual meaning. Therefore, ironically, the sooner our surface fabric falls apart officially, by our public admission of the reality of the sacred, the less human suffering will be sacrificed to the depths.

We must welcome the light into the cracks and wounds of our social framework, for this light brings eventual healing and renewal. The songwriter Leonard Cohen expresses this point precisely when he sings:

> Ring the bells that still can ring.
> Forget your perfect offering.
> There is a crack in everything.
> That's how the light gets in.[7]

We have to forget the "perfect offering" and look instead to the flaws and ruptures, the painful openings, for revelations of the spirit. Patrick White recognised this in his *Flaws in the Glass*, where he wrote that the best parts of his personality and art seemed to well up from the flaws in his character.[8]

EARTH SPIRIT, FEMININE SPIRIT

A spirituality that arises metaphorically from below will be a very earthy spirituality. In theological terms, it will be immanental, sacramental, and the opposite of otherworldly, abstract or puritanical. In political terms, it will also be 'down to earth', and the opposite of hierarchical, authoritarian or 'top-down' styles of religious leadership. As such, it might be difficult for conventional religious awareness, which is still primarily puritanical, abstract and hierarchical, to recognise this new religious dimension in psyche, art and society. What we refer to as our 'secular' society may simply be a radically democratic and immanental style of spirituality, which passes unnoticed by our papal or episcopal traditions, too focused on heavenly verticality to notice the mystical transformation of the horizontal domain of everyday experience.

In this new spirituality, the Earth itself will be experienced as celestial and numinous, while ordinary human activity will be experienced in a ritualistic and ceremonial light. Again, conventional religious awareness might decry this as paganism, earth-worship or worse, but this is not so much paganism as panentheism — namely, the presence of the sacred in the created world. In Australian spirituality, the sacred will truly be revealed as the mystery and silence at the heart of everything we do and feel. God in Australia will not be proud, haughty or exalted but, rather, everyday, horizontal and earthly. Australian religious experience will restore the horizontal arm of the Christian cross, that arm that is smaller and less pronounced than the vertical axis, which announces our redemptive flight to the heavens above. Through the horizontal axis, we gain religious insight into embodiment, creation, manifestation and community, understanding that this world, not just the world to come, is sanctified and dignified through the presence of the Holy Spirit.

The revelation of the sacred in this country will also be profoundly feminine. The feminine face of God is creational, embodied and immanental. The God who is inside nature and who acts as a source of revelation within natural phenomena is traditionally imagined in religions and mythologies as a goddess, the feminine aspect of the divine. To emphasise this feminine dimension means that we have revealed and unconcealed the feminine aspect of God the Father. In the Godhead, gender is very diffuse, with feminine and masculine becoming one in the true experience of God. But in Jewish thinking, the feminine aspect of God has become synonymous with God's intimate presence in creation. The female symbol of God, the shekinah, derives from the Hebrew verb *shakhan*, 'to dwell', which is used in numerous texts that speak of God's dwelling among the people.[9] In Christianity, the figure of Mary, who intercedes and reveals on our behalf, bringing compassion and grace into the world, is this same feminine aspect, as is the *descending* movement of the Holy Spirit, as conceived in the experience of Pentecost.

Australia is, as Aboriginal cosmology knew so well, and as is celebrated in the figure of Kunapipi, a land where spirit dwells in the Earth itself. In the Aboriginal Dreaming, the spirit beings emerge at the dawn of time from the depths of the maternal ground and move upwards from below, just as, in our own time, we feel a spiritual renewal arising from 'below' the threshold of secular consciousness. In all patriarchal cultures and religions, we discover a world-creating spirit descending from on high to bring spiritual quickening to the Earth below. But in either case it is the feminine figure who provides the symbol for that intermediary realm where spirit and earth meet, where *nous* and *physis* interpenetrate to give rise to the soul, the celestial Earth or the creational spirit. Before this feminine religion can be realised, our rigidly patriarchal religion must be softened or even displaced. Perhaps the old church has to be radically humbled so the new feminine spirit can arise in our culture and express itself in our lives.

I have already written a book on the importance of the mother archetype in Australian art and literature,[10] but more work has to be done on the dominance of the mother figure in Australian culture. I have also written a book on the impact of the uprising feminine spirit on men's lives, both within Australia and in all patriarchal societies.[11] Feminism did much to displace patriarchy and reveal the power of the feminine principle, but this movement primarily operated at the sociopolitical level and failed to realise the power of the sacred feminine. Feminist theologians in Australia have come much closer to revealing the revolutionary nature of the new, everyday spirituality. My sense has always been that it is the feminine dimension of religious experience that holds the key to the revolutionary spirit that can bring us into theological relationship with this land. For Christians, Mary and the Holy Spirit are the major catalysts for building a cultural bridge to the Aboriginal world, in which the Earth has been celebrated as feminine for countless millennia. Once again, the Catholic tradition has the advantage here, because the Protestant tradition, at one of its extremes, has viewed the adoration of Mary as idolatrous, and because it is too patriarchal and transcendentalist to allow a significant *rapprochement* between Western religion and Aboriginal cosmology. This is spirit country, and our God is intensely embedded in the material Earth, not as the demon who drives us to materialism (which is the negative and unconscious expression of this archetype) but as the sanctifying presence that allows us to see the transcendent in the ordinary and the divinity in materiality.

SENSUAL SPIRIT

The future religious awareness will be affirmative towards the body and sensuality. The old-style religious philosophy, which separated spirit from matter, and which elevated spirit to unreal heights while down-grading matter to unreal depths, will be replaced by a new attitude that is holistic and non-dualistic. This new attitude will look towards an integration of spirit and matter in the realm of the soul, and will not suffer from a fear-based relationship with the archetypal feminine. It is no accident that the decline of a devitalised church coincided historically with the public rise of sexuality and the so-called sexual revolution of our time. The cultural pendulum had to swing in the opposite direction, to recover balance, because in the nineteenth century especially, it had moved too far in the direction of passionless and chastened spirit, captured perfectly in the moral hypocrisy of the Victorian era.

It suited the dualistic style of the church patriarchs to declare that the spirit is good and sexuality (usually personified as Eve, the feminine) evil, and this construct has lasted for a long time. This debilitating dualism has brought enormous damage to the sexual instinct and to women, who have been identified with sex in the patriarchal mind. A future religious culture will be more sophisticated, subtle and psychological. It will see that it is not sex *per se* but the individual or private will, which separates us from the will of the sacred, that is potentially evil. 'Sin' means falling short, falling away from the will of God, and this is a far more subtle process than historical Christianity has imagined. It is not a clear-cut separation brought about by sexual activity. Sexuality itself serves the life process, which can hardly be viewed as evil. Sexuality can serve the good if it acts in the service of wholeness, and it can serve evil, like any of the instincts or archetypes, if it is manipulated into serving the ego or separate self.

Sex and spirit are not enemies or opposites, but two ends of the one libidinal spectrum. Sexuality is part of the bodily and incarnational fuel that feeds the spirit; in turn, spirit gives sex its direction and meaning. Spirit civilises sex, or *eros*, and allows love, or *agape*, to be born. Poets and mystics have long known about this intimate connection between sexuality and spirituality, and writers such as Blake, Whitman, St John of the Cross and others are brimming with the vitalistic message that spiritual life must be fuelled by sexual passion. The 'war' between sex and spirit is invented by false morality and poor taste. It is only puritans and dualists who shrink from this unitary awareness. It has long been my conviction that Australian experience will contribute to a new, holistic understanding of spirituality and sexuality, mainly because our earthly temper and experiential mode will prevent us from making false separations where there are only dynamic unities.

THE EXPERIENTIAL GROUND

'Experiential' appears to be the other key term or characteristic feature of Australian spirituality. Our 'groundedness' can be interpreted not only as the physical ground of natural existence but also as the psychological ground of human experience. I do not think this makes us 'existential', in the philosophical mode, but, rather, phenomenological, in the sense that we emphasise first the ground of our own experience, and privilege that ground above the realm of abstract knowledge. I do not consider Australians anti-intellectual, just opposed to abstractions that have not yet been verified or supported by our experience. I think this feature of Australian life is something to protect and nurture.

Many people today are talking about the need to experience the sacred, and the word 'experiential' has become a popular term in society. Such references make secularists feel distinctly uncomfortable, because they tend to literalise this term and call to mind pagan masses, occult occurrences or ecstatic conversions. Moreover, some churches also recoil from this popular interest, considering that people have become too demanding in the realm of the spirit, no longer satisfied with the gift of true faith. But people are increasingly less likely to rely on old-style faith. They must have a reason to believe, an impulse to send them forward into spiritual discovery, and when there is some real trigger or significant event, they are then happy to commence a journey into faith. Despite the fears of outsiders, this enabling experience is not necessarily exotic, occult or metaphysically dramatic. It could simply be a sudden intuition of a deeper dimension of the real, or a sense of connection to a world beyond the rational, or a moment of sheer peace in which one's anguish and anxiety is overcome.

We are simply in search of the still small voice within, the inner guide that appears to know more than we know but that we find so difficult to access. We long to move outside the ego and be drawn into the divine will that transcends mere egotism. This is what the thirst for 'experience' is all about; no more content with blind faith or belief, we want to know for ourselves, and there is a real desire in the Australian heart to seek for inner knowing. Once an intuition has been established about a higher will, then we long to foster this connection, through prayer, meditation, study and so on. We then say we are on a 'spiritual journey', and the term often confounds and annoys secularists, who feel angrily excluded. But if we understand 'spirituality' as simply a shift in emphasis from the limited ego to the deeper wisdom within, we might be able to demystify the experience for those who feel shut out from it. Depth psychology, which tracks this journey from ego-orientation to soul-orientation in great detail, can do much to demystify spiritual experiences and to make them seem natural rather than eccentric.

A DIVERSIFIED RELIGIOUS ATTITUDE

By 'Australian spirituality', we do not, of course, refer to the development of a new church or religion. The establishment of a national religion is forbidden by our constitution, and anyway, such an institution would probably become narrow and conformist. Australian spirituality refers to the local or regional spiritual character, which will make its impact upon all religious or spiritual endeavours that take place in the Australian context. Australian spirituality is a spirit of place that will colour and affect everything we do in this country. The world religions practised here will not be superseded by a regional expression of the religious instinct, but they will be powerfully moulded by forces beyond their control. It is the subtlety with which spirit of place works that generates astonishment, and real excitement about future cultural and spiritual prospects.

What I see emerging in this country is not a new religious ideology but a new religious attitude, which respects the diversity of all spiritual expressions. This new attitude will provide the ground for common purpose and shared identity but will not stifle difference or insist upon spiritual uniformity. Our tolerance of diversity and acceptance of plurality will be strengthened by a new cultural epoch concerned with shared meaning, with the various distinct enchantments being loosely federated by a cultural attitude interested in the plural manifestations of the sacred.

Such generosity of spirit can come about only by educating the religious instinct beyond the vulgar phase of religious fundamentalism. This involves deepening our awareness of truth and broadening our capacity for negative capability. In the past, religious truth was often believed to be unchanging, and exclusive to clan or tribe. Our God was a jealous God, who would tolerate no other gods before him. Religious hegemonies and cultures of fear thrived in this atmosphere, and the existence of other religious revelations and traditions made us feel nervous and threatened, anxious to denounce the competing truths as pagan heresies and to bolster the claims of our own, superior tradition. Whether the warring parties were Catholicism and Protestantism, Christianity and Islam or Orthodoxy and Gnosticism, these struggles were always combative and often had tragic results.

But with increased awareness, we understand that the one sacred reality manifests in different ways to different people. No sacredness is free from the constraints of history and culture. Thus, our access to 'absolute' truth is conditioned by a great many relative factors, but this does not make our truth any less true, especially at the symbolic level of reality. We are forced to realise that the mysterious One can reveal itself only in and through the Many. In Australia, our complex history, varied geography and cultural-racial diversity point to the reality of the Many, and we must never allow that sense to be overshadowed by any regime wanting to impose and enforce its version of Oneness. While diversity must remain primary, the existence of other enchantments cannot diminish the passion one feels for one's own. Different traditions and enchantments do not threaten my own truth; rather, they bear testimony to the inexhaustible richness and variety of sacred revelation.

ACKNOWLEDGEMENTS

This book was written between 1996 and 1999, but during that period the chapters were rewritten several times. Many began as scripts for lectures and public addresses and were later extended. This book has been willed into existence by the demand for debate about Australian spirituality, and I would like to acknowledge several of the institutions and societies that have encouraged this project from the beginning, often by commissioning an address that set me to work on the theme of spirituality in a new area of Australian experience.

In Sydney, I am especially indebted to the Religion, Literature and the Arts Project at the Australian Catholic University; the 'Spirit and Place' exhibition at the Museum of Contemporary Art; the Eremos Institute for the Study of Australian Spirituality; the United Theological College at Paramatta; the World Business Academy and the Global Scenarios forum; the Sense of Place Colloquium at the University of Western Sydney; the Theosophical Society; the Australian Association for Transpersonal Psychology; the Australian Association for Psychological Type; and the Australian Association for Religious Education.

In Melbourne, I am grateful for support from the Catholic Education Conference and the Catholic Education

Office; the Anglican Archbishop's Office; the Uniting Church; the Ecumenical Conference; the Gatherings Network; the Centre for Adolescent Health at the Royal Children's Hospital; the Science and Theology Network at the University of Melbourne; the Melbourne International Writers' Week; the Royal College of Psychiatrists; and the Spirituality in the Pub Network.

I also acknowledge the support and interest of the Banyo Centre for Spirituality, Brisbane; the Mildura Writers' Festival; the Jung Societies of Western Australia and South Australia; the Temenos Group, Canberra; and the Outdoor Education Group, Eildon.

There are many groups and societies in Australia attempting to access and articulate the new spiritual awareness that is currently blossoming in our society. This suggests that a cultural metanoia or change of direction is upon us, though as yet, the various groups are not aware of each other's efforts, and often there is an invisible wall between religious and non-religious organisations, even though both are exploring the same field of 'spirituality'.

Various conversations with individuals have been instrumental to the conception and development of this book. Indeed, one could argue that spirituality is still largely an oral culture, maintained and transmitted through dialogue and debate. In today's computer-based society, however, many of these conversations take place on the Internet, which is a fascinating site for spiritual expectation and renewal, since it operates under the powerful and traditional insignia of 'interconnectedness'. I would like to thank my La Trobe University colleagues John Carroll, Rowan Ireland, John Morton, Freya Mathews, Drew Hanlon, Lyn Baker, Stuart Sellar and Bernie Neville for their valuable feedback and support. I am indebted to artists Michael Leunig, Greg Burgess, Robert Dessaix, Janine Burke, Les Murray, Tim Winton and Bruce Dawe for their critical insights and prophetic imagination. For discussions on ecological spirituality,

I am grateful to Peter Adams and Peter Hay of Tasmania, Ian Player of South Africa and Satish Kumar of England; to Monash University colleagues Kate Rigby, Peter Cock, Frank Fisher and Sylvie Shaw; and University of Western Sydney colleagues John Cameron and David Russell.

In the field of religion and theology, my major debt is to Father David Ranson, and I also acknowledge critical feedback and insight from Archbishop Keith Rayner, Archbishop Peter Hollingworth, Bishop Michael Putney, Father Eugene Stockton, Father Frank O'Loughlin, Father Val Rogers, Father Tom Gleeson, Father Tony Kelly, Father Michael Kelly, Father Michael Gilbert, Father Peter Robinson, Brother Mark O'Connor, the Reverend Robert Hoskin, the Reverend Dorothy McRae-McMahon, Sister Veronica Brady, Sister Frances McGuire and Sister Margaret Cain. These clergy and religious do not always agree with my views, and cannot be held responsible for my heretical thoughts, but have contributed in various ways to this project.

I am indebted to conversations and interactions with Aboriginal elders, in particular David Mowaljarlai, OAM, of the Ngarinyin (Kimberley region) and Ilyatjari and Nganyinytja of the Pitjantjatjara (central deserts area), and I thank Hannah Rachel Bell and Diana James for facilitating these exchanges. I would also like to thank Graeme Mundine, Christine Morris, Olga Gostin and Craig San Roque for illuminating discussions on Aboriginal spirituality. For talking over various themes and ideas with me, I thank colleagues Peter Ross, Marion and Peter Carroll, Elizabeth Dryer, Linda Rudge, Jane Magon, and Winifred Wing Han Lamb.

Finally, I am grateful to my publisher, Cathy Jenkins, and editors Alison White and Susannah Burgess, at HarperCollins for their thoughtfulness and editorial excellence.

David Tacey, Associate Professor and Reader
La Trobe University, Melbourne

NOTES

EPIGRAPHS

[1] Lionel Fogarty, quoted on the jacket of Goanna, *Spirit Returns*, Compact Disc, ABC 1998. Based on the poem 'The spirit of one tribe is all', Lionel G. Fogarty, *New and Selected Poems*, Melbourne: Hyland House, 1995, p.30.

[2] Robert Dessaix, 'Some Enchanted Evening', *24 Hours*, ABC Radio, December 1995, p.55.

[3] David Mowaljarlai, 'An Evening of Australian Spirituality', together with Michael Leunig, University of Melbourne, 22 March 1996.

INTRODUCTION: THE RISE OF SPIRITUALITY IN AUSTRALIA

[1] Maryanne Confoy, *Morris West: a Writer and a Spirituality*, Melbourne: HarperCollins, 1997, p.13.

[2] This revising in favour of the sacred is taking place in neo-Marxism (Joel Kovel, *History and Spirit: An Inquiry into the Philosophy of Liberation*, Boston: Beacon Press, 1991); in feminism (Ursula King, *Women and Spirituality: Voices of Protest and Promise*, Basingstoke, UK: Macmillan, 1993); and in psychoanalysis (Neville Symington, *Emotion and Spirit: Questioning the claims of psychoanalysis and religion*, London: Cassell, 1994). Contemporary science, and especially theoretical physics, is a birthing site for spiritual renewal. See especially David Bohm, *Wholeness and the Implicate Order*, London: Routledge, 1980.

[3] Hugh Mackay, quoted in Caroline Jones, *An Authentic Life: Finding Meaning and Spirituality in Everyday Life*, Sydney: ABC Books, 1998.

4   David Tacey, *Edge of the Sacred*, Melbourne: HarperCollins, 1995.

5   Paul Collins, *God's Earth: Religion as if Matter Really Mattered*, Melbourne: HarperCollins, 1995.

6   Aboriginal Elders, *Rainbow Spirit Theology: Towards an Australian Aboriginal Theology*, Melbourne: HarperCollinsReligious, 1997.

7   Nevill Drury and Anna Voigt, *Fire and Shadow: Spirituality in Contemporary Australian Art*, Sydney: HarperCollins, 1999.

8   Caroline Jones, *The Search for Meaning Collection*, Sydney: ABC/HarperCollins, 1995.

9   Veronica Brady, *South of My Days: A Biography of Judith Wright*, Sydney: Angus & Robertson, 1998.

10 Caroline Jones, *Authentic Life*, op.cit.

11 Peter Bishop, *The Myth of Shangri-La*, London: Athlone Press, 1990.

12 Hugh Mackay, *Reinventing Australia*, Sydney: Angus & Robertson, 1993.

13 Steve Biddulph, *Manhood: A book about setting men free*, Sydney: Finch, 1994.

14 See Carol Adams, ed., *Ecofeminism and the Sacred*, New York: Continuum, 1995.

15 See Charlene Spretnak, *States of Grace: The Recovery of Meaning in the Postmodern Age*, San Francisco: HarperSanFrancisco, 1991.

16 John Carroll, *Ego and Soul: The Modern West in Search of Meaning*, Sydney: HarperCollins, 1998.

17 Bernie Neville, *Educating Psyche: Emotion, Imagination, and the Unconscious in Learning*, Melbourne: Collins Dove, 1989.

18 Neville Symington defines psychoanalysis as "a mature natural religion", in his *Emotion and Spirit*, *op. cit.*, p.192.

19 Paul Davies, *God and the New Physics*, London: Dent, 1983.

20 Deborah Bird Rose, *Dingo Makes us Human*, Cambridge: Cambridge University Press, 1992.

21 Tony Kelly, *A New Imagining: Towards an Australian Spirituality*, Melbourne: Collins Dove, 1990.

22 Maryanne Confoy and Dorothy Lee, *Freedom and Entrapment*, Melbourne: Collins Dove, 1995.

23   Kevin Hart, *Trespass of the Sign*, Cambridge University Press, 1989.

24   Anne Pattel-Gray, *Aboriginal Spirituality: Past, Present, Future*, Melbourne: HarperCollinsReligious, 1996.

25   Allison Stringer and Leo McAvoy, 'The Need for Something Different: Spirituality and Wilderness Adventure', *Journal of Experiential Education*, Vol. 15, No. 1, May 1998, pp.13–20.

26   Barbara Stevens Barnum, *Spirituality in Nursing: From Traditional to New Age*, New York: Springer, 1996.

27   Jane Magon, 'Spirituality in Contemporary Australian Art: Some Contexts and Issues in Interpretation', *Artlink*, 18, 1, 1998, pp.38–42.

28   This view was recently put by Morag Fraser, editor of *Eureka Street*, on the ABC television show 'Compass', 21 February 1999.

29   David Millikan (with Nevill Drury), in *Worlds Apart? Christianity and the New Age*, Sydney: ABC Books, 1991, p.4.

30   John Shelby Spong, *Why Christianity Must Change or Die*, New York: HarperSanFrancisco, 1998, p.101.

31   Professor Roy Webb, Vice-Chancellor of Griffith University in Brisbane, in a published statement attending the launch of the fund for the Multi-Faith Centre, December 1998.

32   Patrick White, *The Aunt's Story* (1948), Harmondsworth: Penguin, 1963, p.283.

33   C. G. Jung, 'A Psychological Approach to the Dogma of the Trinity' (1942/1948), *Collected Works* Vol. 11, para.267.

34   John Fisher, 'Spiritual Health, Its Nature and Place in the School Curriculum', unpublished doctoral thesis, Baillieu Library, University of Melbourne, 1998.

35   David Tacey, *Edge of the Sacred*, op. cit.

36   David Tacey, *Remaking Men: The Revolution in Masculinity*, Melbourne: Viking Penguin, 1997.

37   Harold Bloom, *The American Religion: The Emergence of the Post-Christian Nation*, New York: Simon & Schuster, 1992.

38   James Tulip, 'Old time religion has no place in the Australian psyche', *Sydney Morning Herald*, 13 January 1996, p.36.

39   Veronica Brady, 'Review of *Edge of the Sacred*', *Westerly*, No. 3, Spring, 1995, pp.84–87.

[40] Kevin Hart, 'Bringing God back from the dead in a new age of the spirit', *The Age*, 8 July 1995, p.9.

[41] Stephen Pickard, 'The view from the verandah: gospel and spirituality in an Australian setting', *St Mark's Review*, No. 174, Winter 1998, pp.4–10.

1: SPIRITUALITY AND THE RETURN TO MYSTERY

[1] Veronica Brady, 'Called By the Land to Enter the Land', in Catherine Hammond, ed., *Creation Spirituality and the Dreamtime*, Sydney: Millennium Books, 1991, p.40.

[2] William Blake, 'The Marriage of Heaven and Hell' (1793), in G. Keynes, ed., *The Complete Writings of William Blake*, Oxford University Press, 1972, p.151.

[3] Rene Girard, *Violence and the Sacred* (1972), Baltimore: Johns Hopkins University Press, 1977, p.233.

2: AUSTRALIANS IN SEARCH OF SOUL

[1] John Deck, *Nature, Contemplation, and the One*, New York: Larson, 1991, p.49.

[2] John O'Donohue, *Anam Cara: Spiritual Wisdom from the Celtic World*, London: Bantam, 1997, p.119.

[3] David Tacey, 'The Deepening: Spiritual Changes in Australia', in *The Global Scenarios: Developing a Scenario for Australia in an Emerging World*, Canberra: EPAC, 1996, pp.34–37.

[4] Peter Hollingworth, 'Towards a New Spirituality', in *The Global Scenarios*, Canberra: EPAC, 1996, p.50.

[5] Friedrich Nietzsche, *The Birth of Tragedy*, New York: Modern Library, 1968, p.137.

[6] Dennis Altman, *The Age*, 16 September 1993, p.6.

[7] Michael Leunig, *Short Notes from the Long History of Happiness*, Melbourne: Viking Penguin, 1996.

[8] C. G. Jung, 'The Undiscovered Self' (1957), *Collected Works* Vol. 10, para.536.

[9] Patrick White, *Flaws in the Glass* (1981), Harmondsworth: Penguin, 1983, p.144.

[10] *Ibid.*, p.146.

[11] *Ibid.*

3: IN DEFIANCE OF THE SACRED

1   Peter Carey, *Oscar and Lucinda*, Brisbane: University of Queensland Press, 1988, p.389.

2   These same questions are discussed in Bruce Wilson, *Can God Survive in Australia?*, Sydney: Albatross, 1983.

3   Russel Ward, *The Australian Legend* (1958), Melbourne: Oxford University Press, illustrated edition, 1978, pp.16–17.

4   See Alfred Adler, *The Individual Psychology of Alfred Adler*, New York: Basic Books, 1964.

5   David Tacey, *Remaking Men: The Revolution in Masculinity*, Melbourne: Viking Penguin, 1997.

6   Richard Campbell, 'The Character of Australian Religion', *Meanjin*, 36, 2, 1977, pp.178–188.

7   John Shaw Neilson, 'The Gentle Water Bird' (1924), in Cliff Hanna, ed., *John Shaw Neilson*, Brisbane: University of Queensland Press, 1991, p.95.

8   Galarrwuy Yunupingu, quoted in John Morton, 'Aboriginality, Mabo and the republic', in Bain Attwood, ed., *In the Age of Mabo*, Sydney: Allen & Unwin, 1996, p.123.

9   Joseph Furphy, *Such is Life* (1903), Brisbane: University of Queensland Press, 1981, p.66.

10 A. D. Hope, 'Australia' (1939), *Collected Poems: 1930–1970*, Sydney: Angus & Robertson, 1972, p.13.

11 Don Watson, 'Birth of a Post-Modern Nation', *The Weekend Australian*, 24–25 July 1993.

12 A. G. Stephens, in Leon Cantrell, ed., *A.G. Stephens: Selected Writings*, Sydney: Angus & Robertson, 1977, p.395.

13 A. G. Stephens (1904), quoted in Ian Turner, ed., *The Australian Dream*, Melbourne: Sun Books, 1968, p.x.

14 Mircea Eliade, *The Quest: History and Meaning in Religion* (1969), The University of Chicago Press, 1975.

15 Mircea Eliade, *The Sacred and the Profane*, New York: Harcourt, Brace & World, 1959, p.203.

16 Patrick White, *The Vivisector*, London: Cape, 1970, p.612.

17 James Tulip, 'Old time religion has no place in the Australian psyche', *Sydney Morning Herald*, 13 January 1996, p.36.

18 Barbara Thiering, 'Preface', in Veronica Brady, *A Crucible of Prophets: Australians and the Question of God*, Sydney: Theological Explorations, 1981, p.x.

19 See Manning Clark, *A History of Australia, Volume I* (1962), Melbourne University Press, 1979, p.15f.

20 Patrick White, *The Solid Mandala* (1966), Melbourne: Penguin Books, 1977, p.145.

21 Mircea Eliade, *The Sacred and the Profane*, *op. cit.*, p.204.

22 Michael Morwood, *Tomorrow's Catholic: Understanding God and Jesus in a New Millennium*, Melbourne: Spectrum Publications, 1997. See also Paul Collins, *Papal Power*, Melbourne: HarperCollins*Religious*, 1997.

23 Mircea Eliade, *The Quest*, *op. cit.*, pp.iii–iv.

24 Veronica Brady, *A Crucible of Prophets*, *op. cit.*, p.2.

25 Leonie Kramer, '*The Tree of Man*: An Essay in Scepticism', in W. S. Ramson, ed., *The Australian Experience*, Canberra: Australian National University Press, 1974.

26 Leonie Kramer, 'Patrick White's Gotterdammerung', *Quadrant*, 17, May/June 1973, pp.8–19.

4: SPIRIT AND PLACE

1 Leonie Kramer, ed., *The Oxford History of Australian Literature*, Melbourne: Oxford University Press, 1981, p.15.

2 Miriam-Rose Ungunmerr, 'Dadirri', in Eugene Stockton, *The Aboriginal Gift: Spirituality for a Nation*, Sydney: Millennium Books, 1995, p.181.

3 I have argued a case for the dominance of the earth archetype in Australia in *Patrick White*, Melbourne: Oxford University Press, 1988, and *Edge of the Sacred*, Melbourne: HarperCollins, 1995.

4 David Mowaljarlai and Jutta Malnic, *Yorro Yorro: Spirit of the Kimberley*, Broome: Magabala Books, 1993, p.53.

5 Les Murray, 'Equanimity' (1983), in *Collected Poems*, Melbourne: William Heinemann, 1994, pp.179–181.

6 A. D. Hope, 'Australia' (1939), in *Selected Poems*, Sydney: Angus & Robertson, 1992, p.71.

7   Les Murray, 'Noonday Axeman' (1965), *Collected Poems, op. cit.*, pp.3–6.

8   Manning Clark, *A History of Australia*, Vol. 1, Melbourne University Press, 1962, p.15.

9   Chris Wallace-Crabbe, 'Melbourne', in John Barnes and Brian McFarlane, eds, *Cross-Country: A Book of Australian Verse*, Melbourne: Heinemann, 1988, p.280.

10   Aime Cesaire, *Discourse on Colonialism*, New York: Monthly Review Press, 1972, p.11.

11   Matthew Fox, in Catherine Hammond, ed., *Creation Spirituality and the Dreamtime*, Sydney: Millennium, 1991, p.11.

12   Rainbow Spirit Elders, *Rainbow Spirit Theology: Towards an Australian Aboriginal Theology*, Melbourne: HarperCollins, 1997.

13   Eugene Stockton, *The Aboriginal Gift: Spirituality for a Nation*, Sydney: Millennium Books, 1995.

14   John Paul II, *The Pope in Australia: Collected Homilies and Talks*, Sydney: St Paul Publications, 1986, p.4.

15   Aboriginal elder from the Kowanyama people, quoted in conference brochure for 'Healing Our People', the Institute of Criminology conference in Alice Springs in 1991.

16   A. D. Hope, 'Australia' (1939), in *Selected Poems, op. cit.*, p.71.

17   Peter Carey, *Oscar and Lucinda*, Brisbane: University of Queensland Press, 1988, p.389.

18   Judith Wright, 'At Cooloolah' (1955), in *A Human Pattern: Selected Poems*, Sydney: Angus & Robertson, 1990, p.83.

19   This important exhibition was curated by Ross Mellick and Nick Waterlow from the University of New South Wales.

20   Peter Conrad, 'To love or to shove, that is the question', *The Australian*, 3 January 1997, p.4.

21   A similar argument has been explored by Andrew Taylor in *Reading Australian Poetry*, Brisbane: University of Queensland Press, 1987.

22   Les Murray, 'First Essay on Interest', *The People's Otherworld*, Sydney: Angus & Robertson, 1983, p.8.

[23] Patrick White, *The Tree of Man* (1956), Harmondsworth: Penguin, 1977, p.384.

[24] Les Murray, 'Some Religious Stuff I Know About Australia' (1982), *A Working Forest*, Sydney: Duffy & Snellgrove, 1997, p.133.

[25] Les Murray, in Penelope Nelson, *The Poetry of Les Murray*, Sydney: Methuen, 1978, p.2.

[26] Michael Leunig, in *The Search for Meaning: Conversations with Caroline Jones*, Sydney: ABC/Collins Dove, 1992, p.13.

[27] David Mowaljarlai and Jutta Malnic, 1993, *op. cit.*, p.214.

[28] *Ibid.*, p.53.

[29] *Ibid.*, pp.53–4.

[30] Miriam-Rose Ungunmerr, quoted in Eugene Stockton, *The Aboriginal Gift*, *op. cit.*, p.104f.

[31] Les Murray, 'Equanimity', *op. cit.*

5: ABORIGINAL RECONCILIATION AS A SPIRITUAL EXPERIENCE

[1] Les Murray, *Persistence in Folly*, Sydney: Sirius, 1984, p.2.

[2] James McAuley, 'An Art of Poetry', in Leonie Kramer, ed., *James McAuley*, University of Queensland Press, 1988, p.151

[3] C. G. Jung, 'The Complications of American Psychology', *Civilisation in Transition*, para.968.

[4] C. G. Jung, 'Mind and Earth', *Civilisation in Transition*, para.103.

[5] C. G. Jung, 'The Complications of American Psychology', para.979.

[6] Les Murray, 'The Human-Hair Thread', *Persistence in Folly*, *op. cit.*, p.27.

[7] Clare Dunne, *People Under the Skin: An Irish Immigrant's Experience of Aboriginal Australia*, Sydney: Lotus, 1988, p.34.

[8] Jean Gebser, *The Ever-Present Origin*, Athens, Ohio: Ohio University Press, 1985.

[9] Rodney Hall, *A Dream More Luminous than Love: A Trilogy*, Sydney: Picador, 1994.

[10] John Morton, 'Aboriginality, Mabo and the republic', in Bain Attwood, *In the Age of Mabo*, Sydney: Allen & Unwin, 1996, p.123.

[11] Marcia Langton, *Well, I Heard it on the Radio*, Sydney: Australian Film Commission, 1993, p.29.

[12] Les Murray, 'Preface' to *A Working Forest: Selected Prose*, Sydney: Duffy & Snellgrove, 1997.

[13] Julie Marcus, 'The Journey out to the Centre: the cultural appropriation of Ayers Rock', in Gillian Cowlishaw and Barry Morris, eds, *Race Matters: Indigenous Australians and 'Our' Society*, Canberra: Aboriginal Studies Press, 1997, p.47.

[14] Denise Cuthbert and Michele Grossman, 'Forgetting Redfern: Aboriginality in the New Age', *Meanjin* (University of Melbourne), Vol. 57, No. 4, 1998, p.777.

[15] *Ibid.*, p.775.

[16] *Ibid.*, p.774.

[17] Mitchell Rolls, 'The Jungian Quest for the Aborigine Within: A Close Reading of David Tacey's *Edge of the Sacred: Transformation in Australia*', in *Melbourne Journal of Politics: The Reconciliation Issue*, Vol. 25, 1998, p.175.

[18] *Ibid.*

[19] *Ibid.*, p.171.

[20] *Ibid.*, p.177.

[21] Paul Brennan, 'Tourist Eats Native', in *Philosopher* (Sydney), No. 5, May 1997, pp.45–48.

[22] Ken Gelder and Jane Jacobs, *Uncanny Australia: Sacredness and Identity in a Postcolonial Nation*, Melbourne University Press, 1998, p.13.

[23] *Ibid.*, p.6.

[24] David Tacey, 'What Are We Afraid Of?: Intellectualism, Aboriginality, and the Sacred', *Melbourne Journal of Politics*, Vol. 25, 1998, pp.189–194.

[25] Peter Willis, in Max Charlesworth, ed., *Religious Business: Essays on Australian Aboriginal Spirituality*, Cambridge University Press, 1998, p.136.

[26] *Ibid.*, p.139.

[27] Deborah Bird Rose, 'Ned Kelly Died for Our Sins', in Max Charlesworth, ed., *Religious Business: Essays on Australian Aboriginal Spirituality*, Cambridge University Press, 1998, p.106.

[28] *Ibid.*, p.105.

[29] *Ibid.*, p.107.

[30] *Ibid.*, p.114.

[31] *Ibid.*, p.115.

[32] *Ibid.*, p.108.

[33] *Ibid.*, p.117.

[34] Miriam-Rose Ungunmerr, 'Dadirri', in Eugene Stockton, *The Aboriginal Gift*, p.180.

[35] *Ibid.*, p.179.

[36] Deborah Bird Rose (1998), *op. cit.*, p.117.

6: ECOSPIRITUALITY AND ENVIRONMENTAL AWARENESS

[1] Novalis, in Robert Bly, ed., *News of the Universe: Poems of Twofold Consciousness*, San Francisco: Sierra Club Books, 1980, p.1.

[2] Paul Collins, *God's Earth: Religion as if Matter Really Mattered*, Melbourne: Collins Dove, 1995.

[3] Michael Leunig, 'Drawing the line on creativity and other curly issues', *The Age*, 5 August 1995, p.20.

[4] Annie Dillard, *Teaching a Stone to Talk*, London: Picador, 1984, p.70.

[5] David Suzuki and Peter Knudtson, *Wisdom of the Elders*, Sydney: Allen & Unwin, 1997.

[6] Theodore Roszak, *Ecopsychology: Restoring the Earth, Healing the Mind*, San Francisco: Sierra Club Books, 1995.

[7] Grant Watson, *Descent of Spirit*, Sydney: Primavera Press, 1990, p.34.

[8] Mircea Eliade, *Ordeal by Labyrinth*, University of Chicago Press, 1982, p.19.

[9] *Ibid.*, p.56.

[10] *Ibid.*, pp.56–57.

[11] *Ibid.*, p.55.

[12] *Ibid.*, p.56.

7: YOUTH SPIRITUALITY AND OLD RELIGION

1   John 3:8, from *The Jerusalem Bible*.

2   Sandie Cornish, 'Incarnational Faith and Social Transformation', *Conference* (Melbourne), Vol. 15, No. 1, June 1998, p.27.

3   These statistics, and the Sydney and Melbourne surveys, were the subject of a discussion between Philip Adams and B. A. Santamaria on ABC Radio National's 'Late Night Live', broadcast 25 March 1998.

4   Diarmuid O'Murchu, *Reclaiming Spirituality*, Dublin: Gill & Macmillan, 1997, p.2.

5   *Ibid.*, p.12.

6   William Johnston, *Mystical Theology: The Science of Love*, London: HarperCollins, 1995.

7   Tony Kelly, *An Expanding Theology: Faith in a World of Connections*, Sydney: E. J. Dwyer, 1993.

8   Bertolt Brecht, *Life of Galileo* (1940), in Ralph Manheim and John Willett, eds, *Bertolt Brecht: Collected Plays*, Vol. 5, New York: Vintage Books, 1972, p.23.

9   Frank O'Loughlin, 'Society, Church and Change', *Conference* (Melbourne), Vol. 15, No. 1, June 1998, p.16.

8: RELIGION AND THE NEW PARADIGM

1   A. N. Whitehead, quoted in Bruce Wilson, *Can God Survive in Australia?*, Sydney: Albatross, 1983, p.6.

2   Brian Zinnbauer, 'Religion and Spirituality: Unfuzzying the Fuzzy', *Journal for the Scientific Study of Religion* (Utah), 1997, Vol. 36, No. 4, p.561.

3   David Millikan (with Nevill Drury), *Worlds Apart? Christianity and the New Age*, Sydney: ABC Books, 1991, p.5.

4   John Spong, *Christianity Must Change or Die*, New York: HarperSanFrancisco, 1998.

5   Peter Hollingworth, 'Towards a New Spirituality', in John Wilson, ed., *The Global Scenarios: Developing a Scenario for Australia in an Emerging World*, Canberra: EPAC, 1996, p.50.

[6] Sallie McFague, *The Body of God: An Ecological Theology*, Minneapolis: Fortress Press, 1993, p.14.

[7] *Ibid.*

[8] *Ibid.*

[9] *Ibid*, p.xi.

CONCLUSION: CONTOURS OF AUSTRALIAN SPIRITUALITY

[1] Goanna, *Spirit Returns*, Compact Disc, ABC, 1998.

[2] Ruth Benedict, *The Chrysanthemum and the Sword*, Boston: Houghton Mifflin, 1946, p.222ff.

[3] Robert Dessaix, 'Some Enchanted Evening', *24 Hours*, ABC Radio, December 1995, p.55.

[4] Frederick Turner, *The Culture of Hope: A New Birth of the Classical Spirit*, New York: The Free Press, p.157.

[5] Robert Dessaix, 'Some Enchanted Evening', *op. cit.*, p.55.

[6] Veronica Brady, 'Review of *Edge of the Sacred*', *Westerly*, No. 3, Spring 1995, p.87.

[7] Leonard Cohen, 'Anthem', *The Future*, Compact Disc, Columbia, 1992.

[8] Patrick White, *Flaws in the Glass* (1981), Harmondsworth: Penguin, 1983.

[9] Elizabeth Johnson, *She Who Is: The Mystery of God in Feminist Theological Discourse*, New York: Crossroad, 1995, p.85f.

[10] David Tacey, *Patrick White: Fiction and the Unconscious*, Melbourne: Oxford University Press, 1988.

[11] David Tacey, *Remaking Men: The Revolution in Masculinity*, Melbourne: Viking Penguin, 1997.

INDEX

and outdoor education 3;
and shamanism 114, 168;
and wilderness experience 24,
180–3
ecology of the soul 166–170
education 3, 6, 8–12, 24, 52, 57,
81, 160, 187–9
Eliade, Mircea 13, 79, 86, 87, 90,
98, 179–182
Eliot, T.S. 109
eternity and time 22, 36–8, 40, 55,
74, 119, 215
evil and darkness 2, 14, 100,
128–31, 154–61, 172, 217–20,
259

fascism 2, 231
feminism 1, 21, 32, 63, 81, 89,
103, 174, 188
feminine 32, 102–4, 171–5, 231–5,
255–9
Fisher, John 4, 12
Fogarty, Lionel xi, 237
Fox, Matthew 104
Freud, Sigmund 33, 84, 137
Freudian psychology 35, 84, 219
Furphy, Joseph 69, 77,

Gandhi, Mahatma 61
Gebser, Jean 140
Girard, Rene 37
Griffiths, Bede 13, 199

Hall, Rodney 86, 121, 140, 142,
179, 237
Harpur, Charles 86
Hart, Kevin 14, 86
health 3, 6, 9, 10, 24, 46, 52, 61,
64, 165–6, 168, 176, 246–7
Hinduism 53, 211, 226
Hollingworth, Peter 53–4, 226–7
Hope, A.D. 77, 86, 97, 107–8,
248
Horne, Donald 85

Islam 53, 148, 171, 211

Johnston, George 85
Jones, Caroline 3, 5, 67
Judaism 26, 63, 148, 175, 180,
211, 226
Jung, C.G. 10, 13, 16, 35, 60, 61,
63, 84, 135, 144, 178
Jungian psychology 36, 130, 190

Kelly, Ned 85, 155–8
Kelly, Tony 200
Kuhn, Thomas 35

Lawson, Henry 69
Leunig, Michael 4, 60, 87, 90, 113,
168, 237

Mackay, Hugh 3
Magon, Jane 4
Marxism 1, 20–1, 29, 85, 152, 160
McAuley, James 86, 126
McFague, Sallie 232–5
meaning and truth 6, 12, 30,
35–40, 45–8, 57, 65, 87, 109, 128,
166, 187, 196, 202, 208, 243–7
media 5, 56, 128
meditation 24, 32, 53, 59, 63, 199
Merton, Thomas 199, 204
Millikan, David 6, 220
Mithraism 49
morality 9, 14, 25, 37, 40, 126–34,
148, 155–61, 164, 198, 217–20
Morton, John 143
Morwood, Michael 87
Mowaljarlai, David xi, 93–4, 96,
114–18, 142, 160, 250
Murray, Les 4, 86, 89, 91, 97–8,
109, 111–13, 117–22, 138, 142,
146, 152, 236–7

Nganyinyta and Ilyatjari of the
Pitjantjatjara 250–1, 266
Neilson, John Shaw 71, 86, 89,
98, 142
Nietzsche, Friedrich 55
nihilism 19, 37, 110, 202, 210
Nolan, Sidney 85

O'Donohue, John 41
O'Loughlin, Frank 204
O'Murchu, Diarmuid 192–3

Pickard, Stephen 14, 252
political correctness 93–4, 128,
  146–52, 159–61, 249–51
politics 6, 10, 24, 28–9, 36, 38, 47,
  66, 70, 77, 81, 83, 123–34,
  146–61, 186–9
postmodernism 3, 21–2, 33–4, 89,
  109, 150, 210, 238
prophetic mode and insight 13,
  25–8, 38, 87–8, 91, 98, 239, 254
psychoanalysis 1, 24, 214
psychopathology 40, 44, 45–6,
  58–61, 84–6, 113, 128, 144, 165,
  179

Rahner, Karl 29, 211
Ranson, David 251
redemption 2, 22, 61, 70, 102,
  120, 128, 134, 155, 161, 172, 195
re-enchantment 3, 5, 32–8, 43, 48,
  145, 171, 173, 179–85, 242–63
religion 7, 8, 10, 14 24–38, 40–64,
  68–73, 95, 100–6, 127–33,
  155–61, 162–4, 168–74, 189–211,
  212–35, 241–2;
  and community 25, 28, 34,
    40–1, 205–11, 213–14;
  and 'death of God' 22, 38, 100,
    102, 110, 120, 202;
  decline of 8, 14, 15, 25–8, 47,
    53–5, 61–4, 68–73, 78–9,
    101–6, 112, 122, 189–96, 241;
  and idolatry 24, 258;
  and literal thinking 29–32, 33,
    72–3, 219–20, 227, 241;
  and mystery 19, 24–32, 44, 68,
    79, 189, 197–201, 221;
  and mysticism 12, 13, 24, 62, 73,
    103, 114, 167, 199–202;
  and new paradigm 34–8, 168,
    220–35;

and new spirituality 13–16, 21,
  26, 35, 87, 90, 122, 168–70,
  189–94, 197–202, 213, 221–35,
  255–63;
and resistance to change 16,
  25–9, 202–3, 220–35;
and sin 195, 217–20, 259
religious: ancestry 15, 33, 34, 104,
  140, 142, 170, 178, 246;
  awareness 12, 13, 34, 35–8,
    60–61, 118, 145, 208;
  education 11, 29–32, 190–6, 198;
  emotion 2, 5, 17, 54, 62, 238;
  faith 18, 30–2, 36, 58, 63, 190,
    195, 203, 220;
  fundamentalism and
    intolerance 10–12, 19, 25,
    30, 33, 34, 36, 55, 63, 66,
    72, 229, 262;
  instinct 2, 25, 79, 262;
  language 23, 38, 82, 95, 127,
    150, 195–6, 220, 240, 253;
  metanoia and conversion 29,
    61–3, 145;
  persecution 26, 29, 67
Ricketts, William 136
Ricouer, Paul 92
rituals and rites of passage 28, 41,
  46, 49, 53, 75–6, 88, 119, 132,
  155, 169, 176, 197
Rose, Deborah Bird 153–61

sacrifice 45, 48–51, 61, 66,
  125–33, 145, 214
science 9, 29–33, 59, 81, 171, 196;
  new 3, 9, 33, 169
Sculthorpe, Peter 4, 87
secular materialism 1, 4–5, 7,
  28–9, 33–35, 43, 56, 65–9,
  73–80, 84–6, 119, 146–52, 209;
  end of 6, 8–9, 13, 15, 18, 21, 209;
  and envy 18;
  and humanism 7, 33, 66, 173,
    187;

and postsecular enlightenment 7, 33–8
sexuality, the body, and passion 23, 32, 39–40, 99–103, 107, 218, 221, 231–5, 258–60
Slessor, Kenneth 110
soul 24, 38, 39–45, 50–1, 56, 166
spirit 24, 26–8, 31–35, 38, 40, 57, 80, 87, 88, 93–111, 124–8, 215, 230
spiritual hunger 3, 32, 35, 45–8, 53, 193
spirituality: antifundamentalist 10–12, 25;
  and computer connectivity 20;
  and connectedness 15, 17, 19–20, 28, 107, 111–17, 128, 136, 164–170, 214;
  as deep listening 38, 117, 161;
  defined 17–19, 24–5, 242;
  and embarrassment 22, 44, 88, 186, 239, 243;
  fake 24;
  and identity 40, 55–57, 60, 162–4, 246;
  and loneliness 15–16, 205–9, 213–14;
  as natural state 18, 165;
  negative associations of 1, 23–4, 33–4, 146–52, 165;
  New Age 8, 35, 58, 64, 84, 105, 141, 147–8, 170, 177–9, 191–2, 194, 198, 214, 237;
  and personal breakdown and crisis 15, 43, 46, 58–61, 63, 215, 221, 255;
  as public and political issue 2–5, 23, 43–64, 65–92, 123–34, 162–85, 187–9, 219;
  ridiculed and derided 5, 9–10, 18, 21, 23, 26–7, 33–5, 51, 80, 146–52, 165–6;
  as stable foundation 7, 18, 148, 214;

and subjectivity 23–4, 32, 46, 52, 166, 184;
tensions between religion and 13–16, 20, 24–8, 32, 47, 51–4, 61–4, 98–105, 189–211, 212–35, 237, 255;
and transformation 2, 12, 16, 17, 24, 28, 44, 63, 75, 215, 221, 242;
youth 3, 8, 22, 186–211, 218, 227
Spong, Bishop John 6, 223
sport 39, 56
Stockton, Eugene 133, 251
Stephens, A.G. 78–9
suicide 6, 12, 44, 58, 208
Suzuki, David 170

Tacey, David 12–15, 52, 135, 252
Tulip, James 14, 82
Turner, David 152
Turner, Frederick 245

Ungunmerr, Miriam-Rose 95, 117, 159–61
United States 64, 81–2, 141, 178, 213

violence and crime 6, 12, 218–19

Wallace-Crabbe, Chris 99
Watson, Grant 86, 176
Webb, Roy 8
White, Patrick 4, 9, 61–4, 67, 80, 85, 90–2, 110, 112, 136, 236, 239
Willis, Peter 152–3
Winton, Tim 4, 86, 142, 237
Wright, Judith 4, 86, 89, 90, 98, 107–9, 136, 236

Yeats, W.B. 13, 139–40
youth culture 11, 12, 46, 73–8, 186–211, 218
Yunupingu, Galarrwuy 74